Psychoanalysis as an Ethical Process

What role does ethics play in the practice of psychoanalysis and psychotherapy?

For most of its history, psychoanalysis has viewed ethics as a "side issue" in clinical work—occasionally relevant, but not central to therapeutic action. In *Psychoanalysis as an Ethical Process*, Robert Drozek highlights the foundational importance of ethical experience in the therapeutic relationship, as well as the role that ethical commitments have played in inspiring what has been called the "relational turn" in psychoanalysis.

Using vivid clinical examples from the treatment of patients with severe personality disorders, Drozek sketches out an ethically grounded vision of analytic process, wherein analyst and patient are engaged in the co-construction of an intersubjective space that is progressively more consistent with their intrinsic worth as human beings. Psychoanalysis can thus be seen as a unique vehicle for therapeutic *and* ethical change, leading to a dramatic expansion of agency, altruism, and self-esteem for both participants. By bringing our analytic theories into closer contact with our ethical experiences as human beings, we can connect more fully with the fundamental humanity that unites us with our patients, and that serves as the basis for deep and lasting therapeutic change.

This book will be of interest to psychotherapists and psychoanalysts, as well as scholars in ethical theory and philosophy.

Robert P. Drozek, LICSW, is an individual and group psychotherapist in the Adult Center for Borderline Personality Disorder at McLean Hospital. He serves as a teaching associate in the Department of Psychiatry at Harvard Medical School, and as a supervisor of mentalization-based treatment through the Anna Freud Centre and the Borderline Personality Disorder Training Institute at McLean Hospital. He is in private practice in Belmont, Massachusetts.

RELATIONAL PERSPECTIVES BOOK SERIES

LEWIS ARON, ADRIENNE HARRIS,
STEVEN KUCHUCK & EYAL ROZMARIN
Series Editors

The Relational Perspectives Book Series (RPBS) publishes books that grow out of or contribute to the relational tradition in contemporary psychoanalysis. The term *relational psychoanalysis* was first used by Greenberg and Mitchell[1] to bridge the traditions of interpersonal relations, as developed within interpersonal psychoanalysis and object relations, as developed within contemporary British theory. But, under the seminal work of the late Stephen A. Mitchell, the term *relational psychoanalysis* grew and began to accrue to itself many other influences and developments. Various tributaries—interpersonal psychoanalysis, object relations theory, self psychology, empirical infancy research, and elements of contemporary Freudian and Kleinian thought—flow into this tradition, which understands relational configurations between self and others, both real and fantasied, as the primary subject of psychoanalytic investigation.

We refer to the relational tradition, rather than to a relational school, to highlight that we are identifying a trend, a tendency within contemporary psychoanalysis, not a more formally organized or coherent school or system of beliefs. Our use of the term *relational* signifies a dimension of theory and practice that has become salient across the wide spectrum of contemporary psychoanalysis. Now under the editorial supervision of Lewis Aron, Adrienne Harris, Steven Kuchuck and Eyal Rozmarin, the Relational Perspectives Book Series originated in 1990 under the editorial eye of the late Stephen A. Mitchell. Mitchell was the most prolific and influential of the originators of the relational tradition. Committed to dialogue among psychoanalysts, he abhorred the authoritarianism that dictated adherence to a rigid set of beliefs or technical restrictions. He championed open discussion, comparative and integrative approaches, and promoted new voices across the generations.

Included in the Relational Perspectives Book Series are authors and works that come from within the relational tradition, extend and develop that tradition, as well as works that critique relational approaches or compare and contrast it with alternative points of view. The series includes our most distinguished senior psychoanalysts, along with younger contributors who bring fresh vision. A full list of titles in this series is available at www.routledge.com/mentalhealth/series/LEARPBS.

1 Greenberg, J. R., & Mitchell, S. A. (1983). *Object relations in psychoanalytic theory.* Cambridge, MA: Harvard University Press.

Psychoanalysis as an Ethical Process

Robert P. Drozek

Routledge
Taylor & Francis Group
LONDON AND NEW YORK

First published 2019
by Routledge
2 Park Square, Milton Park, Abingdon, Oxon OX14 4RN

and by Routledge
52 Vanderbilt Avenue, New York, NY 10017

Routledge is an imprint of the Taylor & Francis Group, an informa business

British Library Cataloguing in Publication Data
A catalogue record for this book is available from the British Library

Library of Congress Cataloging in Publication Data
Names: Drozek, Robert P., 1979- author.
Title: Psychoanalysis as an ethical process/Robert P. Drozek.
Description: Abingdon, Oxon; New York, NY: Routledge, 2019. | Series: Relational perspectives | Includes bibliographical references and index.
Identifiers: LCCN 2018045755 (print) | LCCN 2018047766 (ebook) | ISBN 9781315160368 (Master) | ISBN 9781351662284 (Adobe) | ISBN 9781351662277 (ePub) | ISBN 9781351662260 (Mobipocket) | ISBN 9781138064447 (hardback: alk. paper) | ISBN 9781138064454 (pbk.: alk. paper)
Subjects: LCSH: Psychotherapy–Moral and ethical aspects. | Psychoanalysis–Moral and ethical aspects. | Psychotherapist and patient.
Classification: LCC RC455.2.E8 (ebook) | LCC RC455.2.E8 D76 2019 (print) | DDC 174.2/968914–dc23
LC record available at https://lccn.loc.gov/2018045755

ISBN: 978-1-138-06444-7 (hbk)
ISBN: 978-1-138-06445-4 (pbk)
ISBN: 978-1-315-16036-8 (ebk)

Typeset in Times New Roman
by Swales & Willis, Exeter, Devon, UK

MIX
Paper from responsible sources
FSC® C013056

Printed and bound in Great Britain by
TJ International Ltd, Padstow, Cornwall

"When I ask myself why I always have striven honestly to be considerate of others and if possible kind to them and why I did not give this up when I noticed that one is harmed by such behavior and is victimized because others are brutal and unreliable, I really have no answer."

—Sigmund Freud (1915a)

"Theory, too, is a work and product of sublimation. If it loses vitality because it has become too remote from concrete experience, or because we no longer make the effort required to understand the presence of abstraction and theory in the life of our science (as of any science) and in our clinical work, we are in danger of losing the subject matter along with the theory."

—Hans Loewald (1988)

"It is probably a mistake to expect any great innovator to really grasp the revolution he or she is participating in. Since the theoreticians are standing in one world view and struggling to give birth to another, they cannot possibly envision what the full fruition of their efforts will be."

—Stephen A. Mitchell (1998)

Contents

Foreword

Peter Fonagy

I have to confess, in the interests of total transparency, that I took Robert Drozek's manuscript on holiday with me. I think I was anticipating a slightly different, perhaps a more leisurely and light-hearted, journey through the ethical complexities of the intensive psychotherapeutic practice that is psychoanalysis. Not that ethical issues should ever be taken lightly. And not that anyone would think that at a time when ethical failures at the highest level affect all of us so profoundly.

Yet I was not anticipating one of the most rigorous and scholarly explorations of the process of therapeutic change in insight-oriented therapeutic endeavors. And that was what awaited me with suntan lotion and the obligatory prosecco. The ambition of the book, which again I feel somewhat hesitant to confess dawned on me gradually as I turned its pages, is nothing short of a compelling attempt to update our understanding of the psychoanalytic change process in the light of the relational turn in psychoanalysis (e.g., Aron, 1996; Benjamin, 1995; Harris, 2005; Mitchell, 1993, 1997; Stern, 1997).

Drozek takes an intriguing approach to this ambitious task. I have to admit that, had I been inclined to take on such a mission, it is most unlikely that I would have rooted it in moral philosophy. Having read this important work, I cannot think of a better way to have grounded the undertaking than in the ethical realignment required of both patient and analyst if they are to take seriously that their shared engagement in broader understanding inevitably entails a joint sense of ownership of a subjective experience that neither wholly possesses and which therefore must remain the responsibility of both. This hopefully productive engagement in a joint enterprise does inevitably constitute, as Drozek points out, an ethical change for both.

The dignity of a person is founded on the holistic understanding of the complexity of the motives that drive their actions (Freud, 1905). As such understanding expands across space and time, the boundaries that physically and so inadequately separate minds are lost, or perhaps better put, we unconsciously yet voluntarily set them aside in critical ways (Winnicott, 1958). As self finds itself, it must inevitably accept responsibility for the other, if for no other reason than to assure its continued integrity as a self.

In previous communications I and colleagues have written at length about the alien self (Fonagy, Gergely, Jurist, & Target, 2002). We use this metaphor to describe the oft-discovered phenomenal experience of a split within the sense of self whereby a person experiences something as clearly them but also as contents they feel no moral responsibility for as they experience no sense of control, no sense of agency in relation to it (Freud, 1940). Our clinical experience with individuals with borderline personality disorder led us to speculate that failed mirroring, as described by Donald Winnicott (1971), created a potential for parts of the self to be hijacked by the overwhelming need created in the mind of a child who is a victim of trauma to identify themselves with the aggressor (Fonagy & Target, 2000; Fonagy, Target, Gergely, Allen, & Bateman, 2003). This model, which provides a prototype for disowning intolerable feelings and thoughts into another mind—projective identification by another name—is of course an ethical violation. Not that we have thought about it in this way in our writings. Coming to think of the process of reacquiring the alien part of the self through a bidirectional and mutual process, which accessing one's mental world inevitably entails, is the cornerstone of the intersubjective turn relational psychoanalysis has taken (Fonagy, Luyten, Allison, & Campbell, 2016).

The exuberance of clinical writings embracing postmodern epistemology has made many of us suspicious of the scholarship that ego psychology-influenced object relations theory encouraged us to pursue (Kernberg, 1996). Perhaps Drozek is right that key lessons were lost in moving away from aspects of what is now somewhat patronizingly referred to as the classical tradition in psychoanalysis. In abandoning the ambition to provide a general psychology, psychoanalysis could afford to pick and choose, and, not surprisingly, selected the more evocative and phenomenologically gripping facets of the individual psyche. If we take psychoanalytic psychology seriously as a project, then the concepts with which the author forces us to engage once more occupy pride of place. The issues of culpability, free will, dignity and the potential to genuinely act in the interest of another person can again become central as we contemplate the reason for doing things in the clinical setting, as well as outside it. I agree with Drozek that our theories need updating to take on board these constructs fundamental to human life. The process involves rediscovery rather than discovery, but I agree that this *re*-search is appropriately nested within a relational clinical approach to psychoanalysis.

As someone who has, for a number of decades, been consistently engaged in attempts to tease out the intersubjective roots of self-understanding, and the role of self-understanding in interpreting the actions of others as aligned with the thoughts, feelings, wishes and desires that drive one's own actions, I felt that I had been pursuing the ethical vision that the book declares as its objective. Having reflected on *Psychoanalysis as an Ethical Process*, I am now clearer about the limitations of my earlier position. I agree with Drozek that clinical experience forces us to see ethics as a dialectical enterprise that bridges apparently irreconcilable oppositions, seeing freedom in determinism, subjectivity within objectivity and self within the other. The clinical applications—our capacity to offer a fuller understanding to our patients—is certainly advanced by considering all analytic practice as motivated along ethical lines.

The book makes a major contribution to (a) resolving the complex and fraught relationship between basic principles of moral philosophy and psychoanalysis, (b) offering an extraordinarily insightful and sophisticated review where these ideas interface with psychoanalytic theory-building, and (c) making a brave effort to engage the practitioner side of the readers to help identify in what way their daily practice could be broadened and enhanced by recognizing that our daily work as psychoanalysts is inevitably part of an ethical process.

I did not take this book on holiday to find a major contribution to the body of psychoanalytic knowledge. However, I was challenged by the book, and a major contribution was what I found. The book offers a novel, creative and scholarly understanding of the complexity psychoanalysts willingly but sometimes naively enter into as they engage in long-term intensive psychological therapy with the individuals who have sought their assistance. Drozek provides the clarity of thinking that we all need to be able to engage in this process in a reflective, productive and satisfying way. Drozek has a new fan.

References

Aron, L. (1996). *A meeting of minds: Mutuality in psychoanalysis*. New York, NY: International Universities Press.

Benjamin, J. (1995). *Like subjects, love objects*. New Haven, CT: Yale University Press.

Fonagy, P., Gergely, G, Jurist, E. L., & Target, M. (2002). *Affect regulation, mentalization, and the development of the self*. New York, NY: Other Press.

Fonagy, P., Luyten, P., Allison, E., & Campbell, C. (2016). Reconciling psychoanalytic ideas with attachment theory. In P. Shaver & J. Cassidy (Eds.), *Handbook of attachment* (3rd ed., pp. 780–804). New York, NY: Guilford Press.

Fonagy, P., & Target, M. (2000). Playing with reality: III. The persistence of dual psychic reality in borderline patients. *International Journal of Psychoanalysis*, *81*(5), 853–874.

Fonagy, P., Target, M., Gergely, G., Allen, J. G., & Bateman, A. (2003). The developmental roots of borderline personality disorder in early attachment relationships: A theory and some evidence. *Psychoanalytic Inquiry*, *23*, 412–459.

Freud, S. (1905). Jokes and their relation to the unconscious. In J. Strachey (Ed. and Trans.), *The standard edition of the complete psychological works of Sigmund Freud* (Vol. 8, pp. 1–236). London, UK: Hogarth Press, 1960.

Freud, S. (1940). Splitting of the ego in the process of defense. In J. Strachey (Ed. and Trans.), *The standard edition of the complete psychological works of Sigmund Freud* (Vol. 23, pp. 275–278). London, UK: Hogarth Press, 1964.

Harris, A. (2005). *Gender as soft assembly*. Hillsdale, NJ: Analytic Press.

Kernberg, O. F. (1996). A psychoanalytic theory of personality disorders. In J. F. Clarkin & M. F. Lenzenweger (Eds.), *Major theories of personality disorders* (pp. 106–137). New York, NY: Guilford Press.

Mitchell, S.A. (1993). *Hope and dread in psychoanalysis*. New York, NY: Basic Books.

Mitchell, S.A. (1997). *Influence and autonomy in psychoanalysis*. Hillsdale, NJ: Analytic Press.

Stern, D. B. (1997). *Unformulated experience: From dissociation to imagination in psychoanalysis*. Hillsdale, NJ: Analytic Press.

Winnicott, D. W. (1958). Primary maternal preoccupation. In D. W. Winnicott (Ed.), *Collected papers: Through paediatrics to psycho-analysis* (pp. 300–305). London, UK: Tavistock.

Winnicott, D. W. (1971). Mirror-role of mother and family in child development. In D. W. Winnicott (Ed.), *Playing and reality* (pp. 111–118). London, UK: Tavistock.

Acknowledgments

In exploring the intersection between psychoanalysis and ethics, this book is predicated on the assumption that diverse and seemingly distinct contexts—of thought, emotion, relationships, and culture—can stimulate and enrich each other in exciting, unpredictable, and often generative ways. My personal process of writing this book is indebted to many such communities and contexts, which I feel privileged to acknowledge at the outset of this work.

I am fortunate to have such warm, interesting, and hilarious friends who have supported and sustained me over the years. I feel especially grateful to David Johnson, Anthony Nadler, and Amos Worth for countless discussions about the ideas in these pages—I cannot imagine this book without your friendship, and impressive clarity of mind. To my friends who are *not* clinicians—thank you for putting up with my incessant musings on these topics over dinner, and on roadtrips. Ryan McEnroe has kindly assisted with copy-editing; David Fleming has graciously contributed his keen literary eye and line editing as I prepared the manuscript. And words cannot express my appreciation for David Klee, whose compelling artwork has long adorned the walls of my home and office, and now the cover of my first book as well.

Within philosophy, I would like to thank Neil Weiner for introducing me to the practical utility of the philosophical method, and Erin Kelly for alerting me to its limitations.

Within psychoanalysis, I want to recognize Lew Aron, Steven Cooper, Hazel Ipp, and Karen Weisgerber, whose encouragement throughout my career has given me the confidence to begin developing and sharing my written work. Lew in particular has been something of a shepherd throughout this process, generously offering his time, singular perspective, and incisive feedback as I expanded a couple of papers into the present volume. Peter Fonagy and Anthony Bateman have provided invaluable clinical training and mentorship, offering the clearest, humblest, and most pragmatic application of psychoanalytic principles that I have ever encountered, which continues to serve as the framework for my daily clinical practice.

I feel continuously grateful for my professional community at McLean Hospital, and especially my colleagues in the Adult Center for Borderline Personality Disorder and Training Institute—Lois Choi-Kain, Shauna Dowden, Joe Flores, Amy Gagliardi, and John Gunderson—for demonstrating the absolute necessity of *progress and change* in the psychoanalytic treatment of patients with personality disorders. Through their selfless examples, Hilary Connery, Patricia Diaferio, and Rachel Tester have taught me the importance of always remaining on the front lines in this work. I am particularly thankful to Brandon Unruh, whose friendship, collaboration, and humanistic ethic continuously remind me that, first and foremost, our patients are people just like us, whom we have the true privilege of helping.

My family serves as the emotional foundation for everything that I do. Rose—thank you for loving me so fully, and for challenging me in the exact ways that I need. Margaret and Kipling—your vitality, creativity, and kindness are the brightest spot in my life.

Finally, I would like to dedicate this book to my patients. Thank you for allowing me to know you in this intimate and sacred way, and for enriching my life so fully in the process.

Part I

Psychoanalysis and ethics

Chapter 1

Introduction to an ethical psychoanalysis[1]

Sitting across from my patient Fred, I was overwhelmed by a powerful desire to strike him repeatedly across the face. I saw the image in my mind clearly—me standing over him while he remained seated, hitting him hard with an open hand, over and over again. He did not defend himself in any way; he just sat there while I hit him. While I was no stranger to countertransference feelings of anger and frustration with my patients, I had never before experienced the urge to impact a patient in a specifically *physical* way. And yet I did not feel at all worried I would act on the impulse. It felt simultaneously "mine" and "not mine," intense yet strangely divorced from action.

My mind flickered back to the only time I had ever hit another human being. At the bus stop in junior high, without warning, an older bully had put his arm around me and knocked my legs out from under me, causing me to fall into a mud puddle. Humiliated, filthy, and enraged, I punched him passionately but weakly in the face, only to be pummeled by him in return. That was the last time I had hit (had consciously wanted to hit) another person.

Fred struggled with a long history of homelessness, unemployment, and highly conflictual interactions with others. Now in his fifties, Fred had been homeless for most of the past twenty years, after his wife had divorced him and he was fired from his job as the manager of a restaurant chain. While he sought help through a variety of homelessness programs, he would inevitably get kicked out for getting into arguments with program staff, usually when he refused to comply with rules he saw as arbitrary or irrational. In his early sessions, Fred spent most of his time cataloguing the wrongs that had been done to him throughout the course of his life, also enumerating the impressive successes he had achieved before his ex-wife had divorced him—the single event to which he attributed his downfall.

In listening to these stories, I was struck by the crystalline vividness with which he recalled these decades-old events, as if they had just happened yesterday. I saw these stories as Fred's way of introducing himself to me—*I am a truly exceptional person. My failures are not my fault. I am the victim of an unfair world that has failed to appreciate what I have to offer. Will* you *appreciate what I have to offer?* Despite Fred's prickliness and arrogance, I liked him. In the face of his destitute circumstances, he expressed his deep conviction that he was destined for greatness, a stance I saw as naive, defensive, and endearing. He also related to me with an almost puppy-like desire for approval and attention, which I think made me feel useful, even with the seemingly intractable problems with which he was struggling.

As the therapy progressed, we came to see how Fred's anger was often triggered by scenarios in which he believed other people were seeing him as "stupid," "worthless," or "a failure." By focusing on the other party's wrongs, either verbally or in his mind, he could maintain a sense of himself as worthwhile, valuable, and most importantly, *not bad.* Fred gradually developed the ability to represent the more vulnerable parts of himself—his feelings of loneliness, his sadness that he had not achieved more in his life, his fear that his enemies were right about him. Fred began to see how his anger was serving as a defense against these feelings, distancing him from his sense that there was something deeply and irrevocably wrong with him, and that he was undeserving of love and care from other people.

And yet, despite these new insights, Fred's interpersonal difficulties outside of sessions continued. Each session, he would come in recounting some injustice he had experienced, with minimal recognition of the role he might be playing in these difficulties. From my perspective, Fred seemed more like the perpetrator than the victim in these situations: receiving citations for parking in fire lanes, getting kicked out of restaurants for smoking cigarettes in them, alienating his adult children by cataloguing their mother's negative qualities. The list went on and on. While I worked hard to explore the historical and dynamic dimensions of these patterns, I could not stop myself from judging Fred, and ultimately from wanting to *punish* him for failing to take responsibility for his life. This is where I found myself when I was beset by the fantasy of hitting Fred—simultaneously experiencing a desire to explore and a desire *to act*, a dialectical tension I now see as central to all effective analytic process.

In this book, I examine the complex relationship between psychoanalysis and what is often called "ethics" or "morality."[2] Much like psychoanalysis, ethics can be understood in a diversity of ways. *Merriam-Webster's Collegiate Dictionary* defines ethics quite formally as "the discipline dealing with what is good and bad and with moral duty and obligation" (p. 429). In more colloquial terms, the terrain of ethics encompasses experiences so central to everyday life that they usually escape our notice. We regularly judge certain behaviors as "right" and "wrong," "good" and "bad," whether in ourselves or in other people. We automatically feel like other people are "worth something," that their well-being really matters. At the same time, we feel obligated to behave in ways that promote the well-being of others, and to cultivate tendencies in ourselves (e.g., compassion, kindness, empathy) that *add something* to the lives of others, rather than simply taking from them. Without reflection, we also assume that we possess some freedom of choice in taking such actions, and thus that we are at least partially responsible for performing them, or culpable for *not* performing them. We even apply these ideas to our social and cultural institutions—such as governments, organizations, and companies—believing they are obligated to respect the needs, values, and interests of the people whose lives they touch.

Psychoanalysis has traditionally had a complicated relationship with ethics. Deeply committed to the view of psychoanalysis as an objective science, Freud appeared to feel conflicted about the centrality of ethical experience in analytic practice. By his own admission, the notion of genuinely ethical motivation left him uncharacteristically perplexed:

> When I ask myself why I always have striven honestly to be considerate of others and if possible kind to them and why I did not give this up when I noticed that one is harmed by such behavior and is victimized because others are brutal and unreliable, I really have no answer.
>
> (Freud, 1915a, pp. 189–190)

On the one hand, Freud (1915a) repeatedly affirmed the ethical neutrality of psychoanalysis, stating, "The unworthiness of human beings, including the analysts, always has impressed me deeply, but why should analyzed men and women in fact be better. *Analysis makes for integration but does not of itself make for goodness*" (p. 188; my italics). On the other hand, he could never fully ignore the ethical implications of psychoanalytic treatment:

> We tell ourselves that anyone who has succeeded in educating himself to truth about himself is permanently defended against the danger of immorality, even though his standard of morality may differ in some respect from that which is customary in society.
>
> (Freud, 1917, p. 434)

Freud's conflict about ethics has reverberated throughout the history of psychoanalysis. Our literature abounds with concepts that are clearly relevant to ethics, such as the super-ego, ego ideal, sublimation, and empathy, as well as recent formulations in relational and intersubjective theorizing, such as mutual recognition, mentalization, and the sharing of affective states. Nevertheless, apart from a handful of exceptions (Meissner, 2003; Orange, 2016; Wallwork, 1991), few articles or books explicitly investigate the intersection of psychoanalysis and ethics, and few theorists invoke ethics to elucidate the nature of analytic change. Ethics thus remains something of a "side issue" in mainstream psychoanalysis—important for some patients at some times, but not central to therapeutic action in general. While we have dispensed with the notion of the analyst as an unbiased and neutral observer, we have not yet discarded Freud's notion of analysis as an ethically neutral enterprise. *The prevailing thought seems to be that psychoanalysis leads to psychic integration and expansion of relational possibilities, but it does not necessarily lead to ethical change.*

While the relational turn has opened up the door for an increased recognition of ethical and humanistic concerns in psychoanalysis (Goodman & Severson, 2016), my sense is that there are still some strong theoretical assumptions, about ethics and about psychoanalysis itself, that have long prevented analysts from fully appreciating the essential role of ethics in therapeutic change. This book attempts to explore these assumptions, developing a vision of psychoanalysis that is ethical in a foundational way, while honoring the spirit of the ideas in question. My hope is that this project will help to facilitate a more productive dialogue between psychoanalysis and ethical theory—utilizing the unique resources of each discipline to illuminate the unexplored potentials of the other.

What does psychoanalysis—with its insights into unconscious motivation, developmental processes, intersubjectivity, the intimate and transformative power of the analytic dyad—have to teach us about ethical motivation, ethical behavior, and ethical change? And how might traditional ethical ideas (e.g., altruism, human dignity, conscious experiences of value, the categorical and objective dimensions of moral judgments) further illuminate the process and nature of therapeutic action? Wrestling with these questions entails an element of risk for all parties involved. As in any new relationship, when opening up a dialogue between two relative strangers, each party accepts the possibility of being transformed by the other, often in exciting, unpredictable, and dangerous ways. My assumption here is that philosophy actually *needs* psychoanalysis in order to address some longstanding problems in the history of ethics, and that psychoanalysis requires certain philosophical insights in order to fully realize its clinical potential. I will thus be examining some basic tensions at the heart of both disciplines, in the hopes that wrestling with these matters openly can reveal untapped resources that might mutually benefit both parties.

In these pages, I advance a conception of psychoanalysis as an essentially (rather than peripherally) ethical process, in which the ethical development of both therapist and patient serves as the fulcrum of psychic change. This model follows in the footsteps of the handful of theorists who frame therapeutic action in fundamentally ethical terms, most notably Benjamin (1995), Hoffman (1998), Searles (1979), Slavin and Kriegman (1998), and Bateman and Fonagy (2016). On these views, therapeutic change is not simply "related to" ethical change. Rather, therapeutic change *constitutes* ethical change—they are two sides of the same coin. Accordingly, recent innovations in relational theorizing can be seen as continuing the longstanding philosophical tradition of virtue ethics, in which there exists a basic correspondence between psychological well-being and a person's ethical life (see Chapter 2).

In particular, I sketch out what I call a *dignity-based* vision of psychoanalytic change, wherein analyst and patient are engaged in the co-construction of an intersubjective space that is progressively more consistent with their intrinsic worth as human beings. Analytic work can be viewed as a collaborative, non-linear, iterative process in which both parties come to value Self and Other under a progressively wider range of conditions. Each individual is able to obtain, in the context of this specific relationship, a less-conditional sense of self-esteem and self-worth, and an expanded capacity to value the other person even when she displays qualities we reflexively identify as "bad" or "problematic."

This is obviously quite abstract, and I will flesh out these ideas through extensive clinical examples as we proceed. For now, I want to acknowledge that, in order for such an account to succeed in even a basic way, I will have to accomplish two main tasks—responding to the various objections to this idea of an ethical psychoanalysis, and developing a compelling clinical theory that is able to explain the full range of analytic phenomena, especially those experiences that do not appear to be "ethical" in any straightforward way. I am thus interested in reconceptualizing everyday psychoanalytic practice, which is not traditionally seen as involving ethics at all, as being an essentially ethical process. In this way, I hope to make ethics an *un*-exceptional, rather than unique, psychoanalytic phenomenon.

This project is visually represented in the painting that appears on the cover of this book, *preserving the paradox, a portrait* by the artist David Klee. While the painting is of course an abstraction, viewers might notice the iconic portrait of Sigmund Freud, cigar in hand, integrated with the likeness of eighteenth century German philosopher Immanuel Kant, who is generally regarded as the most important ethical theorist of the Enlightenment, and whom Freud regularly referenced in both reverential and critical terms (Tauber, 2010). The resultant synthesis represents a strange, vibrant, kaleidoscopic tapestry, a complex quilt of color and shape in which Freud and Kant are both clearly visible and yet impossible to distinguish from each other. Freud *is* Kant, and vice versa, in a way that allows both of them to transcend their identities as individual subjects. Similarly, my hope is that, by bringing psychoanalysis and ethics into closer communication with each other, we can allow each discipline to become the fullest version of itself, while simultaneously realizing a novel and clinically useful vision of the human person that would be impossible to achieve without the contributions of both systems of thought.

My interest in these matters dates back to my time in college. I studied philosophy, finding myself absorbed with many of the "big questions" of moral theory. What is the nature, meaning, and source of ethical experience? How do we explain its pervasiveness and seeming universality? Is it ever possible for us to be truly motivated by the needs and interests of other people, or is ethical motivation always reducible to some self-oriented motive? In making moral judgments, are we simply expressing our personal feelings or preferences, or do such judgments reflect some more "objective" standard?

In wrestling with these questions, I was particularly inspired by the ethical theory of the aforementioned philosopher Immanuel Kant. Kant (1785/1997) built his moral system on the notion of human dignity, understood as the "unconditional, incomparable worth" of human beings (p. 42). He attributed this notion to our capacity for freedom—the potential to serve as a source of meaning and value in our deliberations about "what to do" and "how to live." While we can never fully *prove* such freedom, it serves as a foundational dimension of human identity, significantly influencing our sense of ourselves in relation to others. For Kant, since we experience ourselves as a source of meaning rather than simply as receptacles for other people's meanings, we take ourselves to have an intrinsic worth, or dignity. To the degree that we experience other people in an analogous way, we naturally take them to have dignity as well. In this motivational state, we are more likely to be responsive to their desires and interests, and less likely to relate to them exclusively like objects that might either satisfy or frustrate our own preferences.

While studying these matters, I was deeply engaged in analytic psychotherapy, ultimately transitioning into a psychoanalysis. As the process unfolded, I became captivated by the observation that my own therapeutic shifts were accompanied by an increased ability to be motivated by the people in my life—their needs, desires, interests, and experiences. Rather than having to "choose" between my own psychological well-being and responsiveness to others, there seemed to be a strange and surprising correspondence at work here, some basic connection between *therapeutic* change and *ethical* change. In making me a more integrated and "complete" person, psychoanalysis also seemed to be making me a *better* person, in a very particular sort of way. But why should this be the case, and what was this connection even about?

I entered graduate school in philosophy, in large part to tackle these questions head-on. By my second semester, I had started an independent study on Kantian ethics. I wrote my first paper on these topics, utilizing Kant's notion of human dignity and freedom to explain the psychology of ethical development. The professor—a kind, internationally renowned scholar in moral and political philosophy—looked concerned. "This is obviously important stuff," she told me. "It's well-written and interesting, but it isn't *philosophy*." She explained what, on some level, I had begun to sense. In philosophy, I would have to narrow my scope—working to explain and analyze *concepts*, and avoid focusing so much on the phenomenon of change, which inevitably required delving into more "empirical" matters.

Within weeks, I had withdrawn from graduate school, continuing to serve as a teaching assistant while I figured out what I wanted to do with my life. On the advice of a psychiatrist friend who knew of my interest in mental health, I started working as a mental health counselor on an inpatient psychiatry unit at McLean Hospital. It was there that I began learning about relational psychoanalysis. I was fascinated by what seemed to me to be a dramatic overlap between relational theorizing and moral philosophy. In Greenberg and Mitchell's (1983) *Object Relations in Psychoanalytic Theory*, I saw an approach to understanding human motivation that paralleled the age-old philosophical debate between hedonism and altruism—motivation that derived primarily from "inside" the individual subject, as well as motivation that derived primarily from our relationships, from the subjective lives of other people. In Mitchell's (1988) *Relational Concepts in Psychoanalysis*, I read an argument against psychological hedonism as a primary explanation of human experience, and a commitment to expounding an integrated relational model that could progressively reflect the complexity and dignity of the human subject. And then came the work of Jessica Benjamin. In a more compelling way than I could have imagined, Benjamin (1988, 1995) was elucidating the psychological basis for the correlation between psychoanalysis and ethics that had occupied me for the last five years—if "self-development" is fundamentally constituted by our potential to recognize others, then all therapeutic change would necessarily be accompanied by *ethical* change, and vice versa.

I had found my intellectual home. These theorists were not simply traversing the same conceptual terrain as moral philosophers. By diving into the questions that my professor had rightly said were "beyond philosophy" (e.g., human development, unconscious dynamics, the structure of personality, analytic technique and therapeutic action), they were deepening and expanding the whole realm of inquiry. At the same time, I found myself deeply fulfilled by working directly with people who were suffering—not simply by *explaining* human experience, but by playing an active role in helping these patients develop a greater sense of meaning, purpose, and dignity in their lives.

As I entered graduate school and started clinical training, the real-life importance of these matters became immediately alive for me. Over and over again, in every treatment, I saw this basic correspondence between my patients' capacity to access their own subjective worlds, and their capacity to represent and be responsive to the subjectivity of others. But what surprised me is that I soon discovered an analogous process unfolding in myself as well. At some point in every treatment, I found that my personality set constraining limits on our ability to move forward in the therapy—related to the unique dynamic I had unconsciously co-created with this particular patient, but also related to my own history and patterns of self-experience. As we were able to find a way through these matters together, I gained an expanded capability to value myself and my patient under a wider range of conditions—to accept and value parts of myself that had previously been dissociated, and to be motivated by dimensions of my patient's subjectivity that, up until this point, I had not been able to fully recognize and value.

Interestingly, these developments did not "stop" in the therapeutic dyad. I saw that these treatments were having dramatic repercussions on my life outside of the therapy, resulting in an expanded sense of self-esteem, and an increased receptivity to the internal experiences of the people in my life, my loved ones but also complete strangers. Not only was there a potential connection between clinical process and ethical process. I was stumbling onto the possibility that this connection was *bidirectional and mutual* as well, an essential dimension of therapeutic action for both therapist and patient.

Entering a fellowship program at Boston Psychoanalytic Society and Institute, I began trying to put words on these experiences, publishing several pieces in *Psychoanalytic Dialogues*, the journal founded by many of my psychoanalytic heroes. But what if I were just projecting here? How could I be so sure that I was "observing" this mutual correlation between therapeutic and ethical processes, or if I just understood these relationships in this way as a result of my idiosyncratic psychology? The further that I delved into the relational literature, the less this question worried me. If all theory is simply a distillation of the theorist's individual history and subjective world (Atwood & Stolorow, 1979), then the possibility of any "objective" theory is a fiction, a mirage. My work thus became to articulate my own experiences and assumptions, while making sure these ideas remained "answerable" to a number of factors—the psychoanalytic lexicon, the full range of clinical phenomena, and our "everyday" ideas about ourselves as human beings. This is the project I am attempting in this book.

The anti-theoretical slide

I will now try to outline some of the basic assumptions that inform my approach in what follows. First, I am assuming, perhaps controversially nowadays, that our *theories matter* in the practice of psychoanalysis and psychotherapy. I use the term "theory" in its broadest sense here—an abstract idea (or system of ideas) used to explain and describe psychoanalytic phenomena (e.g., mind, motivation, human development, analytic process, therapeutic action, clinical technique). Such theories include our explicit, professionally endorsed models of psychoanalysis, as well as the implicit, idiosyncratic models that direct and inform our most routine interventions (Argyris & Schön, 1974; Canestri, 2006; Sandler, 1983).

Over the past two decades, the psychoanalytic landscape has undergone what might be called an *anti-theoretical slide*, also described by Friedman (2002) as "theory exhaustion" (p. 728). We can observe this shift in a variety of different trends in the literature—the relative predominance of case discussions compared to theoretical papers;

decreased attention to issues of human motivation (Teicholz, 2010); diminished interest in the role of interpretation in therapeutic work; an emphasis on "process over content"; increased appreciation of the ineffable and non-logical dimensions of experience (e.g., paradox, contradiction, dialectics, unformulated experience, ambiguity, mysticism, transitional experiencing), accompanied by an apparent devaluing of explicit and "rational" operations (e.g., logic, reason, language); frequent references to creativity and the creative arts (e.g., literature, poetry, spontaneity, play); the preponderance of first-personal points of view, along with a seeming trepidation about making general and universal statements about human psychology; a preference for elaborating on specific concepts rather than proposing grand theoretical systems; and decreased interest in "meta-theoretical" matters, that is, the study of theory itself and the role that it plays in therapeutic practice.

I see these anti-theoretical developments as being related to epistemological shifts that have been unfolding in psychoanalysis over the past several decades, identified variously as postmodernism, hermeneutics, constructivism, and perspectivism (Aron, 1996a; Hoffman, 1998; Mitchell, 1993; Renik, 1993). On these views, the subjectivity of the analyst plays an irreducible role in structuring the clinical situation, such that there is no purely objective standpoint we can occupy to validate our theories or to generate definitive "psychoanalytic knowledge." Devoid of such a standpoint, and without our formerly unquestioning confidence in Freud's theoretical edifice, it becomes nearly impossible to value theory in the same way. The authority of theory has thus shifted to the authority of *analytic experience itself* (Foehl, 2010). This has led to an antagonism towards theory within psychoanalysis, and especially within certain segments of relational theorizing. For many practitioners, universally formulated theory not only fails to express the complex textures of human experience, but it can *do violence* to that experience, undermining the idiosyncratic qualities of patient, analyst, and the unique relationship they co-create with one another.

While I welcome this commitment to granting experiential process a greater role in psychoanalysis, I am concerned with what I see as an implicit assumption in the above developments—the idea that it is somehow possible to discard our theories and arrive at an analytic perspective that is somehow *atheoretical*. By contrast, I assume that our explicit and implicit theoretical assumptions deeply and irrevocably structure all therapeutic process—our experiences of our patients, what we "hear" when they speak to us, our assumptions about what constitutes unconscious motivation, our sense of *ourselves* in the clinical moment, our perceptions of intersubjective patterns unfolding in the dyad, and our understanding of our own subjective states (e.g., thoughts, emotions, impulses to do or say certain things) in analytic work.

With this position, I am following in the tradition of those theorists who emphasize not just the importance of theory, but its foundational and unavoidable role in psychoanalytic praxis (Cooper, 1996, 2000; Greenberg, 1991; Mitchell, 1988; Schafer, 1983; Spence, 1982, 1987). As Greenberg and Mitchell (1983) observed in the introduction to their classic text:

> Every analyst, even the most rigidly atheoretical, is at least implicitly a theorist. What one hears from a patient is informed by what one knows about living; it is shaped by a theory which the analyst may or may not articulate (even to himself) and which is derived from what he has read (within and without the technical literature), seen, and lived. With the exception only of the most doctrinaire, each analyst's clinical practice rests on a theory which is already a synthesis of information derived from many sources.
>
> (p. 5)

Several years later, Mitchell (1988) emphasized this point further: "There is no unstructured listening, unmediated by theory" (p. 90). More recently, Foehl (2010) proposes, "*We live our theories* in our engagements and they shape the kinds of interactions we have" (p. 60; my italics). Cooper (2010) elaborates on these points helpfully:

> I do not believe that there is such a thing as not using a theory; a more productive way to frame the question involves the degree to which the analyst is aware of his or her theory and the ideals and ideas that direct the analyst's decision making.
>
> (p. 7)

My preference is to conceptualize theory as existing in a dialectical relationship with experiential process, with theory shaping and structuring our moment-to-moment experiences, and experience continuously influencing the shape and content of our theories. I see classical psychoanalysis as collapsing rather than preserving this dialectic, through its failure to allow our unique experiences and observations (e.g., in clinical interaction, in human development) to sufficiently influence the explicit tenets of mainstream psychoanalysis. This is much of what prompted the advent of relational theorizing, which since its inception has privileged the importance of uniqueness and specificity in individual development and therapeutic work (Greenberg & Mitchell, 1983; Mitchell, 1988). My concern is that, in an attempt to avoid the objectivism of classical thought, we have overcorrected somewhat, minimizing the importance of theory and thereby collapsing this dialectic in the opposite direction.

By maintaining an optimal tension between theory and experience, we will remain connected with the foundational role that our theories play in analytic practice, while ensuring that these theories continue to be nourished by our everyday therapeutic experiences and innovations. In support of this position, it is instructive that the relational turn—arguably the most fertile period of psychoanalytic innovation since Freud founded the discipline—was initiated and preceded by a surge of important metatheoretical works in the literature (Greenberg & Mitchell, 1983; G. S. Klein, 1976; Mitchell, 1988; Schafer, 1976; Spence, 1982). When we devote attention to theory *as theory*, we open up the door to new forms of experiencing in the clinical moment.

Anti-objectivism in relational thought

"Objectivity" has become a dirty word in psychoanalysis. As mentioned earlier, part of the anti-theoretical slide involves an implicit injunction against "objective" or "universal" perspectives on human experience. We see this injunction in all areas of relational discourse—an emphasis on specificity over generality in discussions of motivation (Eagle, 1984; Hoffman, 1995); an abandonment of objective theories of technique (Bacal, 2011; Tublin, 2011); a shift away from linear, stage-based models of development (Coburn, 2002; Seligman, 2005); and the proliferation of "experience-near, clinically based conceptualizations" throughout our literature (Foehl, 2010, p. 48). In these ways, relational theorizing has moved towards an *anti-objectivist*, or anti-essentialist, vision of analytic work (Weisel-Barth, 2015).

For our purposes here, *subjective* refers to a standpoint that we see as reflecting or expressing our particular (conscious or unconscious) internal states (e.g., thoughts, emotions, desires), while *objective* refers to a mode where we abstract from our idiosyncratic standpoint to arrive at a more general or "universal" perspective on human life. This amounts to a process-related rather than content-related distinction, indicating different stances we can take towards our own beliefs and attitudes. "Subjective" implies tentativeness, openness to alternative points of view, epistemic humility, and agnosticism about the truth or falsity of our beliefs—*I might be right, but I do not feel completely certain. It is possible that my viewpoint says more about* me *than the way that things really are.* "Objective," on the other hand, implies confidence, a strong sense of certainty, and the belief that our position is "right" or "best" compared to alternatives—*I know what is going on here. This isn't just about me; it's about the* truth *of the situation.*

The tendency to objectivize is so pervasive that it often escapes our notice. Objective beliefs saturate our theories (e.g., about unconscious motivation, about pathology, about technique), as well as the various formulations we naturally endorse *as human beings* outside of the consulting room: our ideas about human nature and "the meaning of life," our assumptions about human suffering (e.g., what causes it, how to address it), our spiritual and religious beliefs, and especially relevant for our purposes here, our notions of right and wrong and "how to live" in the world. Such beliefs play a powerful role in how we experience ourselves in relation to our patients, and in how we respond to the problems that our patients bring to us. This point becomes crucial in moments of impasse, when, as I hope to illustrate in what follows, both parties can unconsciously cling to objective formulations about Self and Other in a way that hinders rather than facilitates intersubjective relatedness.

While I appreciate the embrace of specificity in psychoanalytic process, I take issue with a tacit premise of anti-objectivism—the idea that we are able to avoid making objective judgments in the first place. In my view, in our clinical practice but also in our everyday lives as human beings, we *necessarily* objectivize. As philosophers have long recognized

(H. Bok, 1998; Darwall, 1983; Korsgaard, 1996b, 2009; Nagel, 1979, 1986), we are constantly assuming both subjective *and* objective perspectives on our lives. We see our beliefs as reflecting our particular viewpoints, but we also see them as saying something about the world *as it actually is*, apart from our individual positions.

As D. N. Stern (1985) illustrates, infancy research supports the notion that, starting as early as two to seven months of age, infants "have some abilities to abstract, average, and represent information preverbally" (p. 97). These "Representations of Interactions that have been Generalized" form the pre-symbolic bedrock of our relational lives, perpetually influencing our contemporary experiences and undergoing "continual growth and elaboration" throughout our life cycle (p. 119). At an intellectual and intersubjective level, we are continuously having unique experiences from which we abstract to arrive at more general or universal outlooks on Self and Other.

In proposing that we cannot "shut off" our tendency to objectivize, I am not implying that we can ever occupy any purely objective standpoint. I am simply making the phenomenological point that all of us, whether we like it or not, relate to some of our beliefs *as if* they are objectively correct. This process is unfolding constantly, reflexively, and typically outside of conscious awareness. At this very moment, for example, we are automatically assuming that an external world exists, that *we* actually exist, and that there is an object positioned right in front of us. This applies regardless of whether we consciously endorse constructivist principles. Even the constructivist can relate to her theory as if it is definitively correct, that is, she can assume an objective form of constructivism.

There are significant dangers involved in ignoring our tendency to objectivize. To the degree that we are disconnected from such beliefs, we are more likely to be unreflectively influenced by them, and less likely to utilize them in ways that could potentially be fruitful in therapeutic work. Anti-objectivism can also have a detrimental effect on psychoanalytic discourse more generally. As I see it, the relational turn did not simply lead to a more egalitarian clinical approach—it ushered in a more open and egalitarian approach to *theorizing*, in which we became freer to examine our basic assumptions based on their own merits, not simply dictated by issues of terminology, popularity, political power, and institutional affiliation. If left unchecked, anti-objectivism runs the risk of furthering a new orthodoxy in relational discourse, where uniqueness becomes so idealized that all objective formulations automatically get dissociated as the problematic "not-me" of psychoanalytic experience (see Aron & Starr, 2013). Under these conditions, power can become localized around a handful of concepts that lie unquestioningly beyond reproach (e.g., dialectics, self-states, intersubjectivity, creativity), while notions that lack political backing can become sequestered and calcified. In a highly subtle way, this process can have the effect of stifling creativity and innovation within psychoanalysis, while inhibiting open and honest discourse about our basic assumptions.

Throughout this book, I attempt to maintain rather than collapse the dialectical tension between objectivity and subjectivity. Lew Aron (2015) recently observed in an online colloquium for the International Association for Relational Psychoanalysis and Psychotherapy:

> To me the essence of the relational turn is to make room for multiplicity. We need both universal and particular approaches and they need to be held in tension. In your effort to outlaw universal claims you in fact restrict pluralism and diversity.

Our task thus becomes articulating the subjective and objective assumptions that we bring to analytic practice, without losing sight of the fact that all of these assumptions are distilled representations of our subjective worlds. While we have increasingly recognized the irreducible subjectivity of the analyst, we have not yet fully appreciated that this subjectivity is constituted by subjectively formulated *and* objectively formulated elements. I will thus conceptualize "objectivity" as a dynamic rather than static capacity. Not only do our subjective processes shape our objective beliefs, but our objective beliefs simultaneously shape our subjective worlds, and all of these processes are significantly influenced by the contexts in which we are embedded, from the therapeutic dyad to the broader psychoanalytic culture.

On this view, we can embrace a tragic but real sense of possibility about "the truth" of our theoretical formulations. Recognizing that we can never access any objective perspective from which to verify our beliefs, we always remember that these beliefs might say more about *us* than about "reality." At the same time, since we can never access that perspective, it remains entirely possible that our formulations, to a greater or lesser degree, might reflect things *as they actually are*, although we could never know such a thing.

This epistemology offers the potential for a renewed sense of ambitiousness in psychoanalytic theorizing, liberating us to access and represent the full range of our subjective and objective beliefs, as long as we do so with humility and self-consciousness. I am reminded of my experience whenever I return to the writings of Freud, Melanie Klein, Sullivan, Fairbairn, and Kohut—all seminal theorists who unselfconsciously endorsed more objectivist outlooks on psychoanalysis. While I see these theorists' formulations as expressions of their subjectivity, that does not dampen my sense of exhilaration and even wonder when I re-read these works, or my non-reflective sense that they are getting at something very real, and very important about the human situation, even though I could never verify such a thing. This is the approach to theory that I will be taking throughout this book.

"Bridging the gap" between theory and life

So far I have argued for the foundational importance of theory within psychoanalysis, while highlighting our inescapable tendency to objectivize our particular perspectives. As a final point, I want to emphasize one of the main considerations that will guide me in what follows—the idea that our theories are answerable not just to clinical phenomena, but to our everyday experiences *as human beings* outside of psychoanalysis. Greenberg and Mitchell (1983) were getting at something similar when they proposed that, in addition to Kuhn's (1977) criteria of accuracy, consistency, scope, simplicity, and fruitfulness, a theory should be evaluated based on "how compelling it appears to be, on its underlying vision of human life" (p. 407).

Along these lines, I am especially interested in a handful of ideas, broadly related to the topic of ethics, that I see as fundamental to ordinary human experience.

- *The assumption of freedom.* In our daily lives, we assume that we have some freedom of choice about what actions we take, and how we choose to conduct ourselves in our lives. For this reason, we tend to hold ourselves responsible for our decisions—for what we choose to do, and even what we choose *not* to do.

- *The importance of behavior and consequences.* Outside of our consulting rooms, we operate as if the question of "what to do" and "how to live" in the world really matters. We see this in our personal lives, for example when we seriously consider where we should live, how to raise our children, and how to spend our money. When our friends share their difficulties with us, we do not simply empathize with them and reflect on the meaning of their concerns—we offer our ideas about *what they should do* in the situations in question. Throughout all of this, we never forget that our actions (and inactions) have real consequences in the world, from an ethical perspective (e.g., how much pleasure versus pain a specific action might generate), but also in helping us to achieve our goals and fulfill our human potentials.
- *The notion of dignity.* We take ourselves and other human beings to have a special sort of value in this world—an intrinsic worth or "dignity" as people, not dependent on extrinsic factors like race, appearance, social status, or sexual orientation (Drozek, 2015a, 2015b). This notion expresses our sense that each of us is truly worth something, that our well-being actually matters, and that there is something fundamentally wrong with treating other people exclusively like objects, without consideration to their thoughts, feelings, or desires.
- *The possibility of altruism.* Regardless of our theoretical beliefs about the possibility of altruistic versus selfish motivation, in our daily lives, we tend to operate as if it is possible to be genuinely motivated by the needs and interests of other people (Drozek, 2010a, 2010b). In a situation when we are trying to help someone who is in pain, it *feels like* we are acting in order to alleviate that person's suffering. And when we are struggling, we naturally assume it is possible for others to be motivated by us as well, hence our feelings of hurt and resentment when others are *not* responsive to our needs and desires.
- *The connection between ethical living and psychological well-being.* Often without reflection, we assume there are certain ethical conditions for an experience of psychological well-being

and fulfillment in this world. When we hear about people who have seriously and consistently violated the rights of others (e.g., serial killers, systematic perpetrators of child abuse, members of hate groups who advocate violence against others), it is difficult for us to imagine that these people feel truly and unconflictedly happy and fulfilled in their lives. I suggest that most of us hold such views even if we recognize, at the theoretical level, that ethics vary based on a person's culture and idiosyncratic history. As Kant (1785/1997) observed long ago, "A good will seems to constitute the indispensable condition even of worthiness to be happy" (p. 7).

For ease of reference, I refer to the above constellation of ideas as our *reflexive ethical commitments*. These commitments are not simply superficial "cognitions" or belief states—they constitute a deep part of our practical identities, playing a foundational role in our sense of *what it means to be human*. Most of us hold these beliefs reflexively, that is, we simply assume them, conducting ourselves in our day-to-day lives and relationships *as if* they are true, regardless of our theoretical opinions about the matters in question. My assumption here is that our consciously endorsed theoretical views (e.g., about human nature, unconscious motivation, constructivist epistemology), while important, are unable to eradicate the more "practical" perspectives we automatically assume when we are engaged as active participants in our everyday lives.

In my view, apart from a few notable exceptions I will consider in these pages, there exists a significant gulf between our publicly endorsed analytic theories and these basic ethical commitments. Not only do our theories fail to reflect them, but there are many ways in which our theories and practices can functionally undermine them. This can result in what might be called a *dissociative gap* between our theories and our everyday experiences as human beings, in which ethics gets relegated to a "not-me" dimension of psychoanalytic process. Under these conditions, we can remain less connected to our ethical commitments in daily clinical work, as well as the ethical dimensions of our patients' experiences.

In the best-case scenario, vaguely sensing this disjunction between our professionally endorsed theories and ethical commitments, we reflexively supplement our theories with these commitments, arriving at an implicit, practically oriented amalgam that comfortably reflects our psychoanalytic *and* ethical notions. We are thus able to "stand in the spaces" between psychoanalysis and ethics, but we do so largely without explication or awareness. Our theories emphasize our patients' lack of agency, but we also recognize that our patients also play an active role in shaping their lives. While our theories emphasize exploration of unconscious meaning, we feel comfortable expressing our ideas and concerns about our patients' actions and choices in the real world. Even though our theories conceptualize motivation in primarily intrapsychic terms, we remain attuned to the self-oriented *and* altruistic dimensions of patients' subjectivity. Our theories say little about our patients' value as human beings, and yet we continue to treat them with respect and dignity, believing that, no matter how much they might be struggling, they deserve to lead lives that are meaningful and worthwhile.

Since we are always subsidizing our theories with our ethical commitments, we fail to notice how, at the explicit level, our theories do not necessarily reflect these commitments. Over time, without a professionally endorsed theory to hold us accountable, it becomes much easier to drift away from our natural ethical ideas. We can start to ignore patients' experiences of freedom and agency, instead seeing them as passive victims of their past circumstances and unconscious processes. We can overlook the role that their behavioral patterns might be playing in perpetuating damaging unconscious dynamics, and that alternative behaviors might play in generating new relational possibilities (Wachtel, 2014). We can also minimize the role of altruistic motivation in our patients' lives, tending to consciously frame their wishes and longings along more intrapsychic or "self-oriented" lines. And finally, we can forget the foundational role that *valuing our patients* should play in analytic work. Especially in moments of impasse, we can lose touch with our patients' unconditional worth and value, unconsciously relating to them primarily as vehicles for our own self-oriented motives (e.g., for self-esteem, power, material well-being).

Not surprisingly, all of these tendencies can have a damaging effect on the therapeutic relationship. As noted previously, most of us naturally associate the aforementioned ethical qualities (e.g., freedom, altruism, dignity) with what it means to be human. When we experience our patients as lacking these qualities, we can draw an overly sharp distinction between ourselves as human beings and our patients as human beings. This can lead us to feel less connected to our patients, and, in more extreme cases, even to develop a destructive feeling of superiority over them, as if we are the "healthy" ones in the relationship and that they are lacking, flawed, or deficient in some fundamental way. Insidiously, these attitudes can persist alongside genuine feelings of care and concern for our patients, and they can be unconsciously communicated regardless of our degree of awareness of them.

In the upcoming chapters, I elaborate a model of *ethical psychoanalysis*, which seeks to bridge the gap between our reflexive ethical commitments and our professionally endorsed theories of psychoanalytic practice. By bridging this gap, we will gain access to a fuller range of our subjective states—those that we commonly regard as psychoanalytic (e.g., fantasies, daydreams, countertransference affects and desires), as well as those that historically have resided "outside" of psychoanalysis, such as our ethical judgments of our patients, and our ideas about how they should live. Rather than ignore or subjugate our ethical intuitions, we might further appreciate how these insights constitute analytic phenomena in and of themselves. This viewpoint could deepen our relationships with our patients, enabling us to retain contact with a broader range of their subjective experiences, and to feel more connected to them *as people* throughout the vicissitudes of clinical work. As I hope to illustrate, such a theory could also offer a more pragmatic therapeutic approach, further illuminating the practical utility of analytic thinking for analysts and non-analytic practitioners alike (Aron & Starr, 2013; Renik, 2006; Wachtel, 2014).

"Sorry to change the subject here, but I want to ask you a question that may seem a bit 'out of the blue' . . . Did anyone ever hit you when you were young?"

The impulse to hit Fred had still not diminished. Consciously, I was aware that this fantasy was likely related to some mutually constructed enactment that was emotionally meaningful for both of us. And yet I was starting to feel a little bit desperate, anxious to hear something from Fred to reassure me that this impulse was significantly related to something in *his* experience, and not just mine.

Surprisingly to me, Fred did not seem at all fazed by this question. His father, whom Fred had always described as emotionally distant and perpetually unimpressed with him, had only physically disciplined him on a handful of occasions. In these moments, no matter what he had done, Fred's father would never get angry with him. Even when he was hitting him with a belt, Fred felt like his father was keeping his distance from him—removed, disconnected, and just going through the motions.

Fred described his deep fears about "getting in trouble" when he was a child. He attended Catholic school, and the nuns would send home notes detailing his many transgressions. Fred shared about his intense anxiety bringing home these notes—an almost paralyzing sense of dread that his mother, the only nurturing presence in Fred's childhood, would not love him anymore. Disgusted by his badness, she would abandon him, surrendering him to his father for disinterested punishment.

This all struck me as quite important. Perhaps, I reflected optimistically, there was some strange sort of "corrective emotional experience" operating here. While his father showed him only coldness and apathy, my desire to strike Fred reflected my passionate investment in him, thus offering both of us a new opportunity for real, vibrant, even dangerous contact with one another.

Fred added, as if in response: "One thing is, I couldn't stand anyone slapping me in the face."

"Excuse me?"

"You can punch me in the face—fine. But don't slap me in the face."

Fred proceeded to share one of the most vivid memories from his childhood. Throughout elementary school, Fred had been mercilessly tormented by the school bully. One day on the crowded playground, the bully had tripped him, and Fred sprang to attack. A bloody brawl ensued, until one of the nuns arrived on the scene to break things up.

Blaming Fred for the altercation, the nun pulled Fred up by the collar. Holding him up in front of all the other students, she slapped him hard across the face. Fred was stunned. The nun had not even investigated the situation; she did not care that the bully had started it, that Fred was just defending himself. She had automatically assumed that Fred was solely responsible, that *he* was the bad one. Humiliated and enraged, Fred slapped her right back, hard across the face.

I began to experience an immense sense of relief. I did not fully understand what was happening, but as Fred shared about this early traumatic encounter, it felt like he was partially letting me off the hook. I was not simply an abusive control freak who wanted to beat up my patient. Rather, something important in Fred's psyche had found expression in me. I was being granted a front-row seat to Fred's early experiences of injustice—as the victim of that injustice (through my identification with the other people in Fred's life), but also as its perpetrator, as the nun who wanted to punish Fred, to slap him and humiliate him, for circumstances largely beyond his control.

At the same time, I could not surrender my responsibility for my aggressive impulses here. Like Fred, *I* had sprung to attack the bully who had tripped me. And, regardless of my theoretical exposition on the matter, I wanted to strike Fred now, to punish him and to make him change. As Freud (1925b) famously proposed in a chapter entitled "Moral Responsibility for the Content of Dreams":

> Obviously one must hold oneself responsible for the evil impulses of one's dreams. What else is one to do with them? Unless the content of the dream (rightly understood) is inspired by alien spirits, it is a part of my own being. … I shall perhaps learn that what I am disavowing not only "is" in me but sometimes "acts" from out of me as well.
>
> (p. 133)

As relational authors have increasingly emphasized, enactments require two willing participants, and thus, I would add, two *responsible* ones.

My desire to strike Fred had now fully subsided. We were approaching the end of the hour, and I looked forward to exploring all of these matters further in sessions to come.

And then, without warning, Fred continued. "My wife, she knew that I hated to be slapped."

I looked up. "Oh?"

"At the end of our marriage, when things were really bad, we got into a horrible argument, and she just started slapping me. But not just one time—over and over, over and over again. I was sitting in a chair in the middle of our bedroom. She just stood over me, and *for ten minutes*, she slapped me back and forth across the face. She wanted me to get mad at her, to get some reaction out of me. But I wouldn't give it to her, no matter how hard she tried. After ten minutes, she just got really tired and gave up. Within a few months, she had moved out of the house and filed for divorce. That was the end, that was really the end for me."

I felt like someone had knocked the wind out of me. This scene perfectly mirrored my fantasy of hitting Fred from earlier in the session —him remaining seated, not defending himself, while I stood over him and slapped him repeatedly in the face. While I had accepted the therapeutic relevance of my countertransference experiences in general (e.g., feelings of anger and frustration, a desire to punish Fred, even the impulse to hit him), it was the *specificity* of these scenes that felt disconcerting to me, as if something mystical or otherworldly were at work here.

Of course, the above material can be understood from a range of different perspectives. Rather than share my reflections now, I will return to my relationship with Fred throughout this book, in order to illustrate the model of ethical psychoanalysis I am proposing. My hope is that, by sharing more candidly about clinical and countertransference experiences that receive insufficient attention in our literature (e.g., our desire to influence and control our patients, our judgments about their behaviors, our self-oriented motives, our sense of self-worth and self-esteem in clinical practice), we will be better positioned to appreciate the genuinely ethical dimensions of analytic process and therapeutic change.

Notes

1 Chapters 1 and 6 contain material from the following paper, reused here by permission of Taylor & Francis, LLC: Drozek, R. P. (2018). Psychoanalysis as an ethical process: Ethical intersubjectivity and therapeutic action. *Psychoanalytic Dialogues, 28*, 538–556.

2 While some authors distinguish between "ethics" and "morality," I will follow the philosophical convention here and use the two terms interchangeably.

Chapter 2

A dialectical vision of psychoanalytic ethics

I have proposed that there currently exists something of a "dissociative gap" between our psychoanalytic theories and our everyday ethical commitments. In this chapter, I explore some of the assumptions about ethics that might have prevented us from fully appreciating the importance of ethical experience in clinical practice. Since analytic theorists rarely offer explicit or systematic discussions of these viewpoints, my task here will remain somewhat speculative. My hope is that the suppositions I highlight will "ring true" for the reader, and that they might provide something of an explanation for the absence of attention that ethics has received in the literature. I suggest that, by applying the construct of dialectics that has been compellingly advanced elsewhere in psychoanalysis, we arrive at a vision of ethics that is compatible with psychoanalytic thinking while remaining true to our natural ethical intuitions. Returning to my work with Fred, I try to illustrate what it might look like to apply an ethical frame to the therapeutic process.

Dialectical thinking in psychoanalysis

Among the wealth of innovations in contemporary psychoanalysis, few concepts have been as consequential as the notion of *dialectics*. I borrow the helpful definition of dialectics articulated by Aron and Starr (2013): "A dialectical relationship exists when there is a tension between two types of experience and yet neither can exist without the other, such that when one is figure, the other is ground, but together they comprise a whole" (p. 39). Along similar lines, Ogden (1994) poetically defines dialectical experience as

> a process in which opposing elements each create, preserve, and negate the other; each stands in a dynamic, ever-changing relationship to the other. Dialectical movement tends toward integrations that are never achieved. Each potential integration creates a new form of opposition characterized by its own distinct form of dialectical tension.
>
> (p. 14)

On these views, dialectical elements do not simply contradict each other; they *create each other* through that very act of contradiction. Take, for example, the often-cited polarity between freedom and determinism. Freedom can be understood as our experience of ourselves as a primary cause in our deliberations and actions, while determinism assumes that "the origin or source of our choices and actions [is not] 'in us' but in conditions, such as the decrees of fate, the foreordaining acts of God, or antecedent causes and laws, over which we had no control" (Kane, 2002a, p. 6; my brackets). From a dialectical perspective, this conception of freedom is actually partially defined by determinism—freedom is understood by what it is not, in this case determination by antecedent causes. Similarly, determinism is understood as the *absence* of the notion of a freely choosing subject. Each concept creates and sustains the other—we cannot even think about one idea without, at least implicitly, invoking and negating the other.

These ideas can also be framed in terms of *paradox*, which Paul L. Russell (1973) defines as "something which the *coherency and constancy of the entire rest of the system requires to be both true and not true; a contradiction from which there is no escape without the destruction of the system*" (p. 69). Pizer (1998) elaborates on this construct further:

> Paradox resides in the multiplicity of bounded nuclei within the self, where simultaneously coexisting nuclei (self-states, affects, self–other representations, and so on) reciprocally contradict or negate each other. . . . Paradox cannot be resolved; mutually negating elements continue to coexist, and the negotiating of paradox yields not resolution but a straddling, or bridging, of contradictory perspectives.
>
> (p. 65)

Influenced by Winnicott's work, many contemporary theorists emphasize the value of *preserving rather than collapsing* the tension between dialectically constituted elements (Benjamin, 1995; Ghent, 1992). Along these lines, Winnicott (1971) famously writes:

> My contribution is to ask for a paradox to be accepted and tolerated and respected, and for it not to be resolved. By flight to split-off intellectual functioning, it is possible to resolve the paradox, but the price of this is the loss of the value of the paradox itself.
>
> (p. xvi)

More recently, Aron and Starr (2013) have applied the above ideas to further understand psychoanalytic theory itself. They explore the myriad of ways in which psychoanalysis has historically been characterized by binary thinking—the tendency to frame experience in terms of polarized dualisms (e.g., psychoanalysis versus psychotherapy, male versus female, autonomy versus relatedness, gentile versus Jew), where one term is valued and the other is demonized. Conversely, Aron and Starr advocate that we adopt a dialectical stance towards these binaries—first identifying them, then deconstructing them, and ultimately moving towards theories that maintain rather than collapse the tensions between these opposing terms.

I will be significantly guided by these insights in what follows, adding the few following considerations. First, given the popularity of dialectical thinking in psychoanalysis, it is easy to reify the idea, assuming that dialectics incontrovertibly *exist* between the elements at play. However, this approach fails to appreciate that dialectics is itself a theoretical construct that we use to organize our perceptions and experiences, and to guide clinical decision-making. When we accept the theoretically constituted nature of dialectics, we are called upon to employ the concept more self-consciously, with an eye towards what it means, how it functions, and its strengths and weaknesses in addressing the range of problems that we face in everyday analytic practice.

Second, as Stephen Mitchell (2000a) argued in one of his final papers, "Each writer applies dialectics in his or her own particular fashion" (p. 264). Some theorists employ dialectics to describe processes that exist in tension with one another, while others focus on processes that genuinely *contradict* one another. Many authors examine dialectics between *experiences* (e.g., aloneness versus connectedness, recognition versus assertion, Self versus Other), others consider similar tensions between *concepts* (e.g., intrapsychic versus interpersonal, drives versus relationality, objectivity versus subjectivity), and still others emphasize dialectics between *behaviors or techniques* (e.g., exploration versus suggestion, discipline versus spontaneity). While I support this broad and flexible application of dialectics, I think that we could do a better job at specifying how we are using the term, and in defining the specific processes purportedly involved in such dialectics. In addition to decreasing confusion about dialectics, this would allow us to have a deeper understanding of the processes in question.

Finally, I worry that, in recent years, we have become somewhat indiscriminate in our application of dialectical thinking. Mitchell (2000a) shared in that same paper, "I am a bit wary of paradox being elevated to a sure-fire method for dealing with contradictions. Sometimes contradictions are not worth sustaining but are better off resolved. Sometimes choices are usefully made" (p. 266). It often feels like we are presuming that dialectics are the solution to every major clinical and theoretical problem in psychoanalysis, an assumption that can inadvertently stifle creativity and lead to complacency in theorizing. In contrast with this approach, I suggest that we devote greater attention to the advantages and disadvantages of dialectics in addressing the particular problems we face in therapeutic work. In my view, part of what makes the idea of dialectics so compelling is that it allows us to access a fuller range of our experiences as human beings, and to resolve conceptual dilemmas that have plagued psychoanalysis throughout its history. As I hope to show here, by developing a dialectical vision of psychoanalytic ethics, we are able to respond to the range of objections against ethical thinking in psychoanalysis, and to move towards a therapeutic model that remains in closer contact with our everyday ethical intuitions.

Assumption #1: Ethics concerns primarily behavior, not subjective experience

It is commonly assumed that ethics involves mainly *behavioral* experience—what we do and "how we should live," considered from a moral perspective. In the Western religious tradition, we see this assumption in the Ten Commandments, which enumerate the various actions that "thou shalt" and "shalt not" take in the eyes of God. In secular moral life, we tend to frame ethics in behavioral terms as well: we are obligated to refrain from taking actions that violate the rights of others (e.g., lying, cheating, stealing), and to adopt behavioral approaches (e.g., kindness, generosity, compassion) that actively promote the dignity and well-being of other people. This outlook is also reflected in the Codes of Ethics for both the International and American Psychoanalytic Associations, which outline "expected conduct" and "constraints on behaviors" that should guide us in clinical practice.

On this view, ethics and psychoanalysis are concerned with dramatically different domains. Psychoanalysis focuses on issues of *meaning*, on the conscious and unconscious dimensions of our subjective worlds, not simply on behavioral conformity to some pre-determined system of ethics or morals. It is difficult to see what this behavioral vision of ethics could really offer to a psychoanalytic understanding of the human person. To take this even further, ethics may appear to contradict certain analytic ideals. Historically, psychoanalysis has ascribed a great value to respecting the basic autonomy of the patient, emphasizing an *exploration* of meaning rather than an *imposition* of meaning. Freud (1923c) writes:

> The analyst respects the patient's individuality and does not seek to remould him in accordance with his own—that is, according to the physician's—personal ideals; he is glad to avoid giving advice and instead to arouse the patient's power of initiative.
>
> (p. 251)

To the degree that ethics entails modifying an individual's behavior in accordance with pre-determined principles, ethics could problematically undermine the autonomy of the patient and thus violate a foundational tenet of the psychoanalytic method.

This behavioral conception constitutes an arbitrarily narrow perspective on ethical experience. When we think about ethics in everyday life, we are not simply concerned with others' actions; we are interested in the *reasons* why they take those actions. As Kant (1785/1997) argues, "When moral worth is at issue, what counts is not actions, which one sees, but those inner principles of actions that one does not see" (pp. 19–20). Take the example of someone rushing into a burning building, placing her life at risk to save the child trapped inside. At first glance, most of us would see this as an ethically commendable action. However, if we were to learn afterwards that the rescuer had done this only because she wanted to receive a large cash reward, it would be difficult for us to ascribe the same moral value to the action. In colloquial terms, we do not simply want people to "do the right thing"—we want to them to do the right thing *for the right reasons*.

This brings us directly to the topic of motivation, one of the most widely discussed matters in contemporary moral philosophy. In this book, rather than conceptualize ethics in strictly behavioral terms, I consider ethical experience as involving *the dialectic between behavior and motivation*, encompassing the dynamic and reciprocal connection between the moral worth of our actions and the moral worth of our motives. If we collapse this dialectic and focus only on behavior, then we are left with a superficial and "exterior" conception of ethics that ignores the subjective world of the moral agent, including her desires, emotions, attitudes, and character. On the other hand, if we attend only to the person's subjective processes, then we are less attentive to the ways in which those processes find expression in her actual relationships with others, including how she treats other people and the impact she might be having on their lives.

On this conception, ethics and psychoanalysis have significant areas of overlap. In recent decades, analytic thinkers have increasingly acknowledged the importance of behavior change in clinical technique (Hoffman, 1998; Mitchell, 2001; Wachtel, 1997), expanding the reach of psychoanalysis into behavioral and motivational domains. A dialectical ethics could illuminate the behavioral *and* motivational facets of our ethical lives (e.g., altruism, selfishness, free will, moral character, the link between ethics and human flourishing), while psychoanalysis might utilize its models of subjective experience, along with its intersubjective method of *deepening* that experience, to further illustrate the nature and development of ethical process.

Assumption #2: Ethics involves conscious experience, not unconscious process

We regularly assume that ethics concerns mainly our conscious ideas about right and wrong—what we "should" and "should not" do in our lives. We see this in our everyday understanding of moral deliberation, where the person consciously reflects upon what action she should take compared to alternatives, weighing the considerations for and against different courses of action. This view of consciousness is also present in our ethically relevant notions of *values and ideals*, the deep and guiding principles of our lives, which we usually see as accessible to conscious awareness, and as related to conscious faculties like language, cognition, and rationality.

Conceived in this way, ethics and psychoanalysis concern drastically different modes of experience. Despite the wide variation across specific models, psychoanalysis tends to be interested in *unconscious patterns of meaning* (Mitchell, 1993)—fantasies, wishes, unformulated experience, dissociated self-states and affects, internalized relational configurations —not simply our conscious beliefs about "right and wrong." Once we recognize the pervasiveness and power of unconscious motivation, it becomes difficult to take any ethical phenomenon at face value. That is, we naturally conceptualize ethics as *an expression or derivative* of our preferred model of unconscious process. Ethics thus starts to feel a bit one-sided and superficial, especially compared to the rich and nuanced theories of unconscious meaning at our disposal in psychoanalysis.

By contrast, I assume that ethics involves *the dialectic between consciousness and unconsciousness*. Especially if we conceptualize ethics as encompassing motivation as well as behavior, it seems unnecessarily arbitrary to insist that moral motivation is exclusively conscious. Rather, we might imagine that ethical experience encompasses the full range of moral motives, emotions, attitudes, and values extending across conscious *and* unconscious dimensions, with each dimension reciprocally influencing the other. What this actually looks like, of course, remains an open question. This dialectical vision of ethics is widely represented within analytic philosophy, including in models of non-cognitivism/expressivism, which hold that ethical judgments primarily reflect our non-rational attitudes and emotional states (Ayer, 1936; Gibbard, 1990; Stevenson, 1944); contemporary Kantian theories (Herman, 1993; Korsgaard, 1996a; Wood, 1999), which tend to support Kant's (2012) perspective that "the human being has by nature a propensity to dissemble" (p. 329); and the ethical approach known as *virtue ethics*, which construes morality in terms of the agent's personal virtues or character (Besser-Jones & Slote, 2015), which by its very nature is never fully accessible to consciousness.

The above dialectical conception opens up the possibility for a closer connection between ethics and psychoanalytic thought. As contemporary theorists have begun to appreciate the role of conscious experience in clinical process (Bateman & Fonagy, 2016; Renik, 2006; D. B. Stern, 2015; Wachtel, 1997), psychoanalysis is better situated to utilize the diverse insights of philosophical ethics. Ethics could further describe the conscious *and* unconscious expressions of moral experience, while psychoanalysis could contextualize the fundamental nature of that experience—its developmental and historical antecedents, its relational context, its significance in intersubjective process, and the association between ethical motivation and the non-ethical dimensions of the human personality.

Assumption #3: Ethics focuses excessively on the needs and interests of other people

Ethics, almost by definition, has historically emphasized the role of *other people* in our moral lives. We see this in traditional notions of altruism—our ability to be motivated by the subjectivity of others, and to act in accordance with such motivation. Ethical theories themselves tend to focus on the nature of our obligations towards others, outlining the content of such obligations and hypothesizing about their moral and psychological bases. This is particularly evident in the ethical theory known as "utilitarianism" or "consequentialism," which holds that the moral worth of an action depends on that action's *consequences*, including the amount of pleasure or pain it produces. As philosophers have long recognized (Brink, 2006; Hooker, 2000b; Scheffler, 1982, 1992; Williams, 1973, 1981), such a model constitutes a demanding and highly imbalanced conception of ethics, where the well-being of other parties can significantly outweigh the agent's own desires, needs, and projects. Kagan (1989) observes, "Given the parameters of the actual world, there is no question that [maximally] promoting the good would require a life of hardship, self-denial, and austerity" (p. 360; my brackets).

From this perspective, an ethical frame of reference seems antithetical to analytic work. Psychoanalysis aims at enhancing the patient's sense of well-being, not simply molding her to promote the well-being of others. Historically, psychoanalysis has been rightly skeptical of ethical commands, since these principles can perpetuate problematic tendencies towards masochism, self-negation, and self-hatred. Freud (1925a) maintains that society "has set up a high ideal of morality—morality being restriction of the instincts—and insists that all its members shall fulfil that ideal without troubling itself with the possibility that obedience may bear heavily upon the individual" (p. 219). More recently, in arguing against my theory of psychoanalytic altruism (Drozek, 2010b), Teicholz (2010) reminds us, "There can be 'pathological' degrees of deference to others' feelings and wishes. Such deference in some contexts is no less troubling than an absence of recognition or a closing down against the other's subjectivity" (p. 576).

In contrast with these views, I suggest that we conceptualize ethics as involving *an optimal dialectical tension between Self and Other*. Ethics could thus encompass behavioral and psychological processes involving the dignity and well-being of *all* human subjects, including the moral agent herself. Any ethical approach that downplays the moral status of the agent would problematically minimize the agent's own internal experiences, thus collapsing this dialectic. This recognition has led to an increased interest within philosophy in the notion of obligations to *oneself*—the idea that we have a moral duty to treat ourselves with respect and dignity, and to develop meaningful aspects of our lives that may have no direct link to ethical matters (Crisp, 1992; Denis, 2001; Johnson, 2011; Quinn, 1993; Wood, 2009).

This vision of ethics seems far more consistent with psychoanalytic thought. Ethics could thus deepen our appreciation of not just the rights of others, but of what *we* deserve in our relationships with other people, and in our relationships with ourselves. And psychoanalysis could be uniquely well-suited to explain the *psychological basis* for this dialectic between Self and Other—illuminating how an overemphasis on the needs and desires of others can signify psychic vulnerabilities in oneself, and how an overemphasis on one's own needs and desires can foreclose the potential for intimate, mutual relatedness between equal subjects (Benjamin, 1988, 1995). Perhaps most importantly, unlike philosophical ethics, psychoanalysis could offer a collaborative method for helping us to achieve and maintain an *experiential* dialectic between Self and Other, in which we are able to simultaneously access (and be motivated by) our subjectivity as well as the internal world of another person. For many patients, this might constitute genuinely new ethical terrain, where they are able to experience, often for the first time, a relationship in which they do not have to "choose" between sacrificing themselves and sacrificing the Other (see Chapter 7).

Assumption #4: Ethics is predicated on the assumption of free will

Within philosophy and without, it is commonly assumed that ethical injunctions presuppose the notion of *freedom*. We hear this connection in the axiom "ought implies can"—we judge that someone "should" take a certain action only if we believe that she is *able* to do the thing in question. According to Kant (1793/1998), "If the moral law commands that we *ought* to be better human beings now, it inescapably follows that we must be *capable* of being better human beings" (p. 70). In contemporary philosophy, this idea presents itself in the Principle of Alternative Possibilities, which holds that "a person is morally responsible for what he has done only if he could have done otherwise" (Frankfurt, 1988, p. 1).

Along similar lines, philosophers argue that some of our most common emotional states (e.g., gratitude, resentment, admiration) are predicated on the concept of freedom (P. Russell, 1995; Strawson, 1974; Wallace, 1994). For example, if I feel resentful at someone for saying something unkind to me, in the heat of the moment, I am usually assuming that the person was free to take another course of action. Correlatively, if I believe that someone is naturally *not* capable of free choice (e.g., in the case of certain forms of psychosis, catatonia, or intellectual disability), it becomes difficult for me to hold that party *responsible* for the unkindness (Van Inwagen, 1983). As Thomas Nagel (1986) observes, "We cease to resent what someone has done if we cease to see the alternatives as alternatives for him" (p. 125).

Psychoanalysis, however, has long problematized the notion of freedom. Freud (1919b) famously announced "the illusion of Free Will" (p. 236), declaring that "psycho-analysts are marked by a particularly strict belief in the determination of mental life" (1910a, p. 38). But such determinism is not relegated to classical thinking. More recently, the prominent relational theorist Steven Cooper (2010) has affirmed, "Freedom is, of course, an illusion. Psychoanalysis is such a radically bold and ultimately indigestible idea because it shows us how understanding this clinical 'fact' is about as close to freedom as we are going to get" (p. 129).

Seen in this light, psychoanalysis and ethics are based on contradictory premises. As the philosopher John Riker (1997) explains, the assumption of a dynamic unconscious necessarily undermines our conscious experience of freedom:

> With the discovery of the unconscious, we found that humans cannot be masters of themselves, for they are thoroughly entangled in economic, conceptual, linguistic, and emotional webs which their cultures and childhood histories weave around and through them. Insofar as ethics proclaimed the possibility that we could be masters of our destinies, it perpetrated an illusion—a crucial illusion, a powerful illusion, an illusion on which the West was built, but an illusion, nonetheless. This illusion made us too responsible, for it held that all humans have control over their own personal destinies and can be anything they want to be, and, therefore, have no reason not to be morally ideal.
>
> (p. 101)

By naively assuming the possibility of freedom, ethics ignores the extent to which we are determined by factors beyond our immediate control—our histories, our unconscious processes, and the relational contexts in which we are inescapably embedded.

In contrast with these views, I presume that ethics encompasses *the irresolvable dialectic between freedom and determinism*. We do have an experience of ourselves as free and undetermined, whether that involves the "big questions" of human existence (e.g., what to do for work, how to conduct ourselves in our relationships, how to raise our children), or the more mundane decisions we face on a daily basis, such as whether to wash the dishes now or wait until after dessert. This awareness leads to a sense of responsibility in our lives—how we behave, what we make of ourselves, and to some degree, the consequences of our actions. And yet, upon reflection, it is impossible to ignore the range of factors (e.g., emotional, historical, social, cultural, unconscious) that influence and even *determine* us, a perspective that makes it difficult to feel like we are fully in charge of anything at all.

Rather than try to sort out which of these standpoints is "right" or "true," thus resolving this tension, I propose an ethical stance that holds the truth of both of these contradictory outlooks—leaving space for genuine freedom while recognizing the tragic impossibility of such freedom (Mitchell, 1988, chapter 9). This dialectical approach overlaps with important currents in contemporary philosophy, such as the position known as compatibilism, which attempts to show how *both* freedom and determinism can be true (H. Bok, 1998; Dennett, 1984; Watson, 2004; Wolf, 1990), as well as constructs of libertarian free will, which recognize the inherent contradiction between determinism and freedom, while supporting the idea that some actions and choices can be genuinely free (Ginet, 1990; Kane, 1996, 2002b; O'Connor, 2000).

On this model, psychoanalysis and ethics have significant areas of productive convergence. Especially as relational authors have devoted increased attention to issues of agency and freedom (Fonagy, Gergely, Jurist, & Target, 2002; Frie, 2008; Gentile, 2010; Rustin, 1997; Slavin, 2010; Weisel-Barth, 2009), psychoanalysis has become better situated to utilize the insights of philosophy on the nature and phenomenology of choice. Ethics could thus further reveal something about the experience of freedom, the impact of that freedom on our sense of identity, and the possible connection between free will and morality. Psychoanalysis, however, could help to elucidate the nature of pathological compulsion, the impact of development on the growth of our agentic capacities, and therapeutic techniques for helping people achieve an increased sense of agency and meaning in their lives.

Assumption #5: Ethics involves objective and universal formulations about human experience

In everyday life, we frequently assume that ethics involves *objective rules and principles* about our moral lives. Empirical research suggests that "individuals tend to regard ethical statements as clearly more objective than social conventions and tastes, and almost as objective as scientific facts" (Goodwin & Darley, 2008, p. 1339; see also Nichols & Folds-Bennett, 2003; Nucci, 2001; Nucci & Turiel, 1978). As the philosopher James Rachels (1998) illustrates, this idea of objectivity is deeply infused in the phenomenology of ethical experience:

> When we judge something to be good or bad, we do not understand ourselves merely to be venting our emotions—if we wanted to do that, we could just say that we like it or dislike it. Nor do we understand ourselves merely to be applying the standards of our society—after all, we know that our society's standards could be misguided. Instead, we mean to be saying something that is objectively true, independently of our feelings and social conventions. One way of expressing our ordinary understanding is to say we assume there are moral facts.
>
> (p. 2)

So if I happen to believe that "Murder is wrong," I usually do not assume it is simply wrong *for me* to murder someone; I tend to think that murder is wrong *in general*, regardless of the person doing it. R. M. Hare (1963) argued that this is an essential feature of ethical thinking, which he saw as both *prescriptive* and *universal*, applying to all people under identical morally relevant circumstances. This is particularly evident in ethical theories themselves, which tend to focus on universal principles that justify our more specific moral intuitions (Williams, 1981, 1985).

In light of these observations, psychoanalysis and ethics seem to endorse contradictory epistemologies. As discussed in Chapter 1, contemporary analysts have largely rejected the notion of objectivity, instead advancing a postmodern epistemology embracing perspectivism, constructivism, and the irreducible role of the analyst's subjectivity in generating analytic knowledge (Aron, 1996a; Hoffman, 1998; Mitchell, 1993; Renik, 1993). This shift has equalized the balance of knowledge and power between analyst and analysand, resulting in a model of clinical process more consistent with the patient's dignity (see Drozek, 2015b). Ethics could appear to undermine these epistemological gains, threatening the contemporary emphasis on egalitarianism, collaboration, and humility on the part of the analyst. Along these lines, Weisel-Barth (2015) has recently taken issue with my proposal that we naturally assume that our patients are worthwhile, on the grounds that this viewpoint is "essentialist" and "objectivist": "I don't ... believe that all people are 'worthy' in the concrete, objective sense" (p. 465).

In contrast with this objectivist approach, I maintain that ethics includes the dynamic and reciprocal dialectic between objective *and* subjective formulations about moral value. Here, we would acknowledge the irreducible role that our subjective values play in structuring our ethical lives, including our experience of values we automatically see as "objective." At the same time, we would recognize the impact that these objective values play in shaping our internal worlds, never losing sight of the possibility that, while some of our values *might* be objectively true, we could never verify such a thing from any impartial standpoint. Whenever we negate either of these perspectives (e.g., by definitively affirming the objective status of some value, or by categorically proclaiming the subjective nature of all values), we collapse this antinomy and minimize an essential dimension of ethical experience.

This dialectical vision parallels several developments in contemporary philosophy, including the theory known as moral particularism, which eschews absolute moral principles and embraces the contextuality and variability of ethical conduct (Dancy, 2004; Hooker & Little, 2000); "mixed" models of moral relativism, which recognize relativistic dimensions of moral practices while highlighting notable similarities among these practices across cultures (S. Bok, 1995; Copp, 1995; Donnelly, 2013); and recent normative ethical approaches like feminist ethics and care ethics, which deemphasize some objective processes (e.g., rationality, impartiality) while reconceptualizing ethics in terms of intersubjective capacities for empathy and care (Jaggar, 2000; Held, 2006; Noddings, 2013; Stohr, 2015).

Understood in this way, psychoanalysis and ethics might be able to have a mutually beneficial relationship with one another. By rejecting "radical relativism" and acknowledging that there are objective constraints on our clinical formulations, relational constructivists are acknowledging that psychoanalytic knowledge contains *both* subjective and objective elements (Aron, 1996a; Hoffman, 1998; D. B. Stern, 1992). Ethics could thus offer insights into the possibly objective dimensions of our moral lives, including the notion of universal human rights, the nature and content of moral motivation, and hypotheses about the *source* of ethical experience (e.g., rationality, the phenomenology of freedom, the reflective structure of consciousness, social embeddedness, "moral intuition," feelings of pleasure and pain in ourselves and others). Psychoanalysis, on the other hand, could bring its expertise in subjectivity to these arenas, clarifying the role of subjectivity in shaping our objectively formulated values, as well as the impact of relational domains (e.g., familial, cultural, therapeutic) on our internalization and enactment of purportedly "objective" values and principles.

Assumption #6: Ethics results in an overly restrictive vision of psychological health

Thus far, we have reviewed psychoanalytic objections to ethics in general, especially concerning ethical theory's suppositions about the nature of mind, motivation, and knowledge. But when we apply the ethical frame of reference to the analytic process itself, a whole new class of objections emerges, centering on the idea that a primarily ethical perspective seems dramatically inappropriate for clinical practice. Consider the proposal, as I will argue in this book, that therapeutic action centers on the expanded development of the patient's ethical capacities. This seems to imply the assumption of *health as moral goodness*, in which ethical experience serves as a necessary condition for psychological health. From this standpoint, however we happen to conceptualize ethics (e.g., the ability to maximally promote others' well-being, the capacity to treat other people as ends-in-themselves, the possession of a virtuous character) sets the standard for what qualifies as "healthy" or "psychologically well."

The approach that has expounded this position most extensively is the branch of philosophy known as *virtue ethics*, which conceptualizes ethics in terms of the agent's character, personality, and motivational capacities. Theories of virtue have a long and distinguished tradition in the history of both Eastern and Western thought, including the writings of Plato, Aristotle, Confucius, Xunzi, Saint Augustine, and Thomas

Aquinas (see Besser-Jones & Slote, 2015). In fact, prior to the advent of psychology and psychoanalysis in the late nineteenth century, virtue ethics stood as the most sustained attempt to tackle questions about the nature of human well-being. Many such models center on the ancient notion of *eudaimonia*, understood as "happiness, flourishing, or a good human life" (Van Zyl, 2015, p. 183). A central tenet of virtue ethics is that flourishing is dependent on ethical virtues (e.g., honesty, generosity, the capacity for empathy and care), such that the possession of such virtues helps to facilitate the person's own sense of well-being, and that the absence of these virtues leads to increased suffering for the agent herself.

In recent years, philosophers have devoted increased attention to the relationship between virtue ethics and psychotherapy (Radden & Sadler, 2010; Riker, 1997; Waring, 2016). The philosopher Edward Harcourt (2015) has argued that psychoanalysis, and relational theory in particular, can be seen as a continuation of ancient philosophy's focus on human flourishing. Besser-Jones (2014) has utilized empirical research within psychology to elaborate an innovative model of virtue ethics, in which virtue—"understood to consist in engaging in positive social interaction marked by a mutual level of caring and respect—is the most promising route to the development of eudaimonic well-being" (p. 95).

Despite these natural connections between psychoanalysis and virtue ethics, considered from an analytic viewpoint, an ethical interpretation of health might feel unnecessarily narrow, arbitrarily collapsing the wide range of eudaimonic experiences into an exclusively moral frame. It seems to leave insufficient space for the unique needs and potentials of specific patients, thereby undermining the contemporary commitment to uniqueness, creativity, and individuality in the therapeutic encounter (Bacal, 2011; Foehl, 2010; Tublin, 2011). Furthermore, this ethical vision can lead to an overly formulaic conception of psychoanalysis. If all clinical work results in the same singular outcome (i.e., expanded ethical capacities), then the analytic process becomes essentially linear and pre-determined, a depiction that undercuts our current understanding of psychoanalysis as non-linear, "messy," and inherently unpredictable (BCPSG, 2010; Coburn, 2002; Seligman, 2005).

These objections presume that ethics is primarily a *content-related* field of inquiry—that it involves determinate factors (e.g., specific behaviors, particular circumstances in the world, traits of character, moral guidelines or principles) possessing either positive or negative moral value. When applying this content-related ethical model to psychoanalysis, the hypothesized content of ethical experience sets an objective standard for health and well-being. It is this assumption—that ethics has definitive, largely inflexible content—that has perhaps most hindered us from recognizing the utility of ethics in everyday clinical practice.

By contrast, I assume that ethics encompasses the dynamic, bi-directional dialectic between *content* and *process*. By process, I mean *the moral agent's complex motivational investments in herself and others, real or internal.* On this model, the content of our ethical beliefs significantly structures the nature of our motivational investment in our relationships, while these investments, reciprocally influenced by (largely implicit) intersubjective dynamics unfolding between Self and Other, extensively structure the content of our ethical beliefs.

To express this idea more colloquially: ethics does not simply concern "what" we value—it also concerns *how* we value, and each dimension of ethical experience reciprocally shapes and constitutes the other. We cannot even think about "something we value" without simultaneously considering *how* we value that thing. Correlatively, we can never imagine "how we value" without considering the *what* that we are valuing.

These process-related observations overlap substantially with the focus of contemporary ethical theory, which illuminates the *form* rather than exclusively the content of ethical valuing. In addition to recognizing the foundational distinction between positive and negative value, philosophers have extensively examined the distinction between intrinsic versus extrinsic value (Bradley, 2006; Moore, 1912, 1922, 1959; Ross, 1930), conditional versus unconditional valuing (Kant, 1785/1997; Korsgaard, 1983), objective versus subjective values (Nagel, 1970), "agent-relative" versus "agent-neutral" values (Parfit, 1984), and internal versus external reasons for action (Williams, 1981).

This distinction between ethical content and ethical process parallels a widely accepted distinction within psychoanalysis, the distinction between *representation* and *motivation*. In psychoanalysis, we are not simply interested in the content of our patients' internalized representations of Self and Other—the "who, what, when, where" of their past and present relationships. We are curious about the nature of their motivational connection to these representations—the specific desires, needs, affects, and values expressing the unique quality of their subjective investment in their relationships. A picture of psychoanalytic experience ignoring either of these dimensions would be virtually unthinkable in clinical work.

If we accept the idea that ethics involves process as well as content, then our vision of psychological health need not be limited by some fixed conception of ethical goodness, that is, *what* we value. Rather, health could be a function of *how* we value, of dynamic movements in our motivational processes. The exact shape of health could thus be different for each person, or for the same person at different moments in time. However, the *trajectory* of health, its directionality, could have significant commonalities across subjects. Such a model would hopefully reflect the spirit of our everyday ethical experiences, while being flexible enough to encompass the diversity of movements we see in the therapeutic dyad. This is the perspective I will be developing in this book.

Assumption #7: Ethics can have offensive and dangerous clinical implications

We have considered some objections to the proposal that psychoanalysis centers on the patient's ethical advancement. But if we conceptualize health along ethical lines, then illness attains an ethical valence as well. This brings us to the notion of *pathology as moral deficiency.*

On this view, psychopathology would always involve some form of ethical impairment, implying that our patients could be morally compromised *as people* (e.g., struggling with aggressiveness, dishonesty, or self-centeredness), and thus that it might even be "their own fault" that they are suffering.

This conception of pathology appears highly problematic for analytic practice. It depicts our patients as morally inferior, locating all of the "moral authority" in the relationship in the healthy, well-analyzed analyst (Aron, 1996a). In addition to being demeaning and unkind, this position seems clinically dangerous. So many of our patients struggle with an exaggerated sense of responsibility and self-blame, and much of analysis involves helping patients to access and accept parts of themselves they had formerly dissociated and devalued. As Strachey (1934) observed long ago:

> The patient, having become aware of the lack of aggressiveness in the real external object, will be able to diminish his own aggressiveness; the new object which he introjects will be less aggressive, and consequently the aggressiveness of his super-ego will also be diminished.
>
> (p. 143)

An ethical psychoanalysis could thus seem *anti*-therapeutic, since it risks intensifying patients' sense of self-blame and self-hatred.

Interestingly, this line of objection presupposes a vision of ethics as involving a singular, unitary self. *Either* the person is morally compromised, *or* she is morally virtuous—there is no in-between. Conversely, I conceptualize ethics as encompassing *the dialectic between the individual subject and her multiple Selves*. We are able to conceptualize the human person from two broad perspectives—as a single metaphysical entity that persists across time, and as a series of self-states that remain in a state of constant fluctuation and evolution. Accordingly, we could never categorically conceptualize someone as either "good" or "bad," "virtuous" or "vile." Rather, we could think about ethical capacities along a continuum, where any given self-state (or aspect of the personality) could possess ethical value to a greater or lesser degree, expressing a wide range of ethical, non-ethical, and un-ethical elements. Since self-experience is always embedded in a relational context, ethics would remain a fundamentally contextual process, always developmentally constituted, and exquisitely sensitive to the interpersonal surround. At the same time, we would not lose sight of the fact that these self-states comprise the subjectivity of a *real moral agent*, with her attendant belief that *she* (not simply some part of herself) is fundamentally responsible for making choices that reflect the value she ascribes to herself and others.

This dialectical conception shares commonalities with important approaches within both psychoanalysis and contemporary philosophy. In recent years, philosophers have increasingly espoused theories affirming the idea that we can be single subjects with complex, multiply constituted identities (Braude, 1991; Radden, 1996, 2004, 2011; Rovane, 1998; Taylor, 1989). For our purposes here, particularly important is the work of the Kantian ethicist Christine Korsgaard (1996b), who proposes a complex notion of mind as consisting of multiple, overlapping "practical identities" (p. 101), including our identity as human beings *in general*, which gives rise to a sense of moral obligation as normally understood.

Within psychoanalysis, while multiplicity theories have been criticized for minimizing the role of the individual within human experience (Frederickson, 2009; Mills, 2005), my impression is that the most sophisticated of such theories describe mind as constituted by the dialectic between individuality and multiplicity (Bromberg, 1998, pp. 272–275; Davies, 1996, p. 564; Mitchell, 1993, pp. 114–117; D. B. Stern, 1997, pp. 153–156). After all, if health derives from the capacity to "stand in the spaces" between self-states, there must be a *someone* doing the standing. Mitchell (1993) explained helpfully:

> The portrayals of self as multiple and discontinuous and of self as integral, continuous, and separable seem to be at odds, mutually exclusive. They are not. People act both discontinuously and continuously; people organize their experience into both multiple and integral configurations. Any given piece of experience can be looked at and felt both in terms of a particular relational context, a particular self/other integration and, at the same time, in terms of a larger, variegated, singular process that forms itself into different patterns at different times.
>
> (p. 115)

Conceptualized in this way, an ethical psychoanalysis need not conclude that our patients suffer from some grand moral failing. Rather, we simply assume that, whenever we encounter an area of pathological psychological process (e.g., neurosis, compulsions, traumatic dissociation, self-hatred and low self-esteem, lack of meaning and purpose, impairments in capacities for intimacy and mutuality), there is some *unconscious ethical block or impairment* that is pathogenically implicated in the disturbance. This way of thinking says nothing categorical about our patients' ethical capacities *as people*, and so it need not intensify their self-judgments. Further, since it applies equally to ourselves as well as to patients, no party can claim "moral superiority" over the other. For all of us, clinicians as well as patients, our sense of responsibility is balanced by the recognition that ethical experience is always partial, discontinuous, temporary, and context-dependent.

Assumption #8: Ethics is not essentially relevant to everyday clinical practice

I have suggested that, by adopting a dialectical model of ethical process, we arrive at an understanding of ethics that is quite compatible with psychoanalytic thinking. But even if we grant this possibility, we might be left with the impression that ethics still does not sufficiently express what feels most foundational to clinical work. Andrew Harlem (2015) has advanced this position in arguing against my ethical portrayal of psychoanalysis: "A normative or ethical frame around inquiry, with its penchant for self-tightening, has the unpalatable consequence of constricting the ways we imagine the psychoanalytic subject" (p. 461). In addition to emphasizing an at-best peripheral vision of analytic meaning, the ethical approach appears to miss the most compelling aspects of therapeutic process, including issues of personal meaning, self-experience, and our sense of ourselves as subjects in collaborative, intimate contact with other meaning-making subjects. As Mitchell (1993) observed, within contemporary psychoanalysis, "the goal is not the establishment of a rational normality but the capacity to generate a sense of self and relationships felt as important, meaningful, and deeply one's own" (p. 37).

I take this to be perhaps the most powerful argument against an ethical psychoanalysis, one that cannot simply be addressed by invoking a dialectical viewpoint. The remainder of this book can be seen as a sustained attempt to answer this objection. However, even at the start of this inquiry, I do think a provisional response can be offered to support the foundational relevance of ethics to clinical practice. Framed in the broadest of terms, ethics is a fundamentally intersubjective endeavor, focusing on our capacity to be motivated by our subjectivities and the subjective lives of other people (Drozek, 2010b). It seems plausible that, when we are struggling with the sorts of difficulties that characterize pathological psychic process (e.g., neurotic suffering, traumatic dissociation, self-hatred, lack of meaning, difficulties with intimacy), we might also be impaired in our capacities to fully experience and be motivationally responsive to the subjective worlds of Self and Other. In other words, psychopathology might be associated with this particular form of ethical impairment.

It also sounds reasonable that psychoanalysis, conceptualized as an intersubjective method that attends to the conscious and unconscious dimensions of human subjectivity, enables us to be increasingly motivated by these internal domains. Under those conditions, we might be able to gain freedom from the aforementioned challenges—to achieve a greater sense of meaning, purpose, and agency in our lives; to "stand in the spaces" between different parts of ourselves; and to strengthen our capacity for intimacy, mutuality, and vitality in our relationships.

This is all to say that, considered from a certain perspective, *ethical change could actually constitute therapeutic change*, encompassing the full range of clinical phenomena we see in analytic practice. The task of an ethical psychoanalysis would be to articulate a model that encompasses these two broad standpoints, utilizing our basic assumptions about unconscious meaning and therapeutic process to shed light on this essential connection between psychoanalysis and ethics.

A dialectical model of moral worth

On the viewpoint I have been developing here, ethics is a fundamentally dialectical enterprise, encompassing a range of often-contradictory processes that cut across several dimensions of human experience:

- The dialectic between behavior and motivation
- The dialectic between consciousness and unconsciousness
- The dialectic between Self and Other
- The dialectic between freedom and determinism
- The dialectic between subjectivity and objectivity
- The dialectic between content and process
- The dialectic between individuality and multiplicity.

This formulation, while promising for psychoanalytic purposes, does not yet address the question of what *constitutes* moral worth and value.

This is where philosophy comes in. Within ethical theory, this debate has typically been waged between the approaches known as *consequentialism* and *deontology*. Consequentialism, also known as *utilitarianism*, frames moral worth primarily in terms of *human well-being*, variously understood "as pleasure, or as happiness, or as the satisfaction of desire, preferences, or interests" (Rawls, 2000, p. 222). Here, actions are morally "right" or "praiseworthy" to the extent that they contribute to overall personal well-being, or are consistent with some more general behavioral principle that, if followed, maximizes well-being (Bentham, 1776/1988; Hooker, 2000a; Mill, 1861/1979; Singer, 2011). In contrast with this theory, non-consequentialism, also known as *deontology*, "takes right action to be the primary evaluative notion; it recognizes various actions as obligatory, prohibited, or permitted on the basis of their intrinsic natures and independently of the value they produce" (Brink, 2006, p. 381; see Kamm, 2007; Kant, 1785/1997; Nagel, 1970, 1986; Quinn, 1993; Rawls, 1971; Ross, 1930).

In my view, the main strength of consequentialism is its ability to reflect the foundational importance of human well-being in our daily lives, as well as our powerful concern with the real *impact* that our actions have on the well-being of ourselves and others. Deontology, on the other hand, is able to express our sense that there are some actions that are categorically prohibited, even if taking them might result in "the greatest good for the greatest number." For example, many of us feel that, even if torturing a known terrorist might provide information that could save the lives of a dozen potential victims, such an action would still be morally prohibited, since it violates the basic rights of the terrorist herself.

If moral value does not derive strictly from pleasure or pain, what is its source? While different theorists answer this question in dramatically different ways, I will focus on one conception that I find particularly useful in analytic practice—the notion of human dignity, understood as *the intrinsic or unconditional worth of human beings*. This idea has been developed most extensively by Immanuel Kant, perhaps the most influential figure in deontological ethics. As discussed in Chapter 1, Kant (1785/1997) defines dignity as the "inner worth," or the "unconditional, incomparable worth," of human beings (p. 42). According to Kant, human beings

> are called *persons* because their nature already marks them out as an end in itself, that is, as something that may not be used merely as a means, and hence so far limits all choice (and is an object of respect). . . . The practical imperative will therefore be the following: *So act that you use humanity, whether in your own person or in the person of any other, always at the same time as an end, never merely as a means.*
>
> (pp. 37–38)

For Kant, dignity is closely related to the notion of *respect*. When we ascribe unconditional worth to another person, we naturally experience a sense of respect for her status as a separate, independent subject who has rights of her own, apart from our personal desires and agendas. This sets significant limits on how we are permitted to treat ourselves and others. Korsgaard (1996a) clarifies, "In the negative sense, to treat another as an end in itself is to respect her autonomy—to leave her actions, decisions, and ends to her own choice" (p. 193).

But this concept of dignity is not strictly prohibitive—it elucidates why the pleasure and pain of other people *matter* to us. According to Kant (1785/1997), we care about human well-being because we care about human beings *themselves*: "For, the ends of a subject who is an end in itself must as far as possible be also *my* ends, if that representation is to have its *full* effect in me" (p. 39). When we take others to have an unconditional or intrinsic value, we are naturally motivated by their internal states. Korsgaard (1996a) elaborates on this idea thus:

> It is because or to the extent that we regard one another as *persons* that we acknowledge the force of deontological reasons. As persons, others demand that we treat them in ways to which they can consent; as persons, we find we must respond to that demand. But we also express our respect for one another's humanity by sharing in each other's ends. As persons, we have a claim on one another's help when it can readily be given or is desperately needed. It is the status of humanity, as the source of normative claims, that is the source of all value.
>
> (p. 299)

In the history of ethics, much of the debate between deontologists and consequentialists can be seen as an attempt to reduce each form of moral value to the other. Consequentialism seeks to explain our diverse ethical intuitions in terms of well-being, while non-consequentialism explains these phenomena in terms of deontological factors (e.g., dignity, rights, respect for autonomy). However, when developing an ethical model for a dialectically informed psychoanalysis, we are under no philosophical pressure to arrive at one single, overarching source of all moral value. Rather, we might conceptualize ethics as involving *the dialectical tension between human well-being and human dignity.*

On this formulation, ethics involves our natural concern for the well-being of ourselves and others, with "well-being" encompassing the full range of eudaimonic experiences—health, happiness, pleasure, flourishing, and the satisfaction of people's needs, desires, and preferences. At the same time, ethics affirms the basic worth of all human beings, calling on us to express and validate that worth as much as possible, through our actions, choices, interpersonal patterns, and subjective lives. While philosophers have been right to observe that dignity and well-being exist in a state of irresolvable tension with one another, we might also recognize that there are important ways in which these processes *constitute* one another, for example, when the affirmation of the intrinsic worth of Self and Other serves as the most harmonious route to personal well-being and fulfillment. As I will suggest later (Chapters 4 and 6), I see this insight as one of the most important ethical contributions of the relational movement in psychoanalysis.

This dialectically constituted vision of moral value is highly consistent with our conventional assumptions in analytic practice, where we are always concerned with the impact of our choices on ourselves and our patients, while recognizing that "consequences" are not the only ethically relevant factor in our considerations—*our patients' rights matter as well.* In therapeutic work, there is frequently a natural, irresolvable tension between well-being and dignity—whether this be the tension between the patient's dignity and the well-being of entities outside the treatment (e.g., when the patient declines permission to publish clinical material that could benefit other patients struggling with similar difficulties) (Aron, 2016a); the opposition between the patient's well-being and the *clinician's* dignity (e.g., when the patient feels like she desperately needs something that violates the clinician's boundaries and values); and sometimes even the conflict between the patient's *own* well-being and dignity (e.g., when the patient pursues forms of relatedness that, while offering her emotional comfort, could simultaneously undermine her dignity and autonomy).

We also see this dialectic reflected in the ethical codes for both the American Psychoanalytic Association (APsaA) and the International Psychoanalytical Association (IPA). In emphasizing the ethical importance of overall professional competence, and by framing psychoanalysis as a method "to reduce suffering and disability and enhance growth and autonomy," the APsaA is promoting the essential ethical value of our patients' health and well-being. The APsaA also maintains that "the psychoanalytic relationship is predicated on respecting human dignity," outlining a range of practices (e.g., confidentiality, truthfulness, avoidance of exploitation and discrimination) that express a basic attitude of respect for patients and their families. Along similar lines, the IPA stresses the importance of continuous professional development and scientifically informed care, thus endorsing the value of patient well-being, while also affirming the necessity of deontological values such as basic human rights, informed consent, and not acting "in any way which is counter to the autonomy of the patient or former patient."

Clinical illustration

With this model in place, I will try to trace out some of the clinical implications of these ideas. Historically, ethics has found its way into analytic discourse under two sets of circumstances—in the therapeutic dyad, when considering behaviors therapists should *avoid* taking (e.g., lying to our patients, having sexual relationships with them) (Celenza, 2007; Dewald & Clark, 2001; Gabbard & Lester, 1995); and more generally, when exploring issues of social justice, politics, and equality from a psychoanalytic point of view (Layton, Hollander, & Gutwill, 2006; Samuels, 2016; Totton, 2000). While I strongly support these forms of inquiry, I am concerned with the fact that ethics receives so little attention in other areas of analytic thought, for example, in addressing the ethical capacities of clinicians themselves, or the moral dimensions of our patients' experiences. It would be a strange form of dissociation if ethics were relevant only when discussing "boundaries" and "social justice," but for some reason did not apply to the essential aspects of the therapeutic process itself.

Apart from some notable exceptions we will review in Chapter 6, our theories tend to unquestioningly operate under a particularly narrow and concrete notion of ethics—ethics becomes relevant only in overt cases of *injustice*, usually when some behavioral boundary is being violated, either by the moral subject or by an ethically culpable institution. As long as everyone is behaving, then ethics can comfortably remain on the back-burner. However, if we accept the dialectical vision of ethics I have developed here, ethics attains a much broader significance. For example, if we retain the natural tension between behavior and motivation, then ethics applies to all the invisible, ineffable dimensions of therapeutic work, even if analyst and patient are appropriately conducting themselves within prescribed moral boundaries. Furthermore, if we conceptualize ethics as existing along a continuum, then we are less interested in whether or not analyst and patient are doing something "right" or "wrong," and we start to become curious about *the ethical textures and subtleties* of their experiences, recognizing that such processes naturally co-exist with other (e.g., non-ethical, unethical) processes to generate the full complexity of clinical experience.

Returning to my patient Fred introduced last chapter, I want to explore what it might look like to approach the therapeutic relationship through an ethical frame. Specifically, I focus on *my own* ethical participation in that relationship. This is for the sake of clarity and simplicity, but also because I hope to argue for the foundational importance of the clinician's ethical self-reflection as an essential, and insufficiently appreciated, part of psychoanalytic praxis (Cooper, 2010). Throughout, I offer ethical *reflections* about this case, without attempting to draw any definitive conclusions. These deliberations will remain provisional and highly incomplete. For now, I will attend exclusively to issues of ethical meaning rather than analytic meaning, postponing a full consideration of therapeutic process (e.g., involving developmental history, unconscious dynamics, and the bi-directional intersubjective patterns unfolding between us) until later in the book.

When examining my ethical involvement in a piece of clinical work, I ask myself the following sorts of questions.

In what ways do my experiences affirm/contradict the patient's dignity?

Here, I am interested in the extent to which I am able to recognize and experience my patient as intrinsically worthwhile, as well as the extent to which, usually unconsciously and reflexively, I might be undermining that worth. When interacting with Fred, I believe I was often able to value him for "who he was," without consciously wanting to change him, or to alter his experience. Especially over time, I came to value him as a person, to care about him and to be dedicated to him, even as I struggled with feelings of frustration and discouragement about the therapy. I saw this in my overall sense of curiosity about his life and relationships, and in my desire to "know" and "understand" him, independently of the clinical consequences of such knowing. As is typical of many analytic therapies, I also believe that my "respect for his autonomy" significantly structured my manner of participating in our relationship—allowing his goals to direct the treatment, honoring his basic rights (e.g., to privacy, to non-exploitation), encouraging him to share about the topics that felt most meaningful to him, and in general, not trying to "control" his decisions, even if I sometimes disagreed with them and worried about their potentially negative impact on his life.

I also related to Fred in ways that undermined his dignity, for example when I valued him only *conditionally*. I could see this when I became quite emotionally attached to Fred behaving in particular ways. Along these lines, I would feel positively about Fred when he approached our sessions in a specific fashion (e.g., exhibiting an interest in his emotional life, displaying curiosity about his interpersonal tendencies), but especially as the therapy progressed, I could sometimes become frustrated and impatient when Fred enacted other behavioral modes (e.g., focusing extensively on people's defects, rebuffing my attempts to explore his emotional states). Leaving aside the transferential meaning of these patterns, from a strictly ethical standpoint, I believe that I was reflexively endowing Fred with conditional goodness and conditional badness in these moments—valuing him when he satisfied criteria that I automatically assumed were "productive" and "healthy," and ascribing badness to him when he displayed tendencies I saw as more detrimental.

Developing these ideas even further, I also undermined Fred's dignity when I ascribed negative value to him *as a person*. While I never formulated this experience consciously, at certain times in the therapy, I started to feel like there was something *essential* about Fred that was defective or problematic, that I wanted to destroy and obliterate. This, I believe, is what Winnicott (1958) was getting at with his notion of "hate in the countertransference," and this is where I found myself when I felt overwhelmed by the desire to strike Fred in the face—to humiliate and demean him, to affirm his badness for its own sake. These sorts of impulses have an important ethical *and* clinical meaning, which have applicability to psychoanalytic process beyond the unique circumstances of this specific example (see Chapters 6 and 7).

In what ways do my experiences enhance/undermine the patient's health and well-being?

In addition, I am curious about the extent to which I am committed to the health and well-being of my patient, as well as the ways in which I might be undermining that well-being, whether by my own selfishness or maliciousness, or more subtly, by my lack of responsiveness to the patient's subjectivity. For much of the time, I felt quite dedicated to promoting Fred's well-being. As the treatment unfolded, we came to see how Fred struggled with powerful feelings of self-loathing and self-hatred, along with a deep fear that he was unworthy of closeness with others, destined to be alone. Personally, I felt deeply invested in helping Fred with these matters. I wanted him to be relieved of these feelings—to gain a sense of himself as deserving of love and care from others, and to experience genuine closeness with other people, including me.

Behaviorally, this commitment showed itself in my general manner of treating Fred in our sessions—regularly with kindness, compassion, and empathy. I would attempt to see things from his perspective, so that he would feel nurtured and less alone, while also seeking to *validate* Fred, to help him feel like his emotions, desires, and behaviors were understandable and even reasonable, given his history. I also felt dedicated to helping Fred achieve his goals for his life—his desire to escape from homelessness, and to live independently; his longing to find a romantic relationship; and his wish to feel valued in some meaningful project, such as his volunteer work or the odd jobs he would periodically obtain. For me, being committed to Fred's well-being involved my interest in all of these factors, the "internal" and the "external," without ignoring either dimension of his experience.

At the same time, there were ways in which I was motivated *contrary* to Fred's well-being. This came out most clearly in the clinical example reviewed earlier, where there was some part of me that wanted to harm Fred physically, to make him feel some sort of pain. Upon further exploration, I came to identify my *punishing* desires towards Fred, which could sometimes arise in relation to aspects of Fred's personality, especially his challenges empathizing with others, and his tendency to treat his children quite cruelly. While there were many moments when I could experience these qualities with a relatively "neutral" form of curiosity, I also sometimes wanted to make Fred feel guilty and bad about *himself* for having them. Without expressing this verbally, I think these motives impacted my behavior most mostly through a sort of "punitive withdrawal" from Fred—at times, feeling less emotionally connected to him, treating him coldly, exhibiting impatience and mild irritation with him, and experiencing less curiosity in our sessions, less interest in seeing the world from his point of view.

There were also many ways in which, rather than acting contrary to Fred's well-being, I was simply *not responsive* to Fred's subjectivity. At any given moment in the therapy, I was deeply aware that Fred had a range of desires and needs that were largely unformulated and unexpressed, of which neither of us were fully aware, and so it was difficult for me to respond to them or deal with them clinically. Furthermore, while I had my various formulations about how to understand Fred's difficulties (more on that in upcoming chapters), as well as my instincts about how to address these, I never lost sight of the fact that I could never fully "know" what Fred might need from me at any particular time.

I also frequently *chose* not to satisfy Fred's desires. For example, while Fred was gradually able to give voice to his longing that I would "take his side" when we discussed his various interpersonal conflicts, I felt a vague but firm resistance to providing such agreement. While I never explicitly formulated these thoughts at the time, I think I was concerned that gratifying this desire could be at odds with Fred's longer-term well-being, foreclosing a deeper exploration of these patterns (e.g., in his interactions with others, in the transference) that offered the potential for lasting change in his life. I also worried that satisfying this desire could contradict Fred's dignity, implicitly colluding with the idea that Fred needed to be "in the right" in order to have worth and value, rather than helping him to gain access to a *less conditional* sense of self-esteem. Furthermore, since I often did not agree that Fred had been unfairly treated in these situations, satisfying this desire would have felt dishonest and inauthentic, and thus at odds with *my* dignity and integrity in the therapeutic relationship.

In what ways do my experiences affirm/undermine my own dignity?

I also reflect on the ways in which I am able to experience *myself* as unconditionally valuable in the therapy, as having a worth and value independent of my behavior or its consequences. For much of my work with Fred, I believe I had access to such a self-state, taking myself to be worthwhile, lovable, and worthy of closeness with others. In those moments, I did not feel like I had to "earn" my worth by behaving in specific ways—it felt somehow intrinsic to me. Relatedly, even when Fred would relate to me primarily as a vehicle to maintain his self-esteem (i.e., as having only conditional value), I still experienced myself as *deserving* to be treated well, to be valued unconditionally by Fred but also by people in general. Interestingly, when this "unconditionally valuable" self-state was especially prominent, I felt more able to value *Fred* unconditionally, in all of the ways outlined above.

I could also inhabit modes of being that contradicted my dignity, most notably when I started to feel quite concerned about my therapeutic "performance," or emotionally attached to Fred engaging in the process in the ways mentioned above. Along these lines, when I felt like my interventions (e.g., listening, internal reflection, empathic validation, interpretations) were particularly effective, or if it seemed as if Fred was responding positively to the therapy (e.g., when he accessed the more vulnerable dimensions of his personality in sessions), I would begin to feel a range of more "positive" emotions, including comfort, exhilaration, and even joy.

However, when I struggled with insecurities about my ability to help Fred, or if I felt like Fred was not improving in the ways I had hoped, I could encounter a range of more challenging emotions—frustration, self-doubt, impatience, discouragement, and even hopelessness. I believe I was unconsciously ascribing conditional goodness and conditional badness to myself at these times—valuing myself when I "performed well" as Fred's therapist, and ascribing badness to myself when I saw myself as failing in that role. These patterns, I believe, were directly related to my conditional valuing of Fred himself. When I valued myself only conditionally, I could only value Fred conditionally, since I needed him to operate along very specific lines in order to maintain my sense of self-esteem in the treatment.

Earlier I observed there were times when I ascribed badness to Fred as a person, as exemplified by my aggressive impulses towards him. As I see it, this process was directly related to a self-state in which I took *myself* to be bad, but not simply conditionally bad (which offers the possibility of redemption), but *intrinsically* bad—deficient, worthless, unfit for relatedness. While I was not conscious of this in the moment I wanted to hit Fred, I now see this dissociated self-state as the relational "fuel" for my aggressive impulse. Unconsciously regarding Fred as the willful impediment to my self-esteem, I was left with proof of my badness, an experience that stands in direct contradiction with my value as a human being. From the viewpoint of *that* experience, dignity is an illusion, a charade. Rather than endure this unbearable feeling of badness, I projected it onto Fred, thus providing me with a temporary respite from my own worthlessness.

On this view, my "ethical violation" of Fred derived directly from my ethical violation of *myself*. As I will argue later (Chapter 6), I see this mutual ethical violation as the essential ingredient in therapeutic impasse, the "doer" versus "done to" dynamic that has received so much attention in our literature (Benjamin, 2004). *Either* I am bad *or* you are bad, and both of us are desperately engaged in an intersubjective, ethical arms race in order to displace the "burden of the badness" onto the other party (Fairbairn, 1952). For now, it is sufficient to note that my (unconscious) ethical violation of Fred was directly related to my (unconscious) ethical violation of myself.

In what ways do my experiences enhance/undermine my own well-being?

And finally, I consider how this particular therapeutic relationship both enhances and diminishes my personal well-being. In my relationship with Fred, this well-being was strengthened in various ways. In general, I felt highly fulfilled in the work, especially as Fred began to encounter significant improvements in his life—an increased sense of value and self-worth, an expanded ability to access his more vulnerable emotions, closer connections with his children, and achievement of his more concrete goals, such as living in his own apartment for the first time in decades. I also had the impression that Fred really needed me, that I was serving a unique and meaningful role in his life, which in turn made *me* feel important, bolstering my experience of personal value. More concretely, while Fred himself was not paying for the therapy (I was paid by my institution to see him), the therapy was partially contributing to my *material* well-being and all this entails—my home and possessions, the food that I eat, the health of my wife and children, and the self-esteem I derive from helping to "provide for" my family.

There were many ways in which the therapy also detracted from my well-being. In addition to all of the difficult emotions already identified (e.g., frustration, anxiety, discouragement), I was aware of a very limited sense of mutuality in the dyad. At the moment in our treatment discussed earlier, I believe that Fred was interested in using only aspects of my subjectivity, specifically the parts of me facilitating his need to be admired and validated. This meant that there were aspects of myself (e.g., my interest in emotional exploration), and certain modes of relatedness that I deeply valued (e.g., flexibility, mutuality, playfulness), that were unable to be actualized in my interactions with Fred, which naturally set some limits on my well-being and fulfillment in the therapy.

Conclusion: The irreducible responsibility of the analyst

Considered from a psychoanalytic perspective, many of the above experiences might seem highly inappropriate for clinical work. As Bion (2013) famously argued, the analyst should approach each treatment without "memory and desire":

> Desires interfere, by absence of mind when observation is essential, with the operation of judgment. Desires distort judgment by selection and suppression of material to be judged. . . . The psychoanalyst can start by avoiding any desires for the approaching end of the session (or week, or term). Desires for results, "cure" or even understanding must not be allowed to proliferate.
>
> (pp. 136–137)

So much of what I have written above concerns my *desires* in my relationship with Fred—for him to behave in a certain way in sessions, for him to "get better," for his external environment to improve, for *me* to maintain a sense of self-worth in the treatment. Such desires sound problematically similar to what has been called "therapeutic zeal" or unanalyzed countertransference, expressing a stance that, as Weisel-Barth (2015) suggests, is too "judgmental" or controlling for psychoanalysis. They also emphasize *my* subjectivity over the patient's, thus potentially inhibiting a range of processes that seem essential to analytic practice—analytic listening, empathic attunement, open-minded exploration, affective sharing, and respect for the patient's autonomy. This can lead to the sort of countertransference enactments that opened this book, where therapists want to beat up their patients.

These concerns assume that it is possible for the analyst to *not* become invested in changing the patient in specific ways. While psychoanalysis has come a long way towards accepting the "irreducible subjectivity of the analyst" (Renik, 1993), I still think we are laboring under an implicit model of what "should" comprise that subjectivity—namely, an open-minded interest in exploration, and definitely *not* a desire to change or direct our patients in prescribed ways.

As I hope to illustrate in this book, I believe that these sorts of desires and investments are not only consistent with analytic exploration—appreciating these things more fully can actually *facilitate* clinical work, since they help us gain access to important unconscious processes unfolding between ourselves and our patients, opening the door to new pathways of mutual vulnerability in the dyad (Aron, 2016b). I am interested in the notion that it is *impossible* for human beings (either consciously or unconsciously) to suspend their tendency to ascribe different sorts of value to all the intricate dimensions of intersubjective life. We all tend to value (or "prefer," or desire) certain relational configurations between ourselves and others, which means that we become emotionally invested in manifesting specific experiences (e.g., behaving in certain ways, leading a particular type of life, feeling specified emotions, actualizing pre-determined "outcomes" in our relationships), reflexively insisting that *other people* behave in certain ways, display specific qualities, and engage with us in a particular fashion. Usually without awareness, we take our self-worth to be dependent on the realization of such configurations, ascribing badness to ourselves and others when we feel like we are being prevented from actualizing them.

For clinicians, these valued relational configurations are extensively influenced by our professionally endorsed models of technique, analytic process, and therapeutic action. Based on our preferred theoretical model, in intimate interaction with our personal psychologies and the current intersubjective situation, we all tend to value unique dimensions of the psychoanalytic encounter—specific clinical "outcomes" (e.g., a renouncement of infantile libidinal aims, increased self-cohesion, an expanded interpersonal repertoire, an enhanced capacity for mutual recognition, the ability to "stand in the spaces"), particular technical interventions (e.g., interpretation, empathic validation, emotional exploration, self-disclosure, inviting patients to inhabit different self-states simultaneously), and the ideal manner for the patient to approach clinical work (e.g., lying on the couch, free-associating, reflecting on internal states instead of employing behavioral strategies, exhibiting curiosity about the analyst's subjectivity). These ideas, which are often implicit and unformulated, play a powerful role in what has been called the clinician's "psychoanalytic identity" (Wille, 2008), or what Cooper (2016) has recently described as "the analyst's object relationship to the psychoanalytic process."

All of these factors significantly structure the conditions for the therapist's sense of self-esteem, as well as the conditions under which the therapist is able to value her patient. On this model, the clinician is continuously and necessarily ascribing a wide range of values to Self and Other in the therapeutic situation, regardless of her conscious beliefs about how she "should" or "should not" be relating to her patient. This means that, while analytic practitioners might be less *behaviorally* directive than clinicians utilizing other models, they are equally unable to suppress the forms of intersubjective valuing under discussion. *What distinguishes psychoanalytic practitioners is not the degree to which they value particular modes of relatedness with their patients, but their dedication to using the analytic method, with its emphasis on unconscious and transferential processes, to understand these intersubjective patterns, and to cultivate new modes of relatedness more consistent with the dignity and well-being of themselves and their patients.*

This way of thinking has important implications for the ethical dimensions of psychoanalysis. From an ethical vantage point, if we are unable to suspend our tendency to value/devalue our patients, then we are faced with the task of understanding the ways in which our valuing expresses (and contradicts) their dignity and well-being. This is not simply because we value "self-understanding" for its own sake—it is because, to the degree that we conceptualize ourselves as moral beings, we are *ethically obligated* to develop ourselves along moral lines, in order to better express the dignity and well-being of Self and Other in all of our relationships, including our relationships with our patients.

In my work with patients, this means that I am never allowed to privilege analytic "exploration" as an end in itself—I am consistently interested in the issue of therapeutic efficacy. Is the therapy helping to make the patient's life better, either internally or externally? This is rarely an easy question to answer, as there is no categorical formula for such a matter, and it hinges on a notion of "better" that is inextricably value-laden and subjectively constituted. But the practical difficulty of answering such a question does not detract from the fact that I am morally obligated to *wrestle* with it.

I am not suggesting that we should prematurely "pull the plug" if our patients are not improving. Rather, I am assuming that I need to take seriously the possibility that *I* am partly responsible for their continued difficulties, and that a shift in my stance (e.g., internally, behaviorally) could lead to increased change in the therapy. In much the same way that I can never conclude that I am "doing enough" to address problems like world hunger and systemic racism, I am not permitted to rest comfortably in the idea that I am engaged in a non-controversially "successful" treatment. I need to remember that I am *one-hundred percent responsible* for fifty percent of this therapy, and so I must always be asking myself the question—would some alteration in my approach lead to greater improvements in the patient's well-being?

In this chapter, I have started to sketch out what it might look like to consider analytic practice along ethical lines. I have not, however, fully considered the clinical implications of these views, nor have I proposed any "technical" modifications based on these reflections. In the next several chapters, I will explore some theoretical revisions that might be necessary in order to ground a genuinely ethical model of psychoanalysis.

Part 2

Theoretical revisions

In Part 1, I suggested that there exists a significant gulf between our publicly endorsed psychoanalytic theories and our everyday ethical assumptions. But this is not simply a theoretical problem. To the degree that we experience ourselves as ethical beings, there could be important parts of ourselves, and of our patients, unable to find adequate expression in clinical work. In the next few chapters, I explore some revisions that might be made to our models of psychoanalytic motivation in order to address this problem. By paying closer attention to the role of *value* in human life, we can develop more "experience-near" theories that are better equipped to explain and affirm our everyday ethical commitments, most notably about altruism, human dignity, and freedom and responsibility.

Chapter 3

The dilemma of intersubjective motivation[1]

Howard was a 37-year-old Marine Corps Veteran who, after struggling with homelessness and heroin addiction for many years, was finally able to achieve sobriety and, with the help of a VA housing program, obtain his own apartment in the community. At the start of therapy, despite being charming and charismatic and having many acquaintances, Howard's life was virtually devoid of any close relationships. He would spend his days in parks and coffee shops, affably chatting with the passers-by until nightfall, when he would return home to his small apartment, alone. A talented spoken word poet, he was willing to let others admire him and his compositions, but he rarely allowed people to *know* him in a deep or meaningful way.

Throughout our early work together, Howard wore dark sunglasses in all of our sessions. He emphatically asserted that he did not have any problems, and that he did not need anything from anyone else, including me. He spent entire sessions lecturing to me about his theories of spirituality and positive thinking, rarely giving me a chance to make comments or ask him any questions. Howard also spent much of his time criticizing me—my clothing, which was not flamboyant enough; my shoes, which I did not polish frequently enough; my personality, which was too "professional"; and my language, which occasionally included words like "sorry" and "need" and thereby betrayed my weakness as a human being. If I tried to explore the meaning of these criticisms, Howard would impatiently reject my efforts and continue with his monologues, explicitly telling me on multiple occasions, "I don't care what you have to say."

In these interactions, Howard was certainly making an emotional impact on me. I wanted to help him, but I did not know how to do so, especially since the parts of myself that my patients usually find helpful (e.g., my empathy, my efforts to understand, my interpretations) would incur Howard's direct attacks. To avoid conflict in our sessions, I naturally drifted into "appeasement mode," trying to refrain from doing the things that upset Howard (e.g., attempting to explore his experiences, commenting on anything about *him*). These modifications seemed to make Howard feel better about the treatment, but I began to realize that *I* did not feel fully present in our relationship. I felt like I was walking on eggshells with Howard, successfully able to avoid his aggressive attacks, but only at the expense of my sense of agency and competence in the therapy.

In recent years, psychoanalytic theory has increasingly turned its focus to issues of intersubjectivity, initiating what has been called an "intersubjective turn" in psychoanalysis (Gerhardt & Sweetnam, 2001; Gerhardt, Sweetnam, & Borton, 2000, 2003). As others have noted (Aron, 1996b; Beebe, Knoblauch, Rustin, & Sorter, 2005; Cooper, 1996; Natterson & Friedman, 1995), the single term "intersubjectivity" has come to denote a number of distinct theoretical approaches, including Benjamin's (1988, 1995) notion of mutual recognition, Fonagy and colleagues' concept of mentalization (Fonagy, Gergely, Jurist, & Target, 2002), Ogden's (1994) proposal of the analytic third, Daniel N. Stern's (1985, 2004) ideas on the sharing of mental states, Stolorow and Atwood's (1992) field theory of "reciprocally interacting subjectivities" (p. 1), and the dyadic systems view of Beebe and colleagues (Beebe et al., 2005; Beebe & Lachmann, 2002). In this chapter, I consider a dimension of intersubjectivity that has received scant direct attention in the aforementioned literature—the capacity for *intersubjective motivation*, conceptualized here as the ability to be motivated by the subjectivity of another person.

In her groundbreaking paper on the development of intersubjectivity, Jessica Benjamin (1995) suggests that intrapsychically oriented psychoanalytic theories set the "goal of development" too low by focusing on the successful internalization of the child's early caregivers (p. 38), arguing instead that successful development, as well as effective psychoanalytic work, fosters our potential to recognize the other as "a separate and equivalent center of self" (p. 30). I hope to advance this position further, suggesting that intersubjectivity theory itself is setting its sights too low by viewing "recognition" (and related concepts like mentalization and the sharing of mental states) as the primary goal of psychic development, and that further attention should be devoted to the related but distinct idea of intersubjective motivation.

To begin, I outline a general conception of intersubjective motivation, and I argue for the importance of this conception in advancing the relational project within psychoanalysis. Then I review a handful of intersubjective approaches, identifying and evaluating three strategies that might be employed to explain the phenomenon of intersubjective motivation. Finally, using Benjamin's notion of mutual recognition as a starting point, I propose an original model of the intrapsychic conditions for intersubjective motivation, arguing for the development of a comprehensive psychoanalytic theory of motivation that includes intrapsychic as well as intersubjective elements.

Intersubjective motivation and the relational project in psychoanalysis

As mentioned earlier, I define the capacity for intersubjective motivation as the ability to be motivated by the subjectivity of another person. Here, "subjectivity" includes both conscious and unconscious processes and states, including but not limited to thoughts, beliefs, affects, feelings, desires, fantasies, values, and mental representations (e.g., of Self and Other, of drives, of the external environment, of interaction sequences between Self and Other). I use the term "motivation" in a broad sense, referring to the processes determining the contents and qualities of one's entire "mental life" (Freud, 1910a, p. 38), rather than just those operations influencing behavior. Understood in this way, intersubjective motivation implies that another's subjectivity can partially determine the content and quality of our own subjective world. Of particular relevance here is the internal state typically referred to as a *motive* or *desire*. On the above conception, our motives can derive fundamentally and irreducibly from the subjectivity of others.

This presentation of intersubjective motivation can also be recast in more experience-near terms. Assume the aforementioned subjective processes constitute the conscious and unconscious *meaning* that a person ascribes to her experience. The phenomenon of intersubjective motivation could imply our ability to be motivated by the meaning that this person assigns to her experiences, rather than exclusively the meaning we assign to that experience based on our own intrapsychic factors. In other words, it implies the possibility of *intersubjective* rather than strictly intrapsychic meaning. A theory of intersubjective motivation could thus help to illuminate the "other-oriented" dimensions of a wide variety of deeply important and emotionally potent relational phenomena, such as romantic and non-romantic care and concern, self-sacrificing and seemingly altruistic behaviors and motives (Badcock, 1986; Bader, 1996; Kriegman, 1990; McWilliams, 1984; Meissner, 2003; Nagel, 1970; Seelig & Rosof, 2001; Shapiro & Gabbard, 1994; Wallwork, 1991), respect for other human beings, and perhaps even the responsiveness of therapists to their patients.

In focusing specifically on intersubjective motivation here, I am not assuming that, empirically speaking, it is ever possible to be motivated solely by another's subjectivity, or that we ever encounter intersubjectively motivated phenomena in any "pure" form, apart from intrapsychic elements. As Jessica Benjamin (1988) suggests, "Intrapsychic and intersubjectivity theory should not be seen in opposition to each other (as they usually are) but as complementary ways of understanding the psyche" (p. 20). Applying this idea to the present topic of motivation, I suggest that, for any given psychic event, we view the relative influence of intrapsychic and intersubjective motivational processes on a continuum, noting that the presence of one form of motivation need not preclude the influence of the other. From this perspective, the present inquiry is both partial and provisional in nature—partial because it focuses primarily on the intersubjectively motivated dimensions of experience, and provisional because it cannot substitute for a comprehensive psychoanalytic theory of motivation, one that includes intersubjective as well as intrapsychic elements, and that therefore could begin to address the complex and dialectical relationship between these realms. In Chapters 4 and 5, I work to flesh out such a model more fully.

With this conception in place, I suggest that this particular view of intersubjective motivation is essential for the continued development of a genuinely relational approach to psychoanalysis, an approach that, as its defining feature, stresses the "dyadic, social, interactional, interpersonal" notion of mind (Aron, 1996a, p. x). Any psychoanalytic theory should be able to explain the basic sources of human motivation, and any truly relational theory should insist that one of those sources is *other people*, or more specifically the meaning that other subjects ascribe to their experience. Without such an account, mind might be relational in a weak sense, since meaning would concern relationships rather than biological drives, but it would not be relational in the fullest sense, since that meaning would derive from processes that, while fundamentally relational, would also be fundamentally intrapsychic. Here I arrive at the important distinction between relational motivation, which always concerns others but is often reducible to intrapsychic factors, and intersubjective motivation, which is *always reducible to the meaning that other subjects ascribe to their experience.*

At this point in its history, relational theory seems unable to explain intersubjective motivation. To partially argue the plausibility of this point, I review two major sources of motivation in relational thought—relational drives and internalized relational configurations. Following Greenberg (1991), I define a drive as "an unconditioned internal need that motivates all behavior and determines the quality of all experience" (p. 23). On this view, in addition to Freud's sexual and aggressive instincts, there are *relational* drives, such as Fairbairn's (1952) object-seeking libido, Bowlby's (1969) concept of attachment, Mahler and her colleagues' (1975) notion of individuation, Kohut's (1977) need for self-cohesion through processes of mirroring and idealization, Lichtenberg's (1989) attachment-affiliation motivational system, and even Mitchell's (1988) drive towards "the establishment and maintenance of connections with others" (p. 5). Such drives are essentially relational, since they can only be fully defined in terms of our relationships with others. Nevertheless, since these drives imply *our* needs and desires (e.g., for individuation, for self-cohesion, for maintaining relationships), their meaning is ultimately reducible to intrapsychic sources, and so they are unable to account for intersubjective motivation. I do not mean to imply that these needs are excessively selfish or hedonistic, or that drive-based motivation is inconsistent with intersubjective motivation. Rather, I am suggesting that the elucidation of these intrapsychically based drives, while helpful, does little to illuminate how we come to be motivated by intersubjective meaning.

It is not sufficient to simply assert that these drives "naturally" lead to intersubjective motivation, for example by suggesting that, in seeking to establish and maintain attachments with others, we automatically acquire this capacity. The theorist must explain *how* an intrapsychically defined drive leads to that capacity, a project that, I suggest, is destined for failure because such drives occupy a different realm of meaning than the one under consideration here.

A second important source of motivation in relational theory is *relational configurations*, or mental representations of Self-in-relationship-with-Other. While different theorists conceptualize these configurations in considerably different ways (Beebe & Lachmann, 2002; Bromberg, 1998; Greenberg, 1991; Jacobsen, 1964; Kernberg, 1976; Mitchell, 1988; Ogden, 1986; Sandler & Sandler, 1998), such configurations usually contain representations of Self, representations of Other, and representations of the "specific interactions which transpire between self and other" (Mitchell, 1988, p. 33). Understood most generally, these configurations embody the symbolic or pre-symbolic meaning that we ascribe to Self-in-relationship-with-Other (Greenberg, 1991, p. 173).

On this conception, it again seems clear that relational configurations are insufficient to explain intersubjective motivation. On the one hand, these configurations are clearly relational—they derive etiologically from interactions with real others, they pervasively shape our interpersonal behavior patterns and experiences in relationships, and they can be modified and transformed within the context of the analytic dyad (Mitchell, 1988, pp. 289–290). Nevertheless, these configurations are by definition intrapsychic organizers of meaning, specifying the meaning we supply to our interactions but remaining silent on how we are motivated by other people's internal worlds. This point applies to pathological as well as "healthy" configurations, since both specify equally, albeit differently, the intrapsychic contributions of the subject.[2]

The line of criticism I have developed here highlights a central dilemma facing any theorist attempting to explain intersubjective motivation. In order to provide a psychoanalytic account of motivation, the theorist must specify the factors *in the subject* responsible for that motivation. However, in specifying the content of these factors, the theorist inevitably elaborates their intrapsychic rather than intersubjective content. To put the matter another way: we must start "in the subject," but in starting there, we find that we cannot get out. To resolve this dilemma, I now turn to an approach that explores the relationship *between* subjects—intersubjectivity theory proper.

Intersubjectivity theory and the dilemma of intersubjective motivation

To lay the groundwork for a theory of intersubjective motivation, I now review three influential conceptions of intersubjectivity—Fonagy and his colleagues' (2002) concept of mentalization, D. N. Stern's (1985, 2004) ideas on the sharing of mental states, and Benjamin's (1988, 1995) notion of mutual recognition. Since none of these theorists have explicitly considered the topic of intersubjective motivation as defined here, I attempt a creative application of their views, highlighting how each theory might explain this phenomenon and assessing the efficacy of these models at resolving the aforementioned dilemma of intersubjective motivation.[3]

Peter Fonagy's (1991) approach to intersubjectivity centers on the construct of mentalization, defined as "the capacity to conceive of conscious and unconscious mental states in oneself and others" (p. 640). Such mental states are usually *intentional* in nature, such as "goals, emotions, desires, and beliefs" that can be attributed to others in order to explain or predict their behavior (Fonagy et al., 2002, p. 146). It is important to note that mentalization does not simply entail the ability to think about mental states; it implies the capacity to do so with some degree of *accuracy*. Accordingly, Fonagy and his colleagues associate mentalizing with *mind-reading* (pp. 24, 47, 52, 170, 221, 352, 354), employing epistemic terms like knowledge (pp. 27, 30, 35, 287), perception (pp. 11, 54, 287, 356), understanding (pp. 5, 253, 257, 287, 299–300, 354), awareness (pp. 257, 472), and recognition (pp. 58, 353) to designate the mode of accurately representing mental states in oneself and others. I refer to this conception of mentalization as an *epistemic* model of intersubjectivity, since it defines intersubjectivity in terms of our ability to "know" the subjectivity of another (Fonagy et al., 2002, pp. 287–288).

Fonagy and his colleagues stress the deeply intersubjective process that underlies the development of mentalization in the child. Briefly put, when the caregiver possesses the capacity to mentalize, she naturally ascribes mental states to the child and communicates this "unconsciously and pervasively" through her interactions with the child (Fonagy et al., 2002, p. 286). In turn, "the child can see his fantasy or idea represented in the adult's mind, reintroject this, and use it as a representation of his own thinking" (Fonagy et al., 2002, p. 266), a mechanism that ultimately enables the child to ascribe mental states to himself and to other people. Here Fonagy and his colleagues are suggesting that certain *intrapsychic structures*, namely representations of ourselves as mental agents, serve as the necessary condition for the full advancement of intersubjective relatedness, a perspective also endorsed in different ways by other authors (Aron, 1995; Lyons-Ruth, 1999).

When applied to the topic under consideration, this epistemic model gives rise to a primarily epistemic approach to intersubjective motivation. On this view, when we mentalize the subjectivity of another person, we can be motivated by that subjectivity, in light of our accurate perception of its contents. This account offers a possible solution to the dilemma of intersubjective motivation. By drawing the explicit connection between mentalization and intrapsychic structures, it elucidates the factors *in the subject* that might be responsible for intersubjective motivation. Such motivation would be truly intersubjective, since it would derive from the other individual's internal states as accurately represented in the process of mentalization.

Nevertheless, this account seems ill-equipped to explain intersubjective motivation, mainly because the capacity to accurately represent someone's mental states does not necessarily imply the ability to be motivated by those states. Interestingly, Fonagy and his colleagues (2002) make a similar point when they state, "The child may know what the other feels but care little or not at all about this" (p. 30), and when they acknowledge "Even when someone can intellectually conceive of the impact of his or her actions on another person, this may be felt as meaningless, empty of emotional conviction" (p. 476).

Additionally, the epistemic conception of intersubjectivity seems perhaps too abstract and "cold" to explain the topic under consideration. As noted earlier, an intersubjective motivational theory could help to illuminate a wide range of deeply meaningful relational phenomena, such as romantic and non-romantic love, self-sacrificing behaviors and motives, and respect for other human beings. By proposing a primarily epistemic vision of intersubjectivity, Fonagy and his colleagues essentially attribute these phenomena to *the accurate perception of reality*, with "reality" understood as "the mental states of others." While such perception constitutes an important feature of the phenomena in question, it does not address what is perhaps most compelling about these forms of intersubjective relatedness—the fact that they occupy a foundational place in our emotional lives, and that the absence of such experiences can equal psychic death both for our patients and for ourselves.

While Fonagy and his colleagues frame intersubjectivity in terms of the knowledge of mental states, Daniel N. Stern (1985, 2004) defines intersubjectivity in terms of the sharing of mental states, advancing what I call a *participatory* view of intersubjectivity. According to Stern (1985), this faculty begins to develop between seven and nine months of age, when "infants gradually come upon the momentous realization that inner subjective experiences, the 'subject matter' of the mind, are potentially shareable with someone else" (p. 124). These internal states are pre-linguistic, including intentions, affects, and attentional states (Stern, 1985, pp. 128–133).

In his later work, Stern (2004) applies this participatory conception to adults as well, variously defining intersubjectivity as the capacity to experience what other subjects are experiencing (pp. xviii, 22, 75–82); the ability to participate in the experience of another (pp. 76, 81, 94, 176); the capability of feeling what other people are feeling "*as if* from within their skin" (p. 76); and the potential to assume another person's perspective, a phenomenon Stern calls "partially living from the other's center" (p. 81). Following Bråten (1998), Stern (2004) emphasizes further, "It is not a form of *knowledge* about the other, but rather a *participation in the other's experience*" (p. 241; italics added). With this account, Stern clearly distinguishes between intersubjective knowledge, in which we accurately perceive the mental states of another, and intersubjective participation, in which we experience another individual's mental states as that person experiences them.[4]

Stern's participatory model has some important motivational implications. If it were truly possible to share someone's mental states, then such mental states would be naturally motivating for the participating subject. For example, if we could actually experience someone's sadness (and not simply *our own* sadness as triggered by the person), then we could be motivated by that sadness, in the same way we are automatically motivated by mental states that originate in ourselves.

These ideas constitute a participatory solution to the dilemma of intersubjective motivation. By endorsing the innate ability to share mental states, the participatory solution specifies factors *in the subject*—namely the shareable mental states of others—that could inspire intersubjective motivation. Such motivation would be genuinely intersubjective, since it would derive from the subjectivity of other people.

However, the participatory solution fails as an explanation of intersubjective motivation, mainly because it ignores the important role that *difference* can play in such motivation. By framing intersubjective motivation solely in terms of participation, the participatory approach is unable to explain instances in which we accurately perceive another's mental state and are motivated by that state without sharing it. Examples of this phenomenon abound in clinical work. A therapist can perceive what a patient is experiencing and be motivated by that perception in subsequent responses and interventions, but, due to the fact that therapist and patient endow their experience with different meanings, the therapist does not necessarily share the mental state serving as the source of the motivation. According to the participatory solution, such motivation would not even qualify as intersubjective, since it lacks the prerequisite sharing of mental states.

Along these same lines, the participatory model offers an overly homogeneous conception of intersubjective motivation. By placing the sharing of mental states as a necessary condition for intersubjective motivation, this model privileges sameness and underemphasizes difference in this motivation, essentially saying, "The only way that I can be motivated by you is to *be* you," at least at the level of mental states and meanings. In this way, the participatory solution underestimates both the motivated subject and the person serving as the "source" of the motivation—it overlooks the subject's capacity to be motivated by unshared mental states, and it ignores the motivating power of the other's distinct internal world.

In contrast with this approach, we might hope for a theory that embraces the possibility of difference between mutually motivated subjects, by explaining how we can be motivated by meanings other than our own, originating in a subject that is distinct from us. This thought brings us to the work of Jessica Benjamin. Building on D. N. Stern's (1985) description of the infant's participatory capacities, Benjamin (1988, 1995) outlines the development of *recognition,* or our ability to experience another subject as "a separate and equivalent center of subjectivity" (Benjamin, 1995, p. 7). She suggests that, under optimal relational circumstances, children receive recognition from their caregivers while also developing the ability to provide this recognition to others, leading to the possibility of *mutual recognition* between subjects (Benjamin, 1995, p. 30).

On Benjamin's view, recognition involves the simultaneous experience of both the fundamental distinctness and the fundamental similarity of another person's subjectivity, processes Benjamin (1988) calls "the two central elements of recognition" (p. 170). When referring to the basic similarity between subjects, Benjamin employs a handful of concepts seemingly interchangeably, such as equality (1988, 1995, 1998, 2000), likeness (1988, 1995, 1998, 2000, 2004), sameness (1988, 1995, 1998), commonality (1988, 1995), and equivalence (1988, 1995, 1999, 2004).

Like Fonagy and his colleagues, Benjamin frames intersubjectivity in largely epistemic terms. As noted above, with her notion of recognition, Benjamin is highlighting our capacity to know certain facts about the world, in this case the distinctness and similarity of other human beings. Benjamin also repeatedly associates intersubjective relatedness with epistemic ideas, such as knowledge (1988, 1995, 1998, 2000), understanding (1988, 1995, 2000), "seeing" (1988, 1995, 2000), awareness (1988, 1995, 1998, 2004), acknowledgment (1988, 1995, 2004), experience (1988, 1995, 2004), discovery (1988, 1995), perception (1988, 1995, 1998), and sensation (2004). In addition, Benjamin identifies other people with externality (1988, 1995, 1998, 1999), reality (1988, 1995, 1998, 1999, 2004), objectivity (1995), and the "outside" (1988, 1995, 1998, 1999, 2000, 2004). These metaphors imply that, on Benjamin's view of intersubjectivity, other subjects occupy a position analogous to that of "the objective world" in scientific inquiry, and that the foundation of intersubjective relatedness consists in knowing particular facts about those subjects.

Once again, this epistemic approach seems ill equipped to explain intersubjective motivation. We might recognize the fundamental distinctness and similarity of another's subjectivity, but such recognition does not entail our ability to be motivated by that subjectivity. Benjamin (1988) corroborates this idea when she notes that we can cognitively accept someone's separateness without necessarily experiencing empathy for that person (p. 76). However, since Benjamin's concept of recognition is primarily an epistemic metaphor, it is unable to illuminate the intersubjective source of this empathy. Knowledge of facts about others, whether these facts concern the contents of a particular person's subjectivity (e.g., as represented in mentalization) or the more general qualities common to all people (e.g., the basic distinctness and similarity apprehended in mutual recognition), does not explain intersubjective *care* and therefore cannot account for intersubjective motivation.

In addition to these epistemic constructs, Benjamin also endorses what I call a *valuational* conception of intersubjectivity. By "valuational," I simply mean *related to value*, and so a specifically valuational theory grounds intersubjective relatedness in the value that human beings ascribe to one another.[5] Benjamin herself does not distinguish between her epistemic and valuational conceptions; rather, her valuational approach lies embedded in her primarily epistemic theoretical framework. The valuational perspective emerges most clearly in Benjamin's comments about *mutual respect*. Benjamin (1995) highlights the capacity "to respect the other subject as an equal" (p. 8), repeatedly aligning this ability with intersubjective relatedness (1988, pp. 8, 39, 70, 192, 195; 1995, pp. 23n, 38, 90; 1998, pp. 80, 86, 94, 98, 102, 2002, p. 49; 2004, p. 33). Benjamin's construct of respect is essentially valuational in nature. It implies not simply knowing the other but *valuing* the other and that which is known in her. Along these same lines, Benjamin aligns intersubjectivity with a number of other value-laden concepts, such as affirmation (1988, pp. 15, 60; 1995, pp. 39, 125; 2002, p. 44), validation (1988, p. 15), appreciation (1988, pp. 15, 28, 54, 177, 195; 1995, pp. 41, 90; 1998, pp. xiii, 65), and even love (1988, pp. 16, 106; 1995, pp. 41, 46, 172; 1998, p. 91).

These observations cast a different light on Benjamin's suggestion that intersubjective relatedness involves the experience of other people as fundamentally distinct yet fundamentally "equal" or "equivalent." As noted earlier, Benjamin often likens this equivalence to similarity. Given the strong valuational current in Benjamin's theory, this equivalence could also mean equally *valuable*. This interpretation is consistent with Benjamin's own employment of the terms (1988, p. 177; 1995, pp. 6–8, 28, 30, 31, 46; 1999, p. 201; 2004, p. 6), for example when she writes about respecting others as equals (1995, p. 8), and especially when she contrasts domination-based relationships with relationships in which both subjects are recognized as equals (1988, pp. 12, 48, 73, 165, 167, 181, 218, 221; 1995, p. 31; 1998, p. 30). Benjamin would thus be suggesting that intersubjective relatedness implies the capacity to simultaneously recognize other people as fundamentally distinct from oneself, fundamentally similar to oneself, and possessing a value equal to one's own.

These ideas imply a valuational approach to intersubjective motivation. When we endow another person with the same value that we assign to ourselves, we can be motivated by the meaning that *she* ascribes to her experience, rather than by our own intrapsychic meaning exclusively. This perspective provides a compelling solution to the dilemma of intersubjective motivation. It identifies the factor *in the subject* ultimately responsible for that motivation, namely the tendency to ascribe equal value to other human beings. Such motivation would be essentially intersubjective, since its content would derive from the internal states of others. Here, the ascription of value serves as the motivational bridge between subjects, enabling us to be motivationally receptive to intersubjective rather than strictly intrapsychic meaning.

The above presentation constitutes a creative extrapolation on Benjamin's explicit formulations. Since Benjamin herself does not fully elaborate her valuational conception of intersubjectivity, and since she never considers the topic of intersubjective motivation as I define it, it is still unclear what it means to "value" someone in this theory, or what the nature of the connection is between such valuing and intersubjective motivation. I will spend the remainder of this chapter addressing these questions.

The intersubjective relational configuration

Using Benjamin's valuational assumptions about intersubjectivity as a starting point, I now propose an original model of the intrapsychic conditions for intersubjective motivation, a composite structure identified as the *intersubjective relational configuration*. In the next chapter, I return to the topic of *how* this configuration develops. For now, I simply assert that the configuration is a developmental achievement, evolving in the context of a relationship with someone (e.g., a caregiver, an analyst) who herself possesses this configuration and therefore is able to be truly motivated by the mental states of another.

Conceptualizing this configuration as an intrapsychic structure, I specify its content as *unconditionally valuable Self in mutually responsive relation to unconditionally valuable Other.* This configuration consists of both mnemic and valuational components, the first of which are *mnemic relational representations*, defined as representations of the formative relationship as experienced by the subject. Following the theories already considered, I assume these include representations of Self in the formative relationship, representations of the other person in that relationship, and representations of the mutually responsive interactions unfolding between them. These representations can be symbolic and non-symbolic in nature, indicating our past experiences of mutual responsiveness and structuring our expectations for the possible recurrence of these experiences in relationships perceived as comparable (Beebe & Lachmann, 2002, chapter 4).

While the aforementioned representations are primarily mnemic in nature, they are not exclusively *concrete* in nature. We represent both Self and Other as possessing what Benjamin (2000) calls *subjecthood*, or the quality of being a distinct, independent subject who is nonetheless fundamentally similar to other people. In most cases, we possess an "amorphous and fluid" conception of subjecthood (Schafer, 1968, p. 26), usually only formulated in vague terms like "fellow person" or "human being like me."

Even in sum, these mnemic representations are not sufficient to explain intersubjective motivation. As I have argued, knowledge of someone's subjectivity does not necessarily lead to intersubjective motivation. Similarly, memories of past experiences of mutual responsiveness do not always inspire intersubjective motivation in the present. I may remember that I experienced mutual responsiveness in the past, and I may even expect to have such experiences again, but this does not entail my present ability to be motivated by the subjectivity of another, distinct subject. This ability is predicated upon the ascription of *value* to another person.

Accordingly, the second essential dimension of the intersubjective configuration is valuational in nature. Rather than consider this dimension a "property" of the Self–Other representations, I conceptualize value as an *activity* performed by the subject (Schafer, 1976). This conception is closely related to the Boston Change Process Study Group's (BCPSG) theory of *implicit relational knowing*. In contrast with declarative knowledge, which is explicit, conscious, and "represented symbolically in imagistic or verbal form" (D. N. Stern et al., 1998, p. 905), implicit relational knowings are non-conscious, non-verbal, and non-symbolic representations of "ways of being with others" (D. N. Stern et al., p. 903). These representations are procedural rather than declarative in nature (BCPSG, 2008, pp. 128–129), meaning that their content "only becomes manifest in the doing" (Lyons-Ruth, 1999, p. 578). While these representations contain cognitive, affective, and behavioral elements (D. N. Stern et al., p. 905), they primarily represent the *activity* of the subject in relation to others, as exemplified by the BCPSG's (2002, 2005, 2007, 2008) repeated alignment of these representations with procedures, behavioral patterns, and observable interactions between people.

Applying these ideas to the present topic of value, I propose the concept of *implicit valuational representations*, defined as non-conscious, non-verbal, and non-symbolic representations of *ways of valuing others*. As I will explain further in forthcoming chapters, I see the activity of valuing as a distinct and fundamental psychic operation, thus departing from the common tendency in psychoanalytic thought to explain values in terms of affective or drive-based processes (Kernberg, 1976; Lichtenberg, Lachmann, & Fosshage, 1992, chapter 10; Sandler & Sandler, 1998, pp. 24–25).

These valuational representations are closely aligned with the aforementioned mnemic representations. Specifically, they represent the unconditional value we ascribe to the *subjecthood* of Self and Other. Here, rather than assign value to some *aspect* of Self and Other (e.g., physical appearance, particular personality traits, gratifying or non-gratifying interpersonal behaviors), we ascribe unconditional value to Self and Other's basic status of *being a subject*.

For our purposes here, "valuing" is defined solely in motivational terms, as *taking something to be a source of meaning*. Furthermore, to value "unconditionally" simply means *to value under all circumstances*, regardless of the presence or absence of either subjective factors (e.g., thoughts, beliefs, affects, feelings, desires, plans, fantasies) or objective factors (e.g., circumstances or states of affairs in the consensually validated external world, including our own behavior or the behavior of others). Accordingly, when endowed with the intersubjective relational configuration, we mnemonically represent Self and Other in the formative relationship, and we simultaneously take the subjecthood of Self and Other to be a source of meaning, regardless of our particular internal states (e.g., our emotions or desires at the time) or the objective aspects of our lives (e.g., how other people are relating to us, whether or not another person's behavior could negatively affect us).

With this conceptual framework in place, I offer the following explanation for the phenomenon of intersubjective motivation. Since we specifically value the quality of *subjecthood* in these representations of Self and Other, then to the extent that we identify a contemporary person as possessing that same quality, we will ascribe unconditional value to her subjecthood as well. In this way, we will take that individual to be a source of meaning, and so we will be able to be motivated by *the other's meanings* rather than simply our own.

In this model, I am suggesting that intersubjective motivation is predicated upon *unconditional* rather than conditional valuing. When we assign conditional value to someone, we are motivationally receptive to her meanings only when certain subjective or objective conditions are met. In such cases, the operative motivational processes are ultimately dependent on the meaning we *ourselves* ascribe to the aforementioned conditions. Such motivation would be essentially reducible to our own meanings, and so it would be intrapsychic in nature. However, when we assign unconditional value to someone, we are motivationally receptive to that person's meanings regardless of any meanings we might assign to related factors in the situation. In such cases, the motivation would derive from the subjectivity of another, and so it would be truly intersubjective.

The process of intersubjective motivation

Employing the above model, I now propose a broad outline for the process of intersubjective motivation. While I frame this account in chronological and categorical terms, in the actual experience of this motivation, the phenomena described here sequentially usually occur simultaneously and implicitly. For the sake of simplicity, I consider the particular phenomenon of unidirectional intersubjective motivation, in which we are motivated by another person's mental states and not vice versa.[6]

To begin, we identify the other person as possessing the quality of subjecthood. In most cases, we do not explicitly and consciously conceptualize the individual as possessing this quality, for example as being "a distinct subject who is fundamentally similar to me." Instead, our representation of the other's subjecthood is largely implicit in the experience of intersubjective motivation, usually only formulated in vague terms like "fellow person" or "human being like me."

At the same time, we ascribe unconditional value to the individual's subjecthood. This ascription is also non-declarative and non-conscious in nature. Just as the contents of implicit relational knowings are revealed primarily through our interactive patterns, our unconditional valuing of the other is exhibited through a wide range of affective, behavioral, and experiential patterns, marked by a consistent concern for the person and an ability to be responsive to her subjectivity without contradicting the value of our own subjectivity. Phenomenologically, this unconditional valuing commonly takes the form of a general feeling of "respect" for someone, a feeling I suggest is not essentially affective in nature but rather is grounded in the activity of unconditional valuing (see Chapters 4 and 5).

In this state of motivational responsiveness, we start to construct *intersubjective representations*. As I have already suggested, our unconditional valuing of another enables us to be receptive to her subjective meanings. However, this receptivity is always partial, perspectival, and largely shaped by our own intrapsychic factors (Aron, 1996a; Hoffman, 1998; Mitchell, 1993; Renik, 1993). We ultimately incorporate these perspectival meanings into our representations of the other person's subjectivity, leading to intersubjective representations that include dimensions of both our own and the other's meanings. While we are frequently conscious of the content of these representations, the vast majority of them are non-conscious and "unformulated" (D. B. Stern, 1997).

These representations are organized around our representation of the individual's subjecthood. Since we take the *person* to be a source of meaning, and since we represent her subjectivity as a fundamental aspect of her, we take her subjectivity to be a source of meaning as well. Therefore, we do not simply *know* the subjectivity of the other; we are *motivated* by that subjectivity as exemplified in our specific, idiosyncratic intersubjective representations.

This motivation expresses itself in a wide range of psychic phenomena, including our affects, desires, impulses, fantasies, feelings of attunement or connection with others, and conscious or non-conscious beliefs (e.g., about ourselves, about others, about interactions between Self and Other). While we regularly recognize that these phenomena are related to the individual who is supposedly the "source" of the motivation (e.g., in the case of wanting to alleviate another's suffering, or when we feel sad or excited for someone), we are often unaware of the intersubjective origins of these seemingly "intrapsychic" phenomena (Ogden, 1994).

I will now draw a few conclusions based on the above model of intersubjective motivation. I have suggested that intersubjective representations include both intersubjective and intrapsychic elements. This means that the psychic phenomena deriving from these representations (e.g., affects, desires, impulses, fantasies, beliefs) are mutually determined by intrapsychic and intersubjective sources. This assumption is consistent with Freud's (1913) familiar concept of overdetermination, or the idea that any given psychic event arises from "numerous contributory factors" (p. 100). While Freud primarily focused on the intrapsychic, unconscious factors (e.g., drives, wishes, defenses) influencing psychic phenomena, I extend the notion of overdetermination to include intersubjective factors operating at varying degrees of consciousness. Whether or not we are aware of them, both intrapsychic and intersubjective meanings mutually shape the conscious and unconscious dimensions of our subjectivity, producing complex psychic phenomena etiologically derived from both types of meaning.

Furthermore, in the above model, the intersubjective relational configuration stands in a foundational relation to the two other forms of intersubjectivity discussed in this chapter, namely intersubjective knowledge and participation. As noted earlier, the capacity to value other people unconditionally is a necessary condition of our receptivity to their meanings. Since that receptivity is a key element in the construction of intersubjective representations, and since knowledge of another's subjectivity relies on the ability to represent it with some degree of accuracy, intersubjective knowledge seems to depend on the capacity to ascribe unconditional value to other subjects. Expressed colloquially: we cannot truly know someone unless we value her, and there are dimensions of a person's experience that are inaccessible to us until we stand in a respectful, loving relation to her, whom we regard both as an "object of knowledge" and as a "valued subject."

A similar point could be made about intersubjective participation. Since we must know another's mental state in order to participate in it, and since the capacity for intersubjective knowledge depends on the ability to value others unconditionally, intersubjective participation seems to depend on intersubjective valuing as well.

In addition, as an approach to intersubjective motivation, the intersubjective relational configuration seems to sidestep the aforementioned problems with the epistemic and participatory conceptions. As I suggested earlier, by placing intersubjective knowledge as the basis for intersubjective motivation, the epistemic perspective offers an overly cold and scientific vision of the phenomenon in question. In contrast with this view, I am placing the unconditional valuing of others as the basis for the intersubjectively motivated dimensions of our experience. This idea implies less distance between subjects than the epistemic approach, while expressing the care and respect for others that usually accompanies intersubjective motivation. Moreover, by proposing a structural association between our representation of ourselves as unconditionally valuable and our representation of others as unconditionally valuable, the present model emphasizes the important role that valuing others can come to play in the areas of identity and self-esteem, especially in our sense of ourselves as leading lives that are valuable and meaningful regardless of external circumstances.

I also argued that, by placing intersubjective participation as the foundation for intersubjective motivation, the participatory conception of intersubjective motivation problematically blurs the distinction between intersubjectively motivated subjects. Conversely, I am suggesting that the motivated subject ascribes unconditional value *specifically* to the other's status as a fundamentally distinct yet fundamentally similar human being. This means that an appreciation of the distinctness of other subjects is not only consistent with intersubjective motivation—it is a necessary condition for this motivation, an essential element in our ability to be receptive to the meanings that constitute another person's distinct subjectivity.

Clinical illustrations

To support the utility of the concept of the intersubjective relational configuration in clinical work, I will review three facets of this construct—the unconditional valuation of the Self, the unconditional valuation of the Other, and the structural association between valuing ourselves and valuing others—and highlight their therapeutic relevance.

The unconditional valuation of the Self

This facet of the intersubjective relational configuration helps to explain a number of "self-oriented" outcomes of psychoanalysis, including the patient's increased sense of self-esteem, self-acceptance, and self-love; her enhanced feeling that she is living in accordance with her self-respect and dignity; the patient's experience of herself as being valuable and worthwhile regardless of external factors (e.g., her physical appearance, others' opinions of her) and internal factors (e.g., certain affective states) that she formerly associated with her "badness" or "defectiveness"; and the burgeoning capacity of the patient to take herself to be a *source* of meaning throughout the therapy, rather than simply a receptacle for other people's meanings.

The unconditional valuation of the Other

This aspect of the intersubjective relational configuration illuminates some of the "other-oriented" outcomes of analytic work, such as the patient's deepening motivational receptivity to the inner lives of others; her growing capability to "take in" and appreciate what other subjects have to offer; a greater capacity to feel care and concern for others, rather than defensively keeping them at bay; what Kennedy (2010) describes as the patient's increased potential to experience "the emotional impact of the analyst's presence, or subjectivity" (p. 565); and the patient's expanded ability to *respect* the other person, rather than primarily hating that person, fearing the person, or compulsively desiring an idealized version of the person.

The structural association between valuing Self and Other

This idea implies that, as we develop the intersubjective relational configuration, there is an increase both in the conditions under which we value ourselves, and in the conditions under which we value the other subject in the formative relationship. It also means that, to the degree that this configuration is motivationally operative, we ascribe unconditional value *both* to our own subjecthood and to the subjecthood of the other person. As the intersubjective relational configuration exerts greater motivational influence over us, we can achieve a progressive harmony between our motivational responsiveness to our own meanings and to the subjective meanings of others.[7]

To illustrate this association between valuing oneself and valuing others, I will return to my work with Howard. As our treatment unfolded, I searched for ways of being with Howard that felt more authentic to me, in which I could find my voice as Howard's therapist without feeling like I was overwhelming him. I was able to find a partial solution to this problem by sharing more openly about my internal states as Howard conducted his monologues, such as my confusion about how to connect with him, my concern about his lack of connection with others, and my curiosity about the more vulnerable aspects of himself that he never discussed. These sorts of therapeutic "I"-statements seemed far less intrusive to Howard than my earlier comments about *him* or the dynamic between us.

Over time, things began to shift in our sessions. Howard became more able to receive my reflections about him without becoming upset with me, and he also started to share about the parts of himself that, earlier in the treatment, did not exist in any meaningful sense—his desire to be admired, his sense of loneliness, emotions of hurt that came up in his interactions with others, his history of emotional and physical trauma, and, as the therapy progressed, his feelings of appreciation for me and our relationship. One of the turning points in the treatment came when, for the first time, Howard spontaneously took off his sunglasses in the session, revealing eyes that shocked me. I had always imagined these eyes would look hard and cold, defensively shutting out the world. Instead, they looked sad, fragile, and deeply vulnerable, almost like the eyes of a child. At the end of that session, Howard noticed an unopened bottle of Dr Pepper on my desk. He walked up and took it, asking me, "Could I have this?" Stunned, I did not say anything at first. Howard quickly replied, "Good," walking out of the office with my Dr Pepper. By taking off his glasses, he was allowing me to take him in, and by taking my bottle of Dr Pepper, he was permitting himself to take me in.

Without offering a full analysis of all of the changes that unfolded in this treatment, I will focus on the therapeutic significance of what I call the "structural association between valuing oneself and valuing others." To begin, I see this association in my desire to find a way of relating to Howard that was motivationally responsive to *both* of our subjectivities. I could not feel comfortable maintaining a strictly analytic/exploratory/interpretive stance with Howard, since that stance inspired such discomfort in him. Since I was valuing Howard's subjecthood, his discomfort was able to motivate me, inspiring me to seek a new way of relating to Howard that would be less overwhelming to him. However, I also could not feel satisfied with simply submitting to Howard's demands, since doing so contradicted my valuation of *my own* subjecthood. This valuation enabled me to be motivationally receptive to my own meanings, which included my curiosity about his inner life, my desire to see him move closer to others, and my desire to play a role in helping him to achieve that goal.

This structural association is also apparent in the changes Howard underwent in therapy. At the start of treatment, Howard's experience was significantly structured by a relational configuration derived from his childhood relationship with his father, where Self and Other stood in a mutually admiring dynamic with one another, and where he valued only aspects of himself (e.g., strength, self-reliance, self-confidence, "positivity") and aspects of the Other (e.g., admiration for him, flamboyance, assertiveness, professional success). To the extent that this relational configuration was operative, Howard could limit the motivational influence of his other configurations, where he ascribed unconditional badness to himself, and where he endowed himself with *conditional* badness, contingent on factors he associated with his "weakness" and "vulnerability" (e.g., his desire to depend on other people; affects such as loneliness or sadness; his attendance at therapy). Since my "therapist"-characteristics (e.g., my questions, my empathy, my attempts to explore his emotions, my assumption that Howard might need help from me) threatened to *make him bad* by engaging with the more vulnerable parts of him (Bromberg, 2006, pp. 90–91), Howard ascribed me with badness when I exhibited these characteristics, resulting in his criticisms and attacks against me.[8]

Gradually, as Howard encountered my willingness to comfortably reveal the more vulnerable aspects of myself (e.g., through my self-disclosures), and as he experienced my non-judgmental curiosity about similar parts of himself, I believe that Howard constructed mnemic representations of me as valuing him under conditions in which he did not yet value himself (e.g., when he displayed vulnerability or need), and as valuing *myself* under conditions in which he did not yet value me (e.g., when *I* displayed vulnerability). These representations served as the relational template for Howard experiencing the parts of himself that, for most of his life, he had associated with his badness.

This is where the aforementioned "structural association" comes in. Since I continued to be motivationally responsive to Howard's subjectivity under conditions in which he accessed and inhabited his vulnerability, Howard was able to start valuing *himself* under these conditions as well. In turn, his less-conditional valuations of himself affected his valuations of me. As Howard became increasingly able to value himself even when experiencing his vulnerability, he was less likely to devalue me when I attempted to engage with these parts of him. Furthermore, due to my motivational responsiveness in these moments, Howard was also able to value me under a greater variety of subjective and objective circumstances—when he was experiencing his own sensitivity and need, when I exhibited my "therapist"-characteristics, and when (intentionally or unintentionally) I displayed my own vulnerability in sessions. In these ways, Howard was beginning to value both himself and me under a wider range of conditions, as exemplified by his increased sharing about the more vulnerable parts of himself, and by his improved ability to "take in" the parts of me that I brought to the clinical encounter.

As I see it, these processes served as the basis for Howard's gradual construction of the intersubjective relational configuration. Specifically, I believe that Howard was constructing symbolic and non-symbolic mnemic representations of the therapeutic relationship—representations of himself, representations of me, and representations of the progressively responsive interactions unfolding between us. Howard also began to value these representations of Self and Other under a progressively wider range of conditions, including the internal conditions (e.g., the unique thoughts, affects, desires, and feelings he experienced in these moments) and the external conditions (e.g., the interactional sequences unfolding between us in therapy; my behaviors, body language, and expressions in these moments; his perceptions of my emotional states) he associated with our increased responsiveness to one another. As the treatment evolved, I believe that Howard moved towards a place where he could value himself and me less conditionally, thus opening the door for *mutual* intersubjective motivation in the dyad, and ultimately in his relationships outside of therapy.

On the above model of therapeutic action, the possibility of psychic change requires that the therapist be motivationally responsive to the patient's subjectivity and to her own subjectivity (Benjamin, 2004, 2010). Had I not found a way of "being myself" with Howard, I would not have been able to attend to the parts of him that he associated with his badness. I would have remained stuck in the mode of appeasing Howard, and so he would not have had the experiences in therapy that enabled him to start valuing himself (and me) under a wider range of conditions. On this view, respect for oneself and for others is *the basis* for successful analytic work as well as the result of it.

Conclusion: Bridging the gap

In closing, I suggest that most of us, regardless of our consciously endorsed theoretical commitments, assume the possibility of intersubjective motivation in our everyday lives. That is, we naturally and automatically assume that we can be motivated by the needs, desires, and interests of other people and, in our more generous moments, that other people can be motivated by these things as well. In a deep and usually non-reflective way, we value this capacity, and we take the potential for it to be an important part of being human. However, psychoanalytic theory makes no such assumptions, since it lacks a model of mind that is able to adequately explain the phenomenon of intersubjective motivation.

This means that there has been a theoretical void in psychoanalysis, and a significant gap between our professional theories and our everyday assumptions about human motivation (Argyris & Schön, 1974).

This theoretical void can have serious implications for clinical practice. On the most basic level, it can lead us to endorse an overly narrow conception of our patients' psychological worlds. When working with a solely intrapsychic theory of motivation, we tend to conceptualize patients' motives in primarily intrapsychic terms. Accordingly, we might be less attuned to the intersubjectively motivated dimensions of their lives, possibly trying to reduce these processes to theoretically sanctioned intrapsychic meanings. This approach can lead patients to feel deeply misunderstood, as if we are missing something essential in their experiences, or even demeaned, as if we are only recognizing the "sick," childish, or historically determined parts of them.

In addition, when employing an exclusively intrapsychic theory of motivation to understand our patients, we are perhaps less likely to notice the developments in intersubjective motivational capacities that are part and parcel of effective analytic work (Searles, 1979; Winnicott, 1971, pp. 177–185). If we do happen to recognize these developments on some vague level, we lack the theoretical framework necessary to fully appreciate their intersubjective nature, and so we still end up conceptualizing them in intrapsychic terms (e.g., as a greater capacity for sublimation, as decreased conflict between one's wishes and superego prohibitions, as internalization of the good object, as increased cohesion of the self). In these ways, we might underestimate our patients' progress, maintaining a conception of their motivational capacities as more self-oriented than they actually are. Furthermore, to the degree that increased awareness of one's intersubjective motives can enhance one's responsiveness to these motives, we run the risk of inhibiting the continued evolution of our patients' emerging potential for intersubjective motivation.

We are also less apt to recognize the *absence* of intersubjective motivation in our patients when employing an exclusively intrapsychic model. We could therefore be less attuned to the ways that our patients unconsciously close themselves off to other people as a possible source of meaning, meaning which, if accessed, could have a powerful therapeutic impact on a wide range of debilitating symptoms, such as feelings of purposelessness, hopelessness, and self-hatred. Similarly, when operating with a solely intrapsychic theory of motivation, we will be less likely to notice our patients' undeveloped potentials for intersubjective motivation. To the extent that the therapist's vision of patients' potentials facilitates psychological change (Cooper, 2000; Loewald, 1960; Summers, 2000), the narrowness of such theories could thus hinder the development of intersubjective motivational capacities throughout the analytic process.

Finally, when working with an exclusively intrapsychic motivational theory, we often feel less connected to our patients. As noted previously, most of us naturally assume that the potential for intersubjective motivation is inextricably bound up with what it means to be human. Nevertheless, when employing a solely intrapsychic notion of motivation to understand our patients, we frequently fail to recognize that our patients possess this basic human potential. In such cases, we can draw an overly sharp distinction between ourselves as human beings and our patients as human beings. This can lead us to feel less connected to our patients and their experiences, and, in more extreme cases, even to adopt a destructive sense of superiority over our patients, as if we are the "healthy" ones in the relationship and that our patients are lacking, flawed, or deficient in some fundamental way. Insidiously, these attitudes can persist alongside genuine feelings of care and concern for our patients, and they can be unconsciously communicated regardless of our degree of awareness of them.

For many practitioners, the above consequences will not always ensue. That is because many of us engage in what might be called a *compensatory process* in regard to our theories. Intuitively sensing the inadequacies of a solely intrapsychic model, and in an effort to remain connected to our patients, we unconsciously supplement our consciously endorsed conceptions of intrapsychic motivation with our convictions about the possibility of intersubjective motivation, naturally fashioning a common-sense motivational theory that includes both intrapsychic and intersubjective elements. Armed with such a theory, when a patient discusses his desire to express love to his children more explicitly, we listen for the intrapsychically motivated dimensions of his subjectivity (e.g., his wish to provide himself with the nurturance he never received as a child, his attempts to mask and undo his aggression towards the neglectful father of his childhood, his efforts to maintain self-cohesion by strengthening his ties to his children-as-selfobjects, his need to expunge his guilt for not being his mother's savior) as well as the intersubjectively motivated aspects of his experience (e.g., his commitment to meeting his children's emotional needs, his wish to make his daughter happy, his desire to bolster his son's self-confidence).

Rather than try to compensate for the inadequacies of our intrapsychic constructs of motivation, we should begin to *revise* these constructs to accommodate our best clinical intuitions, attempting to build a comprehensive psychoanalytic theory of motivation that encompasses both intrapsychic and intersubjective elements (Shapiro & Gabbard, 1994; Slavin & Kriegman, 1992). Such a model would help to bridge the gap between our professional theories and our natural assumptions about human motivation, helping us to feel closer to our patients and more connected to them as human beings. This model could also address the complex relationship between intrapsychic and intersubjective motivation, both in specific circumstances and, dynamically, over the course of individual development and analytic work. Perhaps most importantly, this theory would categorically encourage us to recognize both the intrapsychically and intersubjectively motivated dimensions of our patients' subjectivity. When operating with such a conception, we would be more receptive to the intersubjectively motivated elements in our patients' experiences, less apt to construe these elements as simply "derivative" of intrapsychic motives, more attuned to our patients' untapped potentials for intersubjective motivation, and more likely to acknowledge the genuine progress in intersubjective motivational capacities that, in my opinion, are central to the therapeutic action of psychoanalysis. I will be working to elaborate such a theory for the remainder of this book.

In this chapter, I have attempted to pursue one aspect of the above project, namely the proposal of a vision of intersubjective motivation that can be integrated with the primarily intrapsychic constructs of motivation that are most common in psychoanalysis. In this way, I have tried to advance the project of relational psychoanalysis in general and intersubjectivity theory in particular. More so than perhaps any other sector of psychoanalysis, intersubjectivity theory has taught us that the ability to recognize other subjects is a cornerstone of individual development and therapeutic change, thereby positioning other human beings as a significant source of meaning in our lives. However, most intersubjective models have ignored the topic of intersubjective motivation, instead conceptualizing intersubjective relatedness in primarily epistemic terms. In so doing, these models have underestimated our potential to be motivated by others, failing to avail themselves of the theoretical and clinical utility of a genuinely intersubjective motivational system.

While I have already suggested that the epistemic approach is unable to explain intersubjective motivation, I will go one step further and suggest that it is inadequate as a general conception of intersubjective relatedness. This notion seems overly scientific in nature, implying that the fundamental intersubjective relationship is between *Knower* and *Known*, and that maturity adheres in the capacity to know a certain segment of reality, namely other subjects. In this way, this conception abstracts what is perhaps most human about intersubjective relatedness—the fact that we *value* other people, that we even love them in a way that is not completely reducible to libido, or object-seeking, or attachment. By bringing this idea into our theories, we bring ourselves closer to our patients, and ultimately help them to move closer to us.

Notes

1 This chapter contains material from the following papers, reused here by permission of Taylor & Francis, LLC: Drozek, R. P. (2010a). "Finding the value" in intersubjective and clinical process: Towards a valuational model of relational motivation: Reply to commentaries. *Psychoanalytic Dialogues, 20*, 582–596; and Drozek, R. P. (2010b). Intersubjectivity theory and the dilemma of intersubjective motivation. *Psychoanalytic Dialogues, 20*, 540–560.

2 The reader might object to my approach by insisting that, in considering sources of motivation (e.g., relational drives, relational configurations) as rooted in the individual subject, I am missing the whole point of relational theory, which necessarily conceptualizes the individual as embedded in a context of relatedness with other human beings. In response to this, I distinguish between a person's *context* and a person's *motivational processes*. In focusing on the latter, I am not denying that all people are necessarily embedded in a context of relatedness. In fact, I affirm that we are so embedded, but that it is also fruitful to explore how we can be motivated *within* this context, namely by intrapsychic meanings on the one hand and intersubjective meanings on the other.

3 I focus on these three theories in particular because of their relevance to the viewpoint that I develop later in this chapter, admittedly ignoring other intersubjective approaches (e.g., intersubjective perspectives on empathy and compassion, Ogden's

concept of the analytic third) that could be equally applicable to the topic of intersubjective motivation.

4 D. N. Stern (2004) cites research on mirror neurons to support this conception of intersubjective participation (see Rizzolatti, Fogassi, & Gallese, 2001). Since these neurons fire in the brain of a person who is observing an action in the same way as if that person were actually *performing* the action, Stern (2004) suggests that they could serve as the neurological basis for our ability to participate in other people's experiences (pp. 78–82).

5 The closest synonym to my term "valuational" is the philosophical term "normative," which means *involving the value of things* (e.g., actions, states of affairs, personal characteristics), and therefore concerns language that is evaluative (e.g., "right" and "wrong," "good" and "bad," "should" and "should not," "justified" and "unjustified") rather than strictly descriptive in nature (see Korsgaard, 1996b; Nagel, 1986, chapter 8; Scanlon, 1998, chapters 1 and 2). Since the concept of normativity has more specific connotations within psychoanalysis (often denoting societal, cultural, and developmental standards), I have coined the term *valuational* to mean "related to value" in general.

6 As Lew Aron (personal communication) helpfully points out, by focusing on our *capacity* for intersubjective motivation, I am highlighting processes that are grounded in the individual subject, and not sufficiently addressing how such processes manifest themselves and evolve in reciprocal dynamics operative *between* subjects. In Chapters 6 and 7, I attempt to expand the frame of this inquiry by introducing and elaborating my notion of the *intersubjective nexus of valuing*, which emphasizes the bidirectional valuational patterns continuously unfolding in all relational dyads, and in which all values are continuously influencing, influenced by, and even *constituted by* the valuational tendencies of the other party.

7 Empirically, this viewpoint disallows the possibility of a subject who values herself unconditionally but is unable to ascribe unconditional value to other people, and therefore who is unable to be motivationally receptive to the subjectivity of others. It also rejects the idea of a subject who ascribes unconditional value to others but is unable to value herself unconditionally. In my experience, patients who are generally incapable of intersubjective motivation (e.g., those with severe narcissistic and borderline problems) usually despise themselves, taking themselves to be fundamentally unlovable and, in my terminology, unconditionally bad. Furthermore, patients who exhibit what Teicholz (2010) calls "'pathological' degrees of deference to others' feelings and wishes" are usually not ascribing unconditional value to the person in question (p. 576), and so they are not truly being motivated by that person's subjectivity. Rather, these patients are often only valuing *aspects* of the other (e.g., attentiveness, admiration, dependency) and valuing themselves only conditionally (e.g., contingent on their ability to appease the other).

8 With these attacks, I believe that Howard was also protecting the parts of himself that he valued unconditionally, and, since he judged many of my attributes as being overly weak, trying to make me into the strong, admiring Other who could provide him with the sort of relationship that he valued most.

Chapter 4

The dignity in multiplicity[1]

Martha struggled with a long history of depression and suicidal thinking. While she had achieved some success in her career as a cardiac nurse, over the past decade, she had found it difficult to hold down a job for longer than one year. She would quickly impress her colleagues with her clinical skills and warm manner with patients, but inevitably the same pattern would repeat itself: falling behind in paperwork, feeling deeply insecure in her interactions with co-workers, arriving hours late to shifts, feeling more insecure and ashamed, and finally failing to show up to work altogether, at which point she would either quit or get fired.

Now in her forties, Martha lived a life of profound isolation. Her only living family member was an older sister, whom she saw as her antithesis—married with several children, emotionally stable, and professionally successful. Martha, on the other hand, had not dated anyone in over a decade, and she spent most of her time alone in her apartment—watching TV, eating junk food, languishing in bed, making endless lists, and moving piles of papers from one surface to another. Feeling abandoned by the world, Martha would start to fantasize about ways to take her life, which gave her a temporary feeling of relief that there might be some escape from this agonizing cycle of meaninglessness.

There are few concepts more central to human life than the idea of *dignity*. This concept underlies a range of near-universal intersubjective experiences—the notion that there are basic human rights, and that all of us deserve to have these rights respected; our aversion to taking actions that might seriously harm others; our feelings of revulsion when confronted with torture and abuse; our sense that there is something fundamentally wrong with treating other people exclusively like objects; and the difficulty we have comfortably treating *ourselves* simply like objects, at least without psychic ramifications. Implicit in these experiences is the assumption of dignity. *Human beings are not just objects. Rather, we have a special sort of worth that is intrinsic and unconditional, that is, not dependent on factors apart from our common humanity.*

Somewhat surprisingly, dignity has not received much attention in the analytic literature. Yet dignity serves as a quietly foundational construct in psychoanalysis, regularly exerting its influence on theory and practice while rarely receiving the recognition it deserves. In particular, as I hope to illustrate in this chapter, concerns about dignity have played a pivotal role in encouraging what has been called the "relational turn" in psychoanalysis. Unfortunately, like the notion of intersubjective motivation considered in the last chapter, relational thought is unable to explain dignity in a satisfying way. By continuing to conceptualize value as deriving from other factors (e.g., needs, affects), we have not yet made sufficient space for the possibility of *intrinsic value* within psychoanalytic thought.

Utilizing concepts from ethical theory and analytic ideas regarding the multiplicity of self-states, I will sketch out a model of psychic experience in which dignity plays a defining role. This model emphasizes the ongoing dialectic between dignity-based processes (in which Self and Other are experienced as unconditionally valuable) and processes in which we experience Self and Other as only *conditionally* valuable, or in cases of pathology, unconditionally bad. I trace out some clinical implications of these proposals, offering a *dignity-based* vision of therapeutic work, in which analyst and patient are engaged in the co-construction of an intersubjective space that is progressively more consistent with their intrinsic worth as human beings.

Dignity and freedom

To begin, I provide some background on dignity from philosophy and political theory, the disciplines that have addressed this topic most extensively.[2] We can distinguish between two views on dignity, the *restricted* and *universal* conceptions. In the restricted view, which was common prior to the Enlightenment, dignity refers to the elevated worth of individuals possessing certain qualities, such as high social status or a "dignified" manner. In the universal view, dignity refers to our ascription of unconditional or intrinsic value to ourselves and others *as human beings*, not dependent on factors unique to specific people or classes of people.

This conception derives most directly from the ethical ideas of the eighteenth century German philosopher Immanuel Kant. As discussed in Chapters 1 and 2, Kant (1785/1997) conceives of dignity as the "unconditional, incomparable worth" of human beings (p. 42). For Kant, dignity is closely related to ethics and morality. As Kant puts it, "A human being ... is not a thing and hence not something that can be used merely as a means, but must in all of his actions always be regarded as an end in itself" (p. 38). When we ascribe *unconditional* rather than strictly conditional value to other people, we experience a feeling of respect for them *as* people. In this motivational state, we are more likely to be motivated by their desires and interests, and less likely to relate to them exclusively like objects that might either satisfy or frustrate our own wishes.[3]

For many of us in the Western democratic world, this view of dignity has become so infused into our shared cultural identity that it is difficult to imagine contemporary life without it. We hear it in the dictum "All men are created equal," according to which no person is "more worthwhile" than another. We see this model of dignity in our notions of human rights and social justice, wherein all human beings deserve to be treated with a basic level of respect and care. Finally, this view is connected to our democratic ideals, in which all people are entitled to a government in which they have a voice, and in which their needs, values, and interests hold some degree of motivating power.[4]

Why do we value ourselves and others in this special way? This question can be approached from multiple perspectives—biological, evolutionary, sociological, and as I hope to illustrate, psychoanalytic. I will focus on the most popular answer to this question within philosophy and contemporary culture—the connection between dignity and *freedom*. Consider this description of freedom by the philosopher Robert Kane (2002a):

> From a *personal* or *practical* standpoint, we see ourselves as free agents capable of influencing the world in various ways. Open alternatives seem to lie open to us. We reason or deliberate among them and choose. We feel it is "up to us" what we choose and how

> we act. … This "up to us-ness" also suggests that the origins or sources of our actions are in us and not in something else over which we have no control.
>
> (p. 5)

In this model, freedom involves experiencing ourselves as a *source* of meaning and value, rather than just a causal byproduct of factors distinct from ourselves. While philosophers emphasize the importance of this capacity in our deliberations about "what to do," freedom extends beyond moments of deliberation—it is a deep part of our identities, encompassing our sense that we are somehow *responsible* for who we are and how we live. Many philosophers posit this freedom as the phenomenological basis for human dignity. Since we experience ourselves as a source of meaning rather than simply as receptacles for others' meanings, we take ourselves to have an *intrinsic* worth, or dignity. To the degree that we experience others in an analogous way, we naturally take them to have dignity as well.

Implicit in this formulation is the psychoanalytically relevant distinction between *subjects* and *objects*. Objects are valued *by* people; they cannot value themselves, other objects, or people. *Subjects*, on the other hand, are unique entities possessing the capacity to *endow* things with value, and it is in virtue of this capacity that we take human beings to have a special kind of value, what I am calling dignity (Aron, 2005, pp. 691–692).

These reflections may not seem particularly relevant to clinical work. After all, our patients often *do not* feel like they are "free," "a source of meaning," or "unconditionally valuable." However, I believe that all of us, even our most impaired patients, have intermittent access to the freedom philosophers are highlighting. Consider the person filled with self-hatred, who struggles with a sense of meaninglessness, who cannot live up to her own standards, who does not even feel like her standards *are* her own. Even this person has moments of the freedom mentioned above: when she feels like genuine possibilities are open to her, and when she feels like *she*—not other people, not past versions of herself, not unconscious parts of herself—is choosing what to do, even if she is only deciding between "going to the store" and "staying home."

The analytic theorist who best articulates these ideas is Irwin Hoffman (1998): "There is a 'space' between the source of influence and its impact, a gap in which I am present as an agent, as a choosing subject" (p. xi). Hoffman refers to this as an "active mode" of experience, in which the subject serves as a "*source* of construction" (1995, p. 107), and as "a responsible, free agent, not merely an organism responding to internal and external pressures" (2000, p. 827).

I refer to this capability as *agentic freedom*. This concept is strictly phenomenological in nature, referring to our *experience of ourselves* as free agents, without implying that we are actually free in any objective sense. This freedom encompasses two key analytic constructs—*subjecthood* and *agency*. First, it entails an experience of oneself as a subject, an "I" that has the ability to reflect on itself as an object (a "me") in a world of other people who can be seen as both subjects and objects (Aron, 2000; James, 1890/1950). This notion of subjecthood includes Benjamin's (2000) view of the person as a distinct, independent subject who is fundamentally similar to other subjects, and Fonagy and colleagues' (2002) model of the self as agent, "the mental processes or functions that underpin representations of the self" (p. 24).

Agentic freedom also implies an experience of *agency*—the capacity to play an active role in co-constructing meaning within relational contexts. Unlike many recent conceptions of agency (Gentile, 2010; Rustin, 1997; Slavin, 2010; Weisel-Barth, 2009), this freedom is not associated with psychological health, nor does it derive from optimal developmental circumstances. Rather, it is grounded in the structure of human consciousness, and so it is accessible to everyone. Since many patients lack a robust sense of freedom at the start of analytic work, and since analysis has such a powerful impact on the experience of agency, we often fail to notice the freedom patients possess independently of clinical intervention, simply in virtue of being human.

Agentic freedom presupposes that the subject possesses what Daniel N. Stern (1985) calls the "verbal self," which encompasses a range of capacities that develop during the second year of life—the acquisition of language; the faculty of symbolic thought; "the capacity to make the self the object of reflection" (p. 165); the ability to refer to Self and Other using verbal labels (e.g., "I," "me"); and the capacity to construct complex representations of oneself in relation to others—as a subject, as an objective entity in a world populated by other objective entities, and as someone performing actions that have been observed as well as imagined. Taken together, these milestones entail an expansion of the child's recognition of *possibility*: "the infant can now entertain and maintain a formed wish of how reality ought to be, contrary to fact" (p. 167). Armed with a sense of oneself as a subject, a sense of oneself as an object, and the ability to imagine, represent, and initiate possibilities beyond the present reality, the child commences to experience herself as a source of meaning, rather than just a recipient of others' meanings. This experience serves as the rudimentary basis for a growing awareness of freedom and dignity.

Dignity and the relational turn

With this conception in place, I want to propose that concerns about dignity have played a central role in inspiring and fueling the advent of relational thinking in psychoanalysis. I will thus be offering something of a historical interpretation of what has been called "the relational turn." I will not, however, be arguing that classical theory is "actually" at odds with human dignity, or that relational thought is more consistent with it.[5] I find this topic less interesting than the question of *how* the dignity idea influences theory development and clinical practice. By focusing specifically on dignity to the exclusion of other concerns, I hope to shine a spotlight onto an under-theorized but foundational area of psychoanalytic discourse.

To begin, I suggest that dignity played a powerful role in relationally oriented theorists' dissatisfaction with classical models of motivation. We hear this dissatisfaction in Fairbairn's (1952) assertion "that a relationship with the object, and not gratification of impulse, is the ultimate aim of libidinal striving" (p. 60); in Winnicott's (1971) insight, "it is not instinctual satisfaction that makes a baby begin to be, to feel that life is real, to find life worth living" (p. 133); and in Mitchell's (1988) criticism, "Freud regards what is distinctively human and special in mankind as a tenuous overlay upon a rapacious, bestial core" (p. 74). A common ethical sentiment runs throughout these comments, which is repeatedly echoed throughout the relational lexicon: *human beings are not simply animals, biological organisms, or inanimate objects*. In my view, relational thinkers have seen such formulations not just as inaccurate or unpersuasive, but as potentially demeaning. By framing motivation in specifically *human* terms—that is, in terms of relationships—these theorists were attempting to construct theories that were more consistent with the dignity of the analytic subject.

Dignity has also played an important role in the epistemological developments accompanying the relational turn. When arguing against the idea of the analyst as a "blank-screen," theorists have been taking issue with an authoritarian conception of the therapeutic situation, in which pathology resides primarily in the patient, and transference consists of the patient "transferring" that pathology/distortion onto the all-knowing analyst (Hoffman, 1998). Relational thinkers have seen this model as contrary to the patient's dignity, especially the parts of the patient aligned with health and non-distorted reality (Aron, 1996a). By highlighting the "irreducible subjectivity of the analyst" (Renik, 1993), these authors have been working to equalize the balance of knowledge and power between analyst and analysand, thereby elaborating a vision of psychoanalysis more consistent with the patient's dignity.[6]

Along similar lines, interest in dignity has contributed to our enhanced recognition of the analyst as a *real person* in the analytic dyad. We observe this recognition in a range of theoretical advances—an increased appreciation of the bidirectional, mutual patterns of influence in clinical process (Beebe & Lachmann, 2002); a growing emphasis on the non-generic and unique qualities of the analyst (Hoffman, 1998); the rise of interventions in which the analyst's subjectivity plays a more explicit role (Davies, 1994); and the loosening of classical strictures on technique, such that analysts are free to intervene in more authentic and creative ways with their patients (Aron & Starr, 2013; Ferenczi, 1932/1988).

With these advances, relational theorists have not simply been highlighting the essential intersubjectivity of analytic work—they have been reacting against the classical tendency to *objectify* the analyst, to frame her as an "analytic instrument" without fully appreciating her status as a unique individual. As Aron (1996a) writes, "Just as psychoanalytic theory has focused on the mother exclusively as the object of the infant's needs while ignoring the subjectivity of the mother, so too psychoanalysis … has considered the analyst only as an object" (p. 75). By emphasizing the importance of the analyst as a real person, relational authors have been working to affirm her *as a source of meaning in the clinical situation*, and thus to construct models more expressive of the analyst's dignity. Interestingly, affirming the analyst's dignity is not just about the analyst—by positioning the analyst as an "equivalent subject" in clinical process, relational theorists have been embracing the idea that the patient's health is dependent on her ability to respect the analyst as a distinct subject, and thus that "individual" well-being is constituted by the ability to honor the dignity of *both* Self and Other (Benjamin, 1995; Drozek, 2010a).

The notion of dignity is also implicit in relational psychoanalysis' evolving commitment to issues of social justice. Neil Altman (1995) suggests that relationally oriented theories are particularly well-equipped to explain "the racial, cultural, and social class status of patient and analyst, as well as the institutional context of their work" (p. 56). This point is displayed prominently throughout our literature, which focuses on justice and equality across numerous domains, including sexuality (Mitchell, 1978), gender (Harris, 2005), race (Leary, 2000; Straker, 2011), culture (Aggarwal, 2011; Ipp, 2010), social class (Gaztambide, 2012), and violence (Young-Bruehl, 2011).

This interest is not simply a reflection of the shared sensibilities of relational analysts—it is related to their endorsement of the universal view of dignity under discussion, which emphasizes the equal worth of all people, and therefore exists in tension with policies and practices that devalue anyone who might be seen as "not me." This endorsement has recently led to a renewed ambitiousness in psychoanalytic theory—the idea that psychoanalysis has a role in transforming not simply the individual person but also our cultural institutions, in a manner that expresses "cooperation, compassion, and concern for the interests of the collective, especially the dignity of each person" (Suchet, 2007, p. 884). Hoffman (2009a) proposes:

> At its best a *critical* rather than *conformist* psychoanalysis should emerge as a bastion in our culture that will stand for human freedom, for the dignity of the individual, for the meaningfulness of community, and for the sacrosanct integrity of every moment of experience.
> (pp. 1064–1065)

Finally, I suggest that dignity is related to another pervasive pattern in relational thought—an aversion to framing experience in universal terms, and a preference for honoring uniqueness in human life. We see this tendency in all areas of relational discourse—an emphasis on specificity over generality in models of motivation (Eagle, 1984; Hoffman, 1995); an abandonment of "objective" presentations of technique (Tublin, 2011); a shift away from linear, stage-based conceptions of development (Coburn, 2002; Seligman, 2005); and the proliferation of "experience-near, clinically based conceptualizations" throughout our literature (Foehl, 2010, p. 48). When arguing against the assumption of "universal" or "innate" motivation, Stephen Mitchell (1988) reflected, "As soon as one establishes a motive as innate, one ironically closes it off somewhat from analytic inquiry and thereby loses the opportunity to deepen an appreciation of its origins and resonances within the individual's particular relational matrix" (p. 62).

By postulating universal drives as the basis of experience, classical thought was positing a *generic and a priori* factor (e.g., libido, aggression) as the main determiner of meaning in human life. I believe that relational thinkers have seen this stance as undermining the dignity of the person—her status as a *unique* source of meaning, co-creating messy, unpredictable patterns of meaning with other meaning-making subjects. By placing a primary emphasis on the analysand's unique relational world, these theorists have been advocating for a conception of psychoanalysis not just more consistent with the dignity of analysands *in general*, but with the dignity of any particular person who might approach the therapeutic process.

Explicit views on dignity in relational thought

As noted earlier, few analytic writers devote extended attention to the topic of dignity. By reviewing some references to dignity throughout our literature, we can begin to consider the specifically psychoanalytic contributions to the dignity idea in human experience.

It is widely accepted that respect for the patient's dignity is the foundation for analytic work. As Thomas Ogden (2005) puts it:

> For me, what is most fundamental to psychoanalysis is the principle that an analyst treats his patient—and all those his patient's life impinges upon—in a humane way, in a way that at all times honors human dignity. This principle is the North Star of psychoanalysis; it

> is a point of reference in terms of which all else is located. When an analyst is not being humane, what he is doing with the patient is not recognizable to me as psychoanalysis.
>
> (p. 19)

For Ogden, the ethical foundation of psychoanalysis is the principle that *the analyst should always honor and respect the dignity of the patient.* This view is mirrored by the American Psychoanalytic Association, whose Ethics Code states "the psychoanalytic relationship is predicated on respecting human dignity." While there are different opinions about what this looks like in practice, most clinicians would agree that it disallows many behaviors understood to be unethical—lying to a patient for one's own gain, physically striking a patient, having sex with someone in treatment with you. The dignity of the person is also implicit in the principle that we should be dedicated to the well-being, growth, and flourishing of our patients. If we did not value our patients *as people*, most likely we would not care about their pleasure, pain, or desires.

A number of theorists emphasize the importance of dignity in human development and motivation. In his "Credo," Ghent (1989) associates dignity with self-worth, positing "a need for a feeling of self-worth, dignity, self-esteem" as a fundamental source of motivation (p. 207). Shengold (1979) invokes dignity when introducing his famous idea of soul murder:

> There is an inherent moral protest in the term. Soul murder is a crime characterized by man's inhumanity to man. One man uses his power over another to crush his individuality, his dignity, his capacity to feel deeply (to feel joy, love, and even hate).
>
> (p. 536)

When the parent persistently acts to negate the child's dignity, the child adopts "a mind-splitting or a mind-fragmenting operation," consciously experiencing the abusive parent as "good" while dissociating the parent's badness, thereby creating a rigidified structural split in the personality (p. 539).

More so than any other psychoanalytic theorist, Peter Shabad gives dignity a foundational role in his model of development. In Shabad's (2001) view, when parents are able to validate the child's unique capacities, the child acquires "a sense of worth or personal dignity, and of having a special part to play within the human community" (p. 193). Conversely, when parents are unable to appreciate the uniqueness of the child—often due to their own narcissism—the child contorts herself to comply with the parents' needs and ideals: "eventually, these children grow up to feel their lives are not their own, but the playthings of powers far greater than themselves" (p. 195). Here, health is characterized by experiencing oneself as worthwhile and creatively free, while pathology is marked by a lack of worth and freedom, and a desperate search for these things that forecloses the possibility of free and creative experiences in relationships.

Drawing parallels between the story of "the incredible shrinking man" and analytic change, Donnell B. Stern (2010) emphasizes the increased dignity that accompanies the process of narrating one's life in the real or imagined presence of another:

> Prior to constructing his tale in the explicit terms of his diary, he has become an object in his own life, a figure suffering chaotic, incomprehensible events for no apparent reason and with little feeling. The emergence of meaning from what has felt to him like senselessness, helplessness, and despair confers agency and therefore dignity. He is once again a subject.
>
> (p. 109)

In Stern's view, dignity is aligned with agency and freedom, the ability to serve as a source of one's own experience. However, such freedom is not associated with the concept of a unified self. Rather, it involves "our freedom to tell many self-stories at once—in other words, our freedom to inhabit multiple states of being simultaneously" (p. 122).

Given that dignity concerns the *worth* of the person, it is understandable that many self psychologists devote attention to the topic (Jacobs, 2008; Ornstein, 1993). As Orange (2013) observes, "Self psychology, with its awareness of the many forms of shame and degradation, has placed the restoration of human dignity in the center of the therapeutic project" (p. 110). Developing these ideas along intersubjective lines, Jessica Benjamin proposes a model in which the dignity of *both* analyst and patient is vital to the therapeutic enterprise. As we saw last chapter, Benjamin's (1995) theory of intersubjectivity is centered on the capacity for *mutual recognition*, our ability to experience the Other as "a separate and equivalent center of subjectivity" (p. 7). Benjamin also frames her ideas in terms of *mutual respect*, or the ability of each subject "to respect the other subject as an equal" (p. 8), which necessarily entails respecting *the differences* between them (p. 23n).

The assumption of dignity is deeply embedded in these insights—as noted earlier, the "unconditional worth" of humanity implies the equal worth of all human beings. In this model, successful development entails the *mutual recognition of dignity*—our ability to value both Self and Other *unconditionally*, in the context of a relationship with another subject who is able to do the same. In her more recent writings, Benjamin (2009) invokes dignity when discussing the importance of the analyst accepting responsibility for therapeutic ruptures, and the role of this approach in restoring mutual recognition in the dyad:

> An important sign of re-opening thirdness is being restored to the capacity to hear multiple voices—I can hear both your voice and mine as can you without one cancelling the other out; I can hear more than one part of yourself, you can hear more than one part of yourself. … It is now possible to recognize the presence of multiple voices and parts of self.
>
> (p. 442)

Benjamin relates this process to the expansion of "agency and responsibility" for patient and analyst (p. 450), also linking it to the dignity of both participants (p. 447; see also Benjamin, 2011). Combining her notion of mutual respect with these newer reflections on multiplicity, we arrive at a radical statement of the role of dignity in the analytic encounter. Not only does psychoanalysis enable patient and analyst to simultaneously experience dissociated parts of themselves in the dyad—this enhanced potential for multiplicity entails an enhancement of freedom for both parties, and an ability to *value themselves and others* while experiencing multiple (potentially contradictory) configurations of Self and Other within oneself and within the relationship. Here we see the dignity *in* multiplicity, an idea I will explore further for the remainder of this chapter.

Dignity as a psychoanalytic construct

I now want to make an observation about the role of dignity in clinical practice, namely that *we naturally assume that our patients are worthwhile, and that they are worthwhile in what might be called an "unconditional" sense.* Even in the messiness of day-to-day clinical work—when we feel bored with our patients, when we are primarily interested in how they are making *us* feel, when they are not doing (or feeling, or thinking) what we want them to, when we feel irritated with them, when we even *hate* them and respond accordingly—we simultaneously assume our patients are worthy of respect and care. This is what I mean by "unconditional" or "intrinsic" valuing—valuing the other person *as a person*, regardless of the other bidirectional, "positive" and "negative" valuing that unfolds continuously and implicitly in the relationship. Such valuing is not exclusively dependent on how we feel about the patient, or on whether our needs are getting met—in the terms I am using here, it is unconditional.[7]

This assumption plays a powerful role in how we approach the analytic process. While we rarely notice the presence of dignity (e.g., a basic level of respect for Self and Other) in our patients' narratives, the *absence or contradiction* of dignity in Self or Other (e.g., profound self-neglect, self-hatred, externally directed rage) makes the analyst's ears perk up: "There is something important to be explored here." We want to understand *why* they feel that way, in light of their history, contemporary experiences, internalized representations of Self and Other, and so on. The presumption of dignity thus serves as the context for our explorations of our patients' various ascriptions of value to themselves and others.

At the same time, we automatically take *ourselves* to have a similar sort of value. In fact, it is because of these assumptions that we seek to resolve the difficult impasses that receive so much attention in our literature. Convinced that *both of us* are worthwhile, we are able to summon the faith that *there must be a way of being together in which the dignity of both participants can be respected.*

As a construct, dignity has some unique features. First, the assumption of dignity makes an often-unacknowledged claim to objectivity. When assuming our patients are worthwhile, we do not feel like we are simply expressing our personal feelings—*"I value you."* We feel like we are making a statement about the patient's *actual* worth—*"You are valuable, even if you don't feel that way about yourself."* If a patient tells us she is bad, evil, and undeserving of love, we do not ask ourselves *if* she is really a bad person: "I really need to get to the bottom of this, so that I can see if she is worthy of respect and care." Rather, when our patients say these sorts of things, *we automatically assume that they are wrong.* Interestingly, when patients affirm they are bad, or that their worth is dependent on some "extrinsic" quality (e.g., appearance, material success), there is little they can say or do to make us agree with them.[8]

There is also an ethical dimension to the dignity idea. Traditionally, analytic concepts are *descriptive* in nature, highlighting the subject's conscious and unconscious processes without explicitly taking a stand on the value of these processes. In contrast, dignity seems to straddle the experiential and valuational realms, describing an experience of worth while also *affirming* that worth. This feature partially explains why dignity has not achieved a place of explicit prominence in psychoanalysis—as an ethical concept, it can appear to fall outside the boundaries of "psychoanalysis proper."[9]

Despite the importance dignity holds in clinical practice, traditional psychoanalytic theories tend to provide an unsatisfying explanation of this concept. Since its inception, psychoanalysis has conceptualized value as a derivative rather than primary phenomenon—we value things that lead to drive satisfaction, or that satisfy our needs. In relational thought, we conceptualize values as deriving from affects—we value things that generate positive feelings in us, whether in our early intersubjective contexts or contemporary lives.[10]

Such explanations do not do justice to our experience of dignity. To say that we value others in this special way because "they satisfy our needs" or "they make us feel good" paints an excessively self-oriented picture of dignity—it sounds thin and even demeaning. This conception also contradicts the insight mentioned earlier, that usually this valuing is not dependent on how we feel, or whether our needs are being met. From our perspective as human beings and not just psychoanalysts, we value other human beings *because they deserve it,* because they are the sorts of beings who *are* valuable.

Furthermore, by positing some extra factor within the subject (e.g., needs, affects) as determining the worth she ascribes to others, this model presents an overly passive view of dignity, neglecting the fact that we regularly feel like *we* are choosing to value ourselves and others in this special way, and that other people can choose to value us as well. This is a disempowering vision of dignity, dissociating the agency involved in dignity out of the subject and placing it into "needs" and "affects" (Schafer, 1976).

In making these arguments, I am not suggesting psychoanalytic *practitioners* believe that all values derive from needs and affects, or that we lack all agency in determining our values. Rather, I am concerned that, by employing the aforementioned derivative conceptions of value, we are inadvertently committing ourselves to *concepts* that undermine the dignity of the person, despite the fact that we are naturally committed to affirming that dignity. To preserve our everyday experience of dignity, we need a psychoanalytic construct that allows for the possibility of derivative *and* intrinsic value, affirming the idea that human beings are the recipients *and* the source of the value we ascribe to one another. Such a construct would be more consistent with the nuanced and dialectical vision of human value we already naturally employ in analytic work.

Psychoanalysis also has difficulty explaining the universality of dignity. Ironically, this is especially true in relational thought, which dispenses with universal drives in favor of a model where "all meaning is generated in relation" (Mitchell, 1988, p. 61). While such a theory can explain why children who receive care and validation develop the ability to ascribe unconditional value to themselves and others, it has difficulty explaining why children who never encounter such things still actualize a sense of themselves as having dignity, an inner resilience enabling them to seek out new contexts more consistent with their worth and the worth of others. Shengold (1979) articulates the problem thus:

> Despite the vulnerability of children and the prevalence of bad parents, a completely successful soul murder is probably rare. Why this should be so *is* mysterious; part of the explanation is innate endowment. What was it that enabled one of my patients with two psychotic parents to become, from age four on, the real parent in the family—a sane caring person who was able to help

> her siblings and even take care of her psychotic parents? I have no adequate answer.
>
> (pp. 549–550)

If all meaning derives from relational experiences, it is difficult to explain how someone who has never been valued still develops a sense of dignity.

The philosophical theories reviewed earlier provide some interesting resources to address this problem. On these views, dignity is related to the phenomenology of freedom—since we experience ourselves as a source of meaning rather than just receptacles for others' meanings, we take ourselves to have an intrinsic worth as subjects. I have suggested that all of us have intermittent access to this experience. These considerations lead to a far-reaching clinical idea—regardless of our patients' degrees of pathology, they can encounter a sense of themselves as intrinsically valuable. This capacity is not dependent on their relational histories—it is grounded in the structure of human consciousness, and so it is open to everyone. The awareness of dignity serves as an unparalleled psychic anchor in therapeutic work, leading patients to believe that, regardless of their histories of abuse and trauma, *they deserve something better in the future.* Psychoanalysis is an intersubjective process by which we help patients transform their beliefs about "what they deserve" into a hope and desire for a previously unforeseen possibility, and ultimately into a genuinely new experience of Self-in-relation-to-Other.

The dignity in multiplicity

I will now try to sketch out the broad outlines of a model of psychic experience and development in which dignity plays a defining role. The model is based on the supposition that all of us have intermittent access to a sense of ourselves as intrinsically valuable. This experience has a powerful impact on the basic *directionality* of intersubjectivity across time, naturally leading us to seek out modes of relatedness in which we take ourselves to have more positive and less conditional value. To the degree that we identify other people as similar to us, there also exists an experiential thrust towards valuing them more positively and less conditionally, such that our actions, feelings, and thoughts are more consistent with their dignity. Dignity thus operates as an almost gravitational force in intersubjective relatedness, a gradient continuously nudging us towards a deeper respect for ourselves and others. This, I believe, is what Dr. Martin Luther King, Jr., was affirming when he said, "The arc of the moral universe is long, but it bends towards justice." At the personal and cultural level, human experience is not, nor can it ever be, ethically neutral. This applies even to so-called "pathological" processes that, on their face, seem to contradict the dignity of Self or Other.

I will first articulate, although not fully defend, some of my basic assumptions. I expand the notion of value beyond its more "conscious" or ethical connotations, defining it simply as *taking something to be a source of meaning*. At the conscious level, we regularly experience ourselves as an "I" ascribing value to aspects of our relational lives, whether we are taking some person, thing, or event to be "good" or "bad," or considering if we "should" or "should not" perform a specific action. Following Mitchell (1988), I conceptualize the unconscious in terms of *relational configurations*, our templates for *what it means to be in relationship* with others. However, I see our motivational connection to these configurations in terms of value: unconsciously or implicitly, we constantly ascribe a range of values (e.g., positive/negative, conditional/unconditional) to representations of our experiences in relationships.

In this model, value holds a primary motivational status—all other psychic phenomena (e.g., cognitions, affects, desires, fantasies) can be seen as expressions of our ascriptions of value to certain ways of being with others, influenced by our embeddedness in past and contemporary relational contexts. If we assume that our valuations are not motivationally dependent on desires and affects, then we open up the possibility of *intrinsic value* within psychoanalysis—we can value other people for their own sake, regardless of how they make us feel or whether they meet our needs.

It is important to draw a distinction regularly blurred in the discussions of dignity reviewed earlier—the distinction between *dignity* and *self-esteem*. Dignity refers to the intrinsic worth *of the human subject*. From the first-person perspective, we encounter this worth intermittently, when we reflexively value ourselves as an "I" that serves as a source of meaning. Self-esteem refers to the positive or negative value we ascribe to ourselves *as Selves* (that is, as objects of the "I") in the relational modes we occupy in intersubjective process. While we implicitly ascribe unconditional value to ourselves *as subjects*, we concurrently ascribe other forms of value to various unique, historically influenced representations of ourselves and others. I suggest that this dialectic between "the value of the Subject" and "the value of Self and Other" lies at the heart of personality development and motivation. In addition to emphasizing the dialectic between different relational configurations or self-states, I am interested in the dialectic *within* our different configurations, specifically between our ascription of unconditional value to ourselves and others *as subjects* and our valuations of Self and Other *as objects*, the latter of which can be more or less experientially consistent with the person's dignity.

As other authors have noted, the child's first relational configurations derive from her unique experiences in early familial contexts. The child gradually comes to value herself and the caregiver in a manner consistent with the caregiver's valuations of herself and the child. These valuations form the basis of the child's earliest relational configurations. As discussed last chapter, when the caregiver is able to value herself and the child unconditionally—when she does not feel like she has to choose between maintaining her dignity and honoring the child's dignity—child and caregiver co-create a mutually responsive dynamic, in which both parties are able to value each other simultaneously (Drozek, 2010b). As the child attains the sense of a verbal self and starts to value herself as a subject, she begins to encounter a flexible and progressive harmony between herself and others as subjects—*"I am at the center of the world, and so are you"*—and herself and others as Selves/objects—*"I am valuable to myself but also to you; you matter to yourself, and you also matter to me"* (Benjamin, 1995). For ease of reference, I refer to this capacity as *dignity-based* experiencing.

However, no caregiver ascribes only intrinsic value to her child. In addition, the caregiver also ascribes unconditional value to *aspects* of the child (e.g., behaviors, affective states, attitudes) and conditional value to the child *herself*, dependent on whether or not she displays qualities the caregiver values. Or she ascribes unconditional *badness* to aspects of the child, and conditional badness to the child when she displays those qualities. Over time, the child adopts similar patterns of valuing, as Sullivan (1953) illustrates with his ideas about "good me" and "bad me."

This conditional valuing of the child is frequently related to the caregiver's valuations of herself—*"I ascribe conditional value to myself, and unconditional value to these parts of myself. I need you to be a very specific sort of person with me, so that I can actualize the parts of myself that have intrinsic worth."*

This conditional valuing is a normative part of human development. In my view, it does not cause serious problems as long as the child also attains the capacity for dignity-based experiencing. Even if we feel like we have to "earn our worth" in various ways, we can access a sense of ourselves in which we are a source of meaning and value *no matter what.* The potential for dignity-based experiencing thus serves as the intersubjective buffer for all of the non-dignity-based processes endemic to human life. Here, psychopathology involves either the *absence* of the capacity for dignity-based experience (as we see in cases of severe trauma and neglect), or impairments in this capacity when another configuration is motivationally prominent (as we see in traditional "neuroses"). Without dignity, desire becomes desperation, insecurity becomes self-loathing, and anger becomes hatred.

To illustrate: when the caregiver cannot value herself and the child simultaneously, or if the child is unable to experience the caregiver as valuing her, the child never encounters a mode of relatedness in which Self and Other have a basic sense of worth. Instead, the child values *parts* of herself (e.g., attractiveness, the ability to perform well in some way, a specific relational stance), taking her worth to be dependent on her ability to actualize those parts. As development unfolds, the child desperately seeks to manifest those qualities the caregiver valued most, and to avoid qualities the caregiver devalued—*"If I am the sort of person who feels these things or behaves in these ways, no one will ever want to be with me."* This is the province of compulsion, when we feel like we have to perpetually work to create a certain vision of reality, and to prevent other visions of reality from materializing. We do this not only to make ourselves worthwhile, but because we believe *this is what it means to be in a relationship.*

Perhaps most tragically, there are instances in which the caregiver devalues the child *as a person.* When the caregiver ascribes badness to herself but lacks the potential for dignity-based experiencing, she can become addicted to modes of relatedness where she constantly situates this badness outside of herself (e.g., in the child), also ascribing value to some aspect of herself realized in these dynamics (e.g., a sense of power, self-righteous rage, externally directed aggression). Here, the caregiver *needs the child to be bad* so that she does not have to be, so that she can access the parts of herself she takes to be most valuable. Under these circumstances, the child can enact tendencies towards self-hatred and masochism we encounter so regularly in clinical practice—she sees *herself* as essentially bad (Fairbairn, 1952), unworthy of relationships with others, while unconsciously valuing the qualities in others (e.g., power, aggression) she associates with her own badness.[11]

As noted earlier, as the child acquires the sense of a verbal self and gains the faculty of agentic freedom, she starts to implicitly value herself as a subject. If her earliest relational configurations contradict the intrinsic value of the Self (e.g., if she ascribes badness or only conditional value to herself), the child encounters an experiential discrepancy between her valuation of herself *as subject* and her valuations of herself *as Self.* This discrepancy manifests itself in the vague but powerful feeling that she deserves something better than the roles that have been forced upon her, *even though she has never experienced anything other than those roles.* This yearning for "something better" does not stem from the child's unique history or from the operation of some drive or need, but from the child's implicit recognition of her dignity, deriving as we have seen from the structure of human consciousness.

The child now finds herself in a dilemma. While she longs for a mode of relatedness more consistent with her dignity, such a mode is not readily available to her. In a creative attempt to resolve this dilemma, the child naturally tries to assume a relational position to which she ascribes *more positive and less conditional* value. This solution takes various forms—granting some other valued relational mode (e.g., with other family members, with peers) increased prominence within her psychic economy; attempting to *negate* the demeaning relational mode, perhaps by avoiding the relationship in question; adopting some valued role she has observed or imagined but never experienced herself; if participation in such a role is not possible for her, occupying this role in fantasy; and experimenting with a valued role formerly held exclusively by the caregiver, as exemplified in Freud's (1920) "fort/da" example and Anna Freud's (1946) theorizing about "identification with the aggressor."

These new configurations then become the individual's primary manner of defending against configurations in which she ascribes unconditional badness or only conditional value to herself.

The sense of dignity also impacts the value we ascribe to others. As noted earlier, when we take other people to be fundamentally similar to us, we naturally ascribe value to them as subjects. If our most prominent relational configurations contradict the dignity of others (e.g., when we ascribe badness or only conditional value to them), then we can encounter an experiential discrepancy between our valuation of them *as subjects* and our valuations of them *as Selves*. This incongruity manifests itself in vague feelings of guilt and shame—"This person deserves more than I am giving her"—as well as chronic feelings of emptiness. While we might try to escape this dissonance in various ways (e.g., by denying the essential similarity between us; by defensively focusing on another's wrongs or defects), such feelings can usually only be alleviated by coming to value the other person under a wider range of conditions, thereby adopting a mode of relatedness more experientially consistent with the other's dignity.

The dialectics of dignity in clinical process

I would now like to share some preliminary reflections about what it might look like to conceptualize psychoanalysis along dignity-based, value-oriented lines. To ground these ideas, I draw on Philip Bromberg's pioneering work on the intersubjective nature of dissociative process. In Bromberg's (2006) view, analytic interaction always involves "the ongoing collision of multiple subjectivities contained within and between patient and analyst" (p. 105), in which both parties mutually dissociate their "not-me" self-states, usually without awareness and always in response to the intersubjective dynamic unfolding between them. According to Bromberg (2010), "It is through the open, joint processing of each partner's not-me experience that the potential for expanded symbolization of self-meaning emerges" (p. 21). Through collaborative exploratory inquiry, both members of the dyad gain access to their previously dissociated experiences. Where the patient had rigidly dissociated her self-states from one another, she gains an expanded capacity to "stand in the spaces" between contradictory self-states, leading to an increased sense of wholeness and "the coexistence of self-continuity and self-coherence across self-states" (2006, p. 27; see also Bass, 2012).

Developing these ideas along the lines I have been proposing, I suggest that analyst and patient are continuously ascribing a range of values to various unique configurations of Self and Other in the therapeutic relationship, in light of their respective histories, psychosocial/cultural contexts, and the intersubjective dynamic unfolding between them in the present moment. While some of these values are symbolically accessible, most of them operate outside the awareness of both participants—we reflexively register the valuational patterns of the other party, which in turn affects the values we ascribe to Self and Other in the next moment, which then influences how the Other values us, and so on in the infinitely complex messiness of clinical process.

Examples of such patterns include valuing Self and Other "only if" we display certain qualities (e.g., attractiveness, intelligence, particular valued attitudes or relational approaches); devaluing Self and Other when we display other qualities (e.g., aggression, obstinacy, self-centeredness); and ascribing badness to ourselves and others *as people*. Both parties' valued configurations often fit together seamlessly for some time, leading to a relative sense of equilibrium within each person and within the relationship. For example, I might automatically ascribe conditional value to myself, dependent on my ability to meet the damaged Other's emotional needs, and conditional value to the other individual, depending on whether she allows me to rescue her. This configuration can mesh naturally with my patient's configuration, in which she ascribes conditional value to herself as compliant and passive, taking her worth to be contingent on the responsiveness of her caretaker.

Such dynamics tend to proceed "under the therapeutic radar," since they allow us to feel valued in ways most comfortable for us. We call such patients analyzable, and we are satisfied with the work. However, to the extent that such dynamics start to experientially contradict the dignity of either party, disruptions in the relationship inevitably arise. When working with patients who lack the capacity for dignity-based experiencing, or when working in areas of the personality where our capacities for mutual respect are diminished, the dyad has a much narrower range of conditions under which Self and Other can be experienced as valuable, and a broader array of conditions under which

Self and Other can be experienced as bad or without value. This is the territory of impasse or enactment—both people feel like their valued modes of relatedness are unavailable to them, and they are far more vulnerable to ascribing badness to Self and Other. *You are bad because you are keeping me from what is most valuable.* Each person feels like she must choose between retaining her dignity and preserving the dignity of the other, a phenomenon Benjamin (2004) aptly calls the split-complementarity of "doer and done to."

In these moments, when conceptualizing intersubjective process in terms of dignity, I am particularly interested in our explicit and implicit ideas about how each party "should" be with the other—behaviorally, affectively, attitudinally, and characterologically. *"I/you can only be good if . . ." "You are/I am bad because . . ."* This is where the analyst's self-disclosures can become such an integral part of the therapeutic process—the starting point for the mutual exploration of the bidirectional valuational patterns that have come to grip the dyad. "When you tell me that we're not allowed to talk about your feelings here, I think I've been judging you a bit, maybe even wanting to make you feel bad for not doing what I assume is best for you. I think I'm afraid that, if we can never talk about how you feel, then my hands are kind of tied, and I'll never be able to help you." And later: "This idea of me 'trying to make you feel bad' and you rebelling against me . . . Does this remind you of anything else that is meaningful for you?" Through the joint exploration and processing of these often-unformulated valuational patterns in analyst and patient, each individual becomes increasingly more able to symbolize her own valuational patterns, also gaining insight into their historical antecedents, the role they play in contributing to the present dynamic, the impact these patterns have on the other person, and the ways in which they might limit the richness of intersubjective experience.

On the part of the analyst, these disclosures serve a transformational as well as a communicative function. Through exploring, identifying, and representing the aforementioned patterns, we progressively express our willingness to value Self and Other in different ways. *These are the conditions under which I have been valuing myself and you up until this moment, but I am opening myself up to the possibility that these valuations might be transformed by our relationship together.* Or, stated somewhat differently: *I am not going to let the person I have been up until now determine what (at this very moment) we can become together.* When we are able to take this step, this can liberate the patient to do the same, such that each party begins to value Self and Other under a wider range of conditions. Returning to my earlier example, I become able to value my patient even when she is not simply the compliant receiver of help (e.g., when she displays aggressiveness towards me), and able to value myself even when I cannot fulfill my role of being the effective caretaker for her. In turn, the patient starts to value me even when I am not the perfectly attuned caretaker, and to value herself when she has internal experiences (e.g., vulnerability, a desire for attention) that she associates with her own badness.[12]

In this view of therapeutic action, each dyad must find a way to co-create a mode of relatedness in which both parties can value the other person under a broader domain of conditions, even when she is displaying qualities to which we reflexively ascribe negative (or only conditional) value. This leads to a mutually responsive and respectful dynamic progressively more consistent with the dignity of both parties. Such a dynamic transcends mutual respect as normally understood. *The capacity to value someone's humanity in general is not the same as valuing Self and Other in all of our multiplicity.* Throughout the work, not only do we come to know Self and Other at a deeper level of complexity (i.e., all of the unique Selves that I am in relation to you, all of the unique Selves that you are in relation to me), not only do we come to respect each other, but we come to *value* Self and Other at a greater degree of complexity, even when that which is known is simultaneously devalued. Here, the ability to "stand in the spaces" between contradictory self-states is directly related to the potential for dignity-based experiencing. When we ascribe unconditional value to Self and Other in all of our evolving complexity, we are able to summon the courage to access experiences that exist in a state of dialectical tension with the dignity of Self and Other.

Clinical illustration

To further elucidate the clinical relevance of these proposals, I will return to my work with Martha. Martha grew up in a highly volatile environment, her father abandoning her family before she was born and leaving Martha and her sister in the care of their emotionally unstable mother. The family lived in a state of filth, with food and clothes strewn about the house and cockroaches perusing the wreckage. She remembers frequently receiving drunken phone calls in the middle of night from her mother, calling from the bar to "say goodbye" before she committed suicide.

Martha identified the powerful feelings of shame with which she struggled in childhood—her belief that there was something intrinsically wrong with her, and that no one would ever want to be close to her. In the face of her mother's neediness and self-absorption, Martha internalized the idea that *she* was never allowed to have any needs or desires. *Under no conditions am I allowed to need or want—my "Needing Self" is bad under all conditions.*

Martha was able to derive some sense of worth from taking care of her mother, who showed warmth and gratitude in these moments. Yet as Martha approached adolescence, she became increasingly resentful of her mother and the circumstances in their household. She threw herself passionately into her studies, fervently working to realize a life for herself outside of their suffocating environment. As she succeeded, Martha experienced a growing internal peace—her recognition that, as long as she excelled, she could access a self-esteem that was reliable, not dependent on the vacillating moods of her mother.

As I heard about these developments, I did not think about them simply as a reflection of Martha's idiosyncratic experiences. Rather, I saw them as an expression of the dialectic between a universal dimension of human subjectivity (Martha's natural awareness of dignity) and the unique ways Martha was *not* valued unconditionally. Martha wanted something more for her life not because of her context but in spite of it—because she had access to a sense of herself as *deserving* something more, which gave rise to an experiential tension between "what is" and "what could be."

Martha's understanding of her difficulties with work attendance began to evolve. At first, Martha attributed these difficulties simply to "my depression." She just could not pull herself out of the warmth and comfort of her bed, which felt like it had a gravitational pull over her. We soon discovered these absences were usually preceded by Martha's relational insecurities—feeling slighted by co-workers, abandoned by her sister, overwhelmed by loneliness, and so on.

Martha increasingly assumed a greater sense of agency in these patterns. What she initially experienced as "depression" became *withdrawal.* By withdrawing from her co-workers and sister, she was attempting to communicate her hurt that she was not important enough in their lives, while inviting them to prove that they valued her. Martha started to see the ways in which she ascribed only conditional value to herself and others in these dynamics, valuing others when they were attempting to "rescue" her, and valuing herself as the passive, damaged party being attended to by others. Martha had come to unconsciously believe that, in order to be cared for, she *had* to assume the role of the damaged Other, which had formerly been occupied exclusively by her mother. While these insights felt "true" to Martha, she was also filled with a deep shame about them, voicing the idea that she should not need this sort of care from others, that she did not even deserve it.

I believe that my assumptions about Martha's worth played an important role in these explorations. In considering the connection between Martha's self-hatred and her history of trauma and neglect, I was implicitly communicating my view that this hatred derived from her pathogenic experiences and not from her inherent worthlessness. Similarly, through my non-judgmental curiosity about Martha's desires for relatedness, I was communicating that *I* valued Martha's Needing Self, and thus that I valued her under a wider range of conditions than she was valuing herself at the time (Strachey, 1934).

The assumption of dignity also helped me feel like I had permission to communicate the value I ascribed to Martha and her relational needs. I remember saying, "When you talk about how much you hate yourself, and how you don't feel like you deserve to be loved, I feel a bit conflicted about how to respond. I want to honor that this is how you feel about yourself, but I also feel like it is important to say that I *do* think you deserve these things, and that it is totally understandable for you to want them." I shared these reflections not to tell Martha she was wrong, or to try to change her mind, but as a sort of self-disclosure of my assumption of her worth—to firmly position myself on the side of Martha's dignity. I suspect Martha felt affirmed by this stance, which I see as the basis for ethically grounded exploratory work.

We came to understand Martha's feelings of loneliness and depression as expressions of her investment in her most valued mode of relatedness, in which the self-sacrificing caretaker tends to the damaged Other. Martha was able to effectively inhabit the role of the caretaker in her work life, but when she was not working, she felt like *neither* role was open to her. She was fundamentally alone, without the possibility of "true" relatedness. This sent her spiraling into the realm of unconditional badness, where the Needing Self was left abandoned by the absent Mother.

I was interested in how Martha described herself during these periods—"needy," "weak," "childish," "manipulative," "irrational." We saw how Martha *used* these words to attack and obliterate her desires for connectedness, thereby transforming herself back into the self-sacrificing child who had no needs. (We commonly employ our conscious values to manage and control our desires and affects. Given the conceptualization of desires and affects as emissaries from our unconscious relational configurations, we are thus attempting to actualize, internally and externally, our most valued modes of relatedness.)

At the start of treatment, Martha presented herself as the model patient—arriving early for appointments, taking an engaged and thoughtful approach to our sessions, gratefully accepting my reflections and interpretations. I felt useful to Martha, and optimistic that I might be able to play a role in helping her to move forward in her life.

It will not surprise the reader that, after several months in therapy, Martha began to show many of the tendencies she had displayed in her work life—arriving thirty minutes late to appointments, cancelling sessions last minute, sometimes missing sessions altogether. When I attempted to explore the issue with Martha, she explained these disruptions in markedly concrete terms. She had simply "forgotten," "overslept," or "felt too depressed." She agreed there were similarities between this pattern and her vocational difficulties, but these parallels were incidental, due to the fact that this was her standard way of operating in the world. There was nothing more to say about the matter.

My curiosity about these absences gave way to feelings of irritation and discouragement about the treatment. How was I going to help Martha if she continued missing our appointments, and if we were unable to talk about possibly the most meaningful pattern unfolding between us? In these moments, in addition to respecting Martha as an independent subject, I believe I was also valuing myself and Martha *conditionally*—valuing myself to the degree that I could rescue her from her unconscious impediments, and valuing her to the degree that she engaged fruitfully in the therapeutic process.

Over time, my relationship to Martha's absences began to shift. While I retained my interest in understanding them analytically, I stopped trying to explore these matters explicitly. I felt less irritated with Martha's inconsistency, accepting it as an unavoidable part of our work together. Gradually, I started experiencing a faith that, in ways I could not anticipate, this would somehow turn out to be fruitful in Martha's life.

One day, I received another phone call from Martha several hours after our appointment time. When I asked if she would like to reschedule for later that week, she declined as usual, stating, "No, let's just do next week." While usually I would not press the matter, for some reason I did not feel like letting it go. I was not angry—I felt strangely excited and remember finding the whole situation a bit comical. Without much forethought, I said, "If you truly don't want to come in, then obviously that is your choice. But I want to let you know I would really be happy to meet with you, if you like." Martha gratefully accepted this offer.

In our next session, Martha expressed her surprise at my giving her a "second chance." She felt like I had not offered her another appointment out of a sense of obligation, but because I cared about how she was doing and *wanted* to see her. I reflected that perhaps she had been wanting this for quite some time—to feel like I cared about her in a way beyond my professional obligations. Due to her shame about this desire, she could only ask for this by withdrawing from me. Martha proceeded to elaborate on her self-criticisms for needing anything from me that did not feel "rational" within the context of a professional relationship.

Over the next several months, Martha increasingly gave voice to her longings for closeness with others. She was able to speak openly about wanting to be liked at work, and her wish to have a closer connection with her sister. She shared her desires and fears about dating again, even creating a profile on a dating website. Within the therapy, Martha was able to verbalize how much she valued our relationship, specifically the experience of being known and validated by another human being. She started arriving on time for our sessions again, rarely cancelling an appointment. Martha's work attendance improved dramatically, and, for the first time in years, she started to follow through on plans to spend time with her sister.

I am interested in conceptualizing Martha's progress in terms of *an expansion of the conditions under which Martha and I came to value each other in the therapy.* Through grappling with my frustration about Martha's absences, I came to value her even when she was stepping outside the role of the "good patient," and to value myself when I could not fulfill the role of the effective therapist. This freed me up to spontaneously be a bit more insistent in offering Martha another appointment. In that moment, I believe I was responding to Martha's as-yet-unformulated desire for *personal* care from me, in this way unconsciously valuing what I have called Martha's Needing Self. In turn, Martha began experimenting with valuing herself even when she was experiencing herself as a needing subject, and valuing me when I was not trying to rescue her.

These transformations led to the co-creation of a genuinely new mode of relatedness between us, in which both of us were able to achieve a less conditional sense of self-esteem, and to value each other under an expanded set of conditions. Martha was coming to learn that she could feel valued by another even when she stepped outside the role of the damaged party, enabling her to rely less rigidly on the aforementioned withdrawal tendencies to entice people closer to her. This led to the improvements mentioned above, which have continued for some time now.

My proposal is that these sorts of developments are not unique to my relationship with Martha, but reflective of the progressive move towards dignity-based experiencing that is central to all effective analytic inquiry. As Martha and I valued Self and Other under a wider range of conditions, we both gained access to the sorts of intersubjective processes regularly associated with *health* in contemporary relational thought—increased mutuality and flexibility in our interactions; the generation of new affective experience between us; a deepening recognition of ourselves *as persons* in relationship with one another; and an expanded sense of ourselves as "real," "alive," "existing," and genuinely free.

Conclusion: Dignity as a foundational value in relational thought

In this chapter, I have suggested that many developments associated with the relational turn were driven not simply by theoretical considerations, but by a shared ethical vision among relational theorists and practitioners—the commitment to cultivating a psychoanalysis more consistent with the dignity of the human subject. This idea is compatible with recent work emphasizing the humanistic dimensions of psychoanalytic thought (Altman, 1995; Aron & Starr, 2013). In closing, I would like to make explicit an assumption largely implicit in the literature considered here—namely, that our theories are partially *answerable to* the intrinsic worth of the person. Greenberg and Mitchell (1983) were getting at something similar when they proposed that, in addition to Kuhn's (1977) criteria of accuracy, consistency, scope, simplicity, and fruitfulness, a theory should be evaluated based on "how compelling it appears to be, on its underlying vision of human life" (p. 407).

To the above list I would add an *ethical* criterion—the extent to which the theory is consistent with and expressive of the dignity of the person. Obviously, there will be disagreement about how a theory might "satisfy" or "violate" such a criterion, and our opinions about such matters will be largely shaped by our own values, culture, theoretical orientation, and personal preferences. Such ethical considerations are already influencing theory development in psychoanalysis, and there is good reason to make these concerns explicit: *how does the theory (or concept) embody the worth of the individual? How might it contradict that worth?* By explicitly attending to such questions, we would be encouraging continuous revision of our theories in order to further reflect the dignity of the analytic subject, an endeavor that could lead to progressively more humane conceptions of psychoanalytic work. Such an approach would constitute an ethically grounded mode of theory construction, privileging care and empathy over disinterested knowledge (Levinas, 1981/1998). We need to respect the people we are trying to understand, in our clinical practice *but also in the theories we espouse.* If a theory or concept can only "explain" an experience by undermining someone's dignity, we have preliminary reason to doubt the explanation itself, on ethical grounds.

Some readers may question the relevance of this point to relational thought. After all, we have come so far, and our theories paint a much more humane picture of human relatedness and therapeutic technique. While I agree with this view, I am not prepared to conclude that relational psychoanalysis is immune to these problems. This position is supported by Mitchell's (1988) main work, where he systematically argued against conceptual tendencies that undermine others' dignity (e.g., portraying human beings as passive, driven by infantile needs, determined by antecedent causes, motivated by universal motivations), tendencies that he illustrated are employed by relationally oriented as well as classical authors (pp. 62, 151–172, 242–243). From the perspective of dignity, not all relational models are created equal. In this pluralistic psychoanalytic landscape, all theories contain diverse elements operating concurrently at multiple levels of discourse, some of which affirm the worth of the person and some of which undermine it.

By explicitly affirming dignity as an overarching value of relational thought, we would be shifting the locus of power from our theories to the worth of our common humanity. This approach naturally sets limits on the authority any theory or idea can attain. The theory's power would not derive from its popularity, history, or political affiliation—it would derive from the theory's ability to explain and affirm the inherent worth of the person, and its power would be limited to the degree that it undermines that worth. In this way, dignity would be serving as a "third term" that mediates our relationships to our theories, simultaneously affirming the value of humanity, whether in ourselves or in the people we are trying to help.

Notes

1 This chapter contains material from the following papers, reused by permission of Taylor & Francis, LLC: Drozek, R. P. (2015a). The dialectics of dignity: Clinical applications: Reply to commentaries. *Psychoanalytic Dialogues, 25*, 472–480; and Drozek, R. P. (2015b). The dignity in multiplicity: Human value as a foundational concept in relational thought. *Psychoanalytic Dialogues, 25*, 431–451.

2 The following constitutes a selective treatment of dignity, highlighting topics that I find most interesting and relevant to relational practice. For a more extensive review of the concept, see Rosen (2012).

3 Within philosophy, Kant has been rightly criticized for endorsing an overly rationalistic and individualistic view of the person. By integrating Kant's phenomenological ideas about dignity and freedom with current analytic ideas regarding multiplicity and intersubjective process, I hope to preserve Kant's humanistic insights while avoiding the aforementioned pitfalls of his model.

4 This notion of dignity places strict limits on tendencies towards prejudice, social injustice, cruelty and indifference to the needs of others, and unfair treatment on the basis of the idiosyncratic qualities that distinguish us from one another, such as race, social status, gender, and sexual orientation. Despite these aspirational implications of the dignity idea, it functions only as an ideal that can never be fully realized, existing in paradoxical tension with the tendency to ascribe only *conditional* or

negative value to Self and Other, as we see in experiences like self-loathing, insecurity, hatred of others, racism, homophobia, and so on.

5 While aspects of classical thought might seem to contradict the person's worth, other features can be seen as affirming that worth, for example its commitment to expanding the freedom of the analytic subject (Fenichel, 1941; Freud, 1923a), and its view of that subject as the (often unconscious) source of her own experiences and meanings (see Kennedy, 1993; Schafer, 1976). Throughout this chapter, rather than categorically affirm or dismiss entire theories, I prefer to focus on the *theoretical strategies and assumptions* employed in specific theories. This constitutes a selective yet progressive approach to theory construction, allowing us to revise those concepts that have outlived their usefulness without abandoning earlier innovations that continue to enrich our practice.

6 This sentiment has manifested itself in the prevalence of "co"-terms in relational thought (e.g., co-construction, co-creation), also leading many theorists to view relational theory as a more democratic or "egalitarian" view of analytic work. As Wachtel (1986) suggests, despite the natural asymmetry of clinical work, "In one sense patient and therapist are assuredly equals—both are 'more simply human than otherwise' and equally deserving of respect and human dignity" (p. 67).

7 In suggesting that we "assume" our patients are worthwhile, I do not want to imply (a) that such assumptions are always consciously or explicitly formulated, (b) that we *only* value our patients positively, or (c) that we *should* only value them positively. As I discuss later, we simultaneously ascribe a wide range of values to our patients (e.g., positive, negative, conditional, unconditional), often unconsciously and always in response to the intersubjective dynamic in the relationship at the time. I see this tension between different types of valuing (within and between members of the dyad) as one of the central dialectics in analytic process, a dialectic that collapses when either party rigidly insists that one or the other person "should" only engage in a particular sort of valuing.

8 Weisel-Barth (2015) takes issue with this proposal, arguing that there is something epistemologically arrogant about assuming that our patients are intrinsically worthwhile: "lacking experience of the person outside the analytic space, I'm just not able to know or judge such a thing" (p. 468). Personally, while I appreciate this embrace of humility, I find it difficult to believe that any of us remain truly agnostic when our patients claim they are bad or evil. Such agnosticism would entail feeling genuinely open to the possibility that our patients do not deserve our care or respect. If I were "neutral" on the matter of my patients' worth, I think I would find it challenging to feel connected with my patients, and to remain dedicated to them in the way that is necessary for safe, vibrant, and sustained analytic inquiry.

9 For those of us with postmodern leanings, this can all start to feel a little uncomfortable. How can we situate an objective, valuational concept within the confines of a contextual, descriptive psychoanalysis? While I find this question fascinating, I will not offer a full answer to it here. As a provisional response, I suggest that affirming dignity does not mean embracing epistemic objectivism across the board. I can affirm the worth of humanity without abandoning the belief that anything else I might say about this worth (e.g., what it looks like empirically, what contradicts it) is necessarily structured by personal, intrapsychic, and cultural factors. In this way, human dignity occupies a position analogous to "the objective world" in Hoffman's (1998) dialectical constructivism—while we strongly believe *that* it exists, we remain perpetually agnostic about the accuracy of our statements about it, since in principle there is no objective standpoint that anyone can occupy to determine the truth value of the statement in question.

10 For examples of need-based models of value, see Fairbairn, 1952; Greenberg, 1991; M. Klein, 1975; Kohut, 1984; Lichtenberg et al., 1992; Sullivan, 1953. For examples of affect-based models of value, see Kernberg, 1976; Sandler & Sandler, 1998; Spezzano, 1993; Teicholz, 2010.

11 We see a similar state of affairs when the caregiver is indifferent or neutral to the child. In many cases, the caregiver fails to ascribe either positive or negative value to the child, leading to minimal interaction with the child and significant neglect of her needs. Since the child takes the caregiver to be a *source* of value, and since the caregiver fails to value the child, the child takes herself to lack value, that is, *she ascribes negative value to herself as a person.* This analysis is consistent with many patients' belief that it is somehow *their* fault they were neglected, and with their vague sense that, if they had been "better" in some way, their caregivers would have been more responsive to their needs and desires.

12 As discussed in Chapter 3, I assume that there is a natural correlation between valuing oneself and valuing others (see Benjamin, 1995; Drozek, 2010a). The conditional valuing of others often implies the conditional valuing of oneself—I value myself only under certain conditions, and I value you when you help me meet these conditions. Similarly, the ascription of badness to others *as people* frequently implies the ascription of badness to oneself—I devalue you in order to escape from my own badness. However, when I am able to value you even if you do not help me satisfy the conditions for my worth, I open myself up to the possibility that *I* can be valuable under a wider range of conditions (e.g., when you are not bolstering my self-esteem). And when I am able to value myself even if I cannot meet the conditions for my worth, I place less pressure on you to make me feel worthwhile, thus opening myself up to valuing *you* under a wider range of conditions (e.g., when you are not complying with my ideal vision of you).

Chapter 5

Value as the native tongue of psychoanalysis

Fred grew up in a large middle-class family, the oldest of twelve children. His mother was kind and mild-mannered, but continuously preoccupied by her extensive responsibilities; he experienced her as never really wanting to engage with him in a meaningful way. Fred's father worked long hours as a carpenter, rarely spending time with Fred or his siblings—he was severe, emotionally cold, and perpetually unimpressed with everything. He would occasionally enlist Fred's help in completing some sort of household project, like fixing their stairs or building a shed. But rather than explain how to complete these tasks, he expected Fred to already know how to do these things, and he would quickly become disgusted with Fred's uncertainty and mistakes. There was no room for error in this relationship—love and attention was based on *efficiency* and *productivity*. As his siblings grew older and more capable, Fred's father began to utilize them for these same projects instead, leaving Fred feeling rejected and deeply inadequate. Fred always felt like his father's love and attention lay torturously just beyond his reach. He could not shake the idea that, if he could do something differently, or somehow figure out a way to *be* different, then his father would finally love him.

Fred remembers struggling with a deep sense of injustice throughout his childhood, feeling like his father would never allow him to achieve agency and self-worth within their family. When he was eight years old, Fred won a kids' shooting contest at the county fair. This was the moment he had been waiting for—finally he had succeeded; finally, he was *the best* at something. Fred vividly remembers the pride and exhilaration he felt as he brought home the prize: a golden retriever puppy. His father reacted with rage, ordering Fred to turn around and bring the puppy back to the fair. Fred begged his mother to intervene, but she deferred, as she always did, to his father's authority. Shocked and devastated, Fred tried to run away, but he had to return home when he realized, humiliated, that he had nowhere else to go, that he needed his family in order to survive.

This pattern continued throughout Fred's adolescence. To earn extra money, Fred started working a part-time job after school in a factory. When his father learned of this, he demanded that Fred surrender most of his earnings towards "room and board." Fred tried to reason with his father, who would not budge, and once again, his mother refused to step in to support him. This calcified one of the overarching themes of Fred's life—he was the victim of a deep injustice, alone and without allies, and unable to take any actions to defend his rights.

Fred struggled with reading and writing all throughout his childhood. His father, perpetually disappointed by Fred's academic performance, recommended that he transfer to a vocational school, as he would never be able to complete college. Despite these challenges, Fred worked tirelessly, graduating high school and gaining admission to a state school, majoring in business. Fred's proudest moment came at his college graduation. His parents were both there, and for the first time Fred could remember, his father told him that he was proud of him, and that he loved him.

This commenced what Fred still regards as the most exciting and fulfilling period of his life. Soon after graduation, Fred was able to secure a job at a popular restaurant chain, quickly rising to a prominent position in management there. He became known for his incisiveness and ruthlessness, able to swoop in and revive a failing location, vanquishing any barriers (and people) that stood in his way.

As he spoke of these matters, I reflected, in an attempt at mirroring, "You felt like a god."

"No," he corrected me, without irony: "I *was* God."

Fred soon met Betsy, the woman who would become his wife. She was not interested in him at first, but he pursued her tenaciously, and she relented. Their relationship progressed quickly; they soon married and had their first child. With all of the money Fred was earning, he was able to buy a house for them, supporting Betsy financially and paying her way through college. He had finally achieved what he had always wanted—a wife, an amazing job, financial success, two beautiful children. Through sheer exertion of will, he had not only *become* his father; he had surpassed him, attaining a sense of worth and value in the process.

After a decade of marriage, Fred's edifice started to show some cracks. Fred's employees and colleagues complained about him, citing his rigidity, arrogance, and critical tendencies as creating a "hostile work environment." Betsy, who had now graduated law school and attained professional success in her own right, began to withdraw from him, cultivating relationships with other attorneys, spending more time outside the home, and ultimately asking for a divorce. Fred was incensed, and he refused—they had made a vow. She had no right to break this promise, to destroy his family. If she insisted on not being involved with him romantically, he would not stand in the way of that. They could just move into separate bedrooms but continue living together in the same house to "keep the family together," for the sake of the children.

For the next five years, Fred became embroiled in a fractious legal battle—devoting all of his energy and resources to preventing this divorce from proceeding, and when this was unsuccessful, to pursuing full custody of their children. This instigated a whole new cast of adversaries onto the scene: lawyers, judges, incompetent teachers, the guardian ad litem. In the midst of these battles, Fred was unable to remain sufficiently engaged at his job, and he was fired for missing work. At the time, he did not care. He simply had to do everything in his power to prevent this from happening. He drained his savings to pay the legal fees, eventually losing the house as well. When all of the money was gone, Fred finally had to give up. Homeless, unemployed, and divorced, he had been soundly defeated by the blind injustice of his life.

Thus far in this book, I have considered two foundational ethical experiences, altruistic motivation and human dignity, and argued for the utility of the concept of *value* in explaining and validating these experiences from a psychoanalytic perspective. Implicit in my reflections is the idea that our theories of motivation *really matter*—that our manner of thinking about what motivates our patients plays an essential role in how we experience and relate to them in everyday therapeutic work.

In this way, I am taking a position that is perhaps no longer self-evident in psychoanalysis. While motivation was a central concern of many of the theorists who inspired the relational turn in psychoanalysis (Fairbairn, 1952; Greenberg & Mitchell, 1983; Kohut, 1977, 1984; Mitchell, 1988; Sullivan, 1953), in recent years, the topic of motivation has lost its formerly held position of prominence in psychoanalytic thought. Few contemporary authors grant extended attention to the topic, focusing more on clinical issues, often without fully articulating their basic assumptions about what constitutes motivation in the cases under discussion. From one viewpoint, this shift in focus is an appropriate corollary to the relational turn. Historically, the issue of motivation has been associated with the individual subject, and so it might seem less central to a relationally oriented psychoanalysis, which necessarily attends to processes unfolding *between* subjects. Furthermore, since motivational concepts have traditionally been framed in "universal" terms, the topic of motivation seems to contradict many postmodern and constructivist currents in relational thought, which stresses instead "the infinite variety in the ways that universal traits or tendencies can be given expression in each individual or dyad" (Teicholz, 2010).

In contrast with these views, I assume that we do not have the option of simply ignoring the topic of motivation in psychoanalysis. Whether we like it or not, we are constantly making assumptions about what motivates ourselves and our patients—we could not eliminate this tendency even if we wanted to. As other authors have noted (Cooper, 1996; Greenberg, 1991; Schafer, 1983; Spence, 1982, 1987), all analytic "observation" is inevitably shaped by our motivational presuppositions, whether these derive from our professionally endorsed models of motivation, our personal analyses, or our informal ideas about "what people need" and "why they do what they do." Even if left unarticulated, these assumptions exert considerable influence over our contributions to clinical process—our experiences of our patients, our emotional responses to them, the content and nature of our interpretations, the non-verbal dimensions of the therapeutic dialogue. This is true even when we try to hold our motivational presumptions lightly. Stephen Mitchell (1988) suggested:

> No matter how much we try to listen to the patient's experiences from within the context of his or her own phenomenology, no matter how scrupulous we are not to superimpose our own theoretical presuppositions on clinical data, to listen is to arrange.
>
> (p. 90; see also Cooper, 2000)

Furthermore, as Jay Greenberg (1991) has argued, our theories of motivation are an essential element of productive analytic practice: "The interpreting analyst needs some construct that gives warrant for assuming that the patient's experience is more than it seems to be" (pp. 126–127). Conceptions of motivation allow us to consider the deeper meaning of our patients' narratives. Without them, we are never able to move beyond patients' conscious understanding of the nature of their difficulties.

If it is neither possible nor advisable to shed our motivational assumptions, then we are faced with the task of articulating and evaluating them. To the degree that our theories of motivation remain unarticulated, we are more likely to be unreflectively influenced by them. As I have argued throughout this book, we naturally associate a range of ethical phenomena (e.g., altruism, human dignity, freedom and responsibility) with "what it means to be human." By retaining models of motivation that inadvertently undermine these phenomena, we can become progressively disconnected from the common sense of humanity that, in my view, serves as the foundation for all effective and humane analytic work.

In this chapter, I would like to consider some of the theoretical and clinical benefits of conceptualizing motivation along valuational lines. In addition to offering a flexible, intuitive, and therapeutically useful approach to motivation, value enables us to remain more connected to our patients, in their suffering but also, on a more fundamental level, as fellow persons participating in a shared human experience.

Value as the "native tongue" of psychoanalysis

In the 1970s, Roy Schafer (1976) published a series of ambitious papers in which he delivered a sweeping critique of the Freudian metapsychology of the day, arguing instead for the adoption of what he called an "action language" in psychoanalysis, which explicitly places "the person as agent ... at the center of psychoanalytic understanding" (p. 361).

Along with several other theorists arguing against the classical edifice at that time (G. S. Klein, 1976; Kohut, 1977; Spence, 1982), Schafer's deconstructive aims were quite effective at weakening the psychoanalytic community's confidence in the Freudian edifice, thereby laying essential groundwork for the paradigm shift towards relational thinking that was soon to come (Greenberg & Mitchell, 1983; Mitchell, 1988). While Schafer's (1976) "action language" never fully caught on, I would like to borrow his phrase about action being the "native tongue" of psychoanalysis, suggesting instead that *value* can be seen as the native tongue of psychoanalysis: "It has remained the taken-for-granted part of the language used by analysands and analysts to develop and formulate interpretations—an ordinary and pre-systemic language that is rather like a necessary but personally unacknowledged servant" (p. 362).

For theoretical purposes, I have defined *value* as "taking something to be a source of meaning." In everyday parlance, we hear value whenever we call things "good" and "bad," "beautiful" and "ugly," "amazing" and "horrible." We apply these sorts of terms to our behavior as well, concluding that we "should" or "should not" make a certain decision, or that a given action is "right" or "wrong." To borrow the distinction made by philosophers, we do not simply *describe* or *analyze* reality—we *evaluate* it.

Not surprisingly, valuational ideas also figure prominently in psychoanalysis. Our patients ask themselves (and us) what they "should" and "should not" do, and they attack themselves when they contradict the valuational standards to which they hold themselves. They ascribe positive and negative value to themselves *as people*, talking about feeling "bad," "worthless," and "dirty," and as the treatment progresses, feeling "worthwhile" and "good" about themselves. They apply these terms to other people as well, calling a new lover "perfect," or an enemy at work "a horrible asshole who just wants to fuck with me." Regardless of the clinician's orientation, these valuations serve as key signposts in clinical work, signifying the areas of our patients' motivational investment and guiding the focus of analytic inquiry.

At the same time, *we* are constantly considering the value of our own contributions to the therapeutic relationship. We ask ourselves how we should think about (and respond to) what is happening between us and our patients, reflections that are only meaningful if we think that some answers are potentially *better* than others. In hindsight, we say to ourselves,

"I'm not sure if I should have said that" or "I think I made the right decision back there." As relational authors have emphasized, we naturally ascribe positive value to some aspects of the therapeutic process and negative value to others—certain ways of being with our patients (Aron, 1991, 1996a; Renik, 1993), the "rituals" and frame of our sessions (Hoffman, 1998; Tublin, 2011; Zeddies, 2001), theories of technique and therapeutic action (Aron, 1999; Cooper, 2010; Greenberg, 1999; D. B. Stern, 2012), our patients' affective and behavioral tendencies (Cooper, 2000; Renik, 1996), and objective aspects of patients' lives outside of sessions (Summers, 2000). These valuations play a central role in our idiosyncratic ways of engaging in analytic practice, influencing our moment-to-moment choices and broader clinical approaches.

Notions of value have also figured prominently throughout the history of psychoanalysis. Value makes its first psychoanalytic appearance in Freud's (1914) concept of the ego ideal, which "finds itself possessed of every perfection that is of value" (p. 94), as well as his construct of the super-ego, which "represents the claims of morality" and "applies the strictest moral standard to the helpless ego which is at its mercy" (Freud, 1933, p. 61). Value is also central to Melanie Klein's (1975) theories of the paranoid-schizoid and depressive positions, which involve the dynamic relationships between "love" and "hate" directed towards various configurations of "good" and "bad" objects: "When a well-marked cleavage between good and bad objects has been attained, the subject attempts to restore the former, making good in the restoration every detail of his sadistic attacks" (p. 265). These Kleinian conceptions of value have been further elaborated by both Jacobsen (1964) and Kernberg (1975, 1976), who advance models centering on the internalization, development, and integration of "good" and "bad" representations of Self and Other.

We observe value in Sullivan's (1953) vision of the self as comprised of "reflected appraisals" (p. 17), involving personifications of "good-me" in satisfying interactions with the tender/"good" mother, and "bad-me" in distressing interactions with the anxious/"bad" mother (pp. 161–162). Fairbairn's (1952) system can be read as perhaps the most comprehensive psychoanalytic theory of value, including the internalization of "good objects" in the form of the super-ego (p. 93n), the internalization and repression of "bad objects" (chapter 3), an explanation of conditional versus unconditional forms of valuing (pp. 66, 93), and his notion of the moral defense, in which the developing child takes "the burden of the badness" onto herself in order to preserve the goodness of her caretakers (p. 65).

Winnicott's (1965) valuational ideas come through most prominently in his discussion of environmental processes, for example in his observations about "good-enough" mothering, which he posits as a developmental condition for the infant's capacity for spontaneous, creative True Self experiencing (chapter 12). Kohut's (1977) formulation of narcissism abounds with notions of value, including his concept of the mirroring selfobject, who provides the child with "self-esteem-enhancing acceptance and approval" (p. 61); his view of the idealized selfobject, who empathically "permits and indeed enjoys the child's idealization of him and merger with him" (p. 185); and his conception of the cohesive self, understood as "the storehouse of self-confidence and basic self-esteem that sustains a person throughout life" (p. 188n). For Kohut, *self-esteem* is an inherently valuational construct, signifying the value that the subject ascribes, or fails to ascribe, to herself.

Value also plays an important role in the attachment-related literature. Value is essential to Bowlby's (1973) description of internal working models, which include the individual's "notion of how *acceptable* or *unacceptable* he himself is in the eyes of his attachment figures" (p. 203; my italics). In contemporary developmental theory, Fonagy and colleagues (2002) employ conceptions of negative value in their notion of the *alien self*, which arises when, in response to profound abuse or traumatization, "the vacuous self comes to be colonized by the image of the aggressor, and the child comes to experience himself as evil and monstrous" (p. 198).

Value also plays an important role in contemporary relational thinking. As noted in Chapter 3, Jessica Benjamin's (1988, 1995) view of mutual recognition is an essentially valuational idea, since it refers not simply to cognitively "knowing" the other person, but to *valuing* the Other, even in the face of her alterity. Thomas Ogden (1986) invokes value in his model of object relations, in which the ego "is under constant pressure from the self-component of the relationship to be transformed into a good object" (p. 157), and the object continues to ascribe *badness* to the Self, in order to preserve the internalized object relationship (p. 160).

With their influential concept of role-responsiveness, Sandler and Sandler (1998) frame transference enactments in terms of value: "The aim of such interactions is to bring about . . . closeness to the primary affective 'good' state or object, and distance from (or obliteration of) the primary affective 'bad', unpleasant state or object" (p. 76).

Elaborating Fairbairn's theory along intersubjective lines, Jody Davies (2004) illustrates the role of value in the projective–introjective mechanisms that characterize both developmental and clinical processes. Not only does the child/patient internalize the parent/analyst's badness to maintain her connection to the caregiver, but then that badness "is projectively evacuated into the other, and the self once again feels a sense of internal goodness, innocence, and sanity" (p. 722). On this model, rather than shifting successively between these two valuational polarities, therapeutic action resides in the dyad's expanded ability "to occupy both good and bad self-states simultaneously" (p. 724; see also Davies, 2006, 2015).

The list of citations here could go on and on. However, despite the importance of valuational ideas in psychoanalytic thought, as I discussed in Chapter 4, psychoanalysis has conceptualized value primarily as a *derivative* phenomenon—we value things that lead to drive satisfaction (Freud, 1933; M. Klein, 1975), that satisfy our needs (Fairbairn, 1952; Greenberg, 1991; Kohut, 1984; Lichtenberg, Lachmann, & Fosshage, 1992; Sullivan, 1953; Winnicott, 1965), or that generate positive emotions in us (Kernberg, 1976; Sandler & Sandler, 1998; Spezzano, 1993; Teicholz, 2010). I see this tendency as a theoretical descendant of the drive-based assumptions of Freud's model, where "value," as embodied in the super-ego, is seen primarily as "the representative of the id" (Freud, 1923a, p. 58). On this view, even if we acknowledge the pervasiveness of value throughout human life, from the perspective of motivation, value is secondary and superficial. As Greenberg (1991) has suggested, "There is . . . nothing good or bad about a relationship that is independent of what the participants want or need from it" (p. 86).

To my knowledge, there are no examples of psychoanalytic theories that explicitly endorse a notion of value as motivationally primary. Rather, while theorists often write "as if" value is primary (e.g., the "good object" versus the "bad object"), when they take a step back from the phenomenology, they end up *explaining* value as deriving from other subjective processes. It is only relatively recently, in the context of the advent of relational thinking in psychoanalysis, that we have been given the conceptual resources to allow for the possibility of value as a foundational source of motivation.

This comes out most clearly in the work of Stephen Mitchell, the theorist perhaps most responsible for the development of what has been called a "drive-free" model of psychoanalysis (Greenberg, 1991). In proposing his vision of motivation, Mitchell (1988) started with the assumption that, most fundamentally, human beings seek relatedness with other human beings (pp. 26, 88–90, 107, 158, 160, 169–170, 197, 222–223, 290). Since the child is seeking "relatedness" rather than pleasure or need-satisfaction, the child becomes motivationally invested in whatever "closest bonds within the family" are available to her (p. 208). The specific form this takes depends on the child's unique relational context, especially "the temperamental givens of the baby and the contours of parental character and fantasies" (p. 275).

Over time, the developing child comes to represent these modes of relatedness in the form of relational configurations, which are intrapsychic representations of what we take to be "the ultimate form of human contact" (Mitchell, 1988, p. 223; see also pp. 150, 205, 207–209, 224, 301; 1993, p. 224; 1997, p. 252; 2002, pp. 49, 52). In Mitchell's view, the child becomes deeply *loyal* to these configurations, naturally seeking to maintain and perpetuate these loyalties in the intrapsychic and interpersonal realms (see, 1987, pp. 406–408; 1988, pp. 11, 28, 88, 102, 165, 169, 172, 237, 273, 276–278, 291, 305; 1993, p. 105; 1998, p. 133; 2000b, p. 123). On this model, relational configurations constitute the subject's foundational motivational templates for *what it means to be in a relationship* with other people (Mitchell, 1988, p. 28).

Even to this day, I do not think that psychoanalysis has fully appreciated the profound implications of this way of thinking about intersubjective experience. Since Mitchell construed relational configurations as the source of all human motivation, *all other motivational constructs are motivationally secondary* in his model. As evidenced by his various clinical examples in *Relational Concepts in Psychoanalysis* (pp. 36–40, 110–111, 114–117, 120–121, 157–158, 166–167, 212–224, 226–234, 271–274, 301–306), Mitchell (1988) saw other subjective phenomena (e.g., needs, affects, impulses, pleasure) as "vehicles for the perpetuation" of these more fundamental loyalties (p. 27).

For this reason, Mitchell (1988) even rejected *relational* theories that posit universal needs whose aims are fixed pre-experientially, such as Fairbairn's dependency needs, Sandler's need for safety, Sullivan's security operations, and Kohut's selfobject needs (p. 62). Along similar lines, Mitchell criticized relational models emphasizing the *self*-oriented dimensions of motivation—such as "self-organization, ego functions, homeostatic regulation of affects, developmental needs, a true or nuclear self, and so on" (p. 9)—while minimizing the centrality of "the self with others" (p. 200).

With the above formulations, Mitchell was proposing what I see as perhaps the purest example of a psychoanalytic theory not based on drives, needs, or affects. Mitchell's success in this project derives from his view of *relational loyalty*, a concept that, unlike other motivational constructs, has no independent motivational content—it has no specific aim, focus, valence, or direction. The notion of "loyalty in general" is conceptually empty; there is only loyalty *to* something, namely to some particular relational configuration. Value works in a strikingly similar way. The idea of "valuing" in general is utterly meaningless; we can only speak of valuing *something*, in most cases some subjective or objective dimension of intersubjective experience. Like loyalty, value is an entirely *processes-oriented*, rather than content-oriented, motivational construct—it simply specifies the quality of our motivational investment (e.g., positive, negative, conditional, unconditional), and the content of the motivation is fully supplied by the unique character of the relational experience in question.

Value is, and has always been, a foundational dimension of psychoanalytic discourse. However, due to our tendency to construe motivation as deriving from other subjective factors, we have failed to grant value a position of fundamental prominence in our theories. By placing relationships as the primary source of motivation, relational thought has offered the resources to explain and validate the essential role of value in everyday human life.

One subject, multiple selves

Before moving forward, I will try to briefly review the model I have outlined so far in this book. On this view, to borrow a helpful phrase from the Boston Change Process Study Group (2010), the "foundational level of psychodynamic meaning" is our ascriptions of value. Here, all other psychic phenomena (e.g., cognitions, affects, desires, fantasies) are expressions of our ascriptions of value to particular ways of being with others, influenced by our embodied experiences and our embeddedness in past and contemporary relational contexts. While this model does not deny the clinical importance of desires and affects, it sees these phenomena as "valuational derivatives," signifying our valued and devalued templates for *what it means to be in relationship* with other subjects, and thereby serving as essential guideposts in analytic practice. We do not value an experience just because it makes us feel good, or because it satisfies our needs or desires. *We desire those experiences that are consistent with our valued modes of relatedness (whether or not they cause us pain), and we want to avoid experiences that mirror our devalued modes of relatedness (even if they offer us the possibility of greater pleasure).* This is what Mitchell was getting at with his theory of relational loyalty—the idea that we are not primarily motivated to generate certain affects (e.g., pleasure versus pain), or to satisfy predetermined needs or drives, but to actualize the optimal possibilities for relatedness we have encountered thus far in our lives.

In affirming the foundational nature of valuing, I am not suggesting that we could ever point to a motivational process completely devoid of desires and affects. Practically speaking, whenever we value something, we usually experience some form of desire or emotion in relation to it. However, as the philosopher Thomas Nagel (1970) has persuasively argued in his seminal work *The Possibility of Altruism*, recognizing that "all motivation implies the presence of desire" does not mean that desire is the ultimate *source* of all motivation (p. 32). Rather, we desire some thing (e.g., a person, a way of life), and feel positive emotions when we imagine it, *because we value that thing*, because we take it to be worthwhile and meaningful.

Consistent with other relational models, I affirm that value is inextricably embedded in intersubjective contexts. Within these contexts, we are constantly involved in reciprocal, two-way interactions with other valuing subjects, who influence (but do not determine) our own valuations, which in turn affect (but do not determine) other subjects' valuations. At the conscious level, we encounter many aspects of our experience quite passively, as simply "happening" to us—events in the external world, the qualities and behaviors of other individuals, and even our subjective states, such as our thoughts, emotions, and desires. At the same time, we all have at least intermittent access to what I call *agentic freedom*—a sense of ourselves as subjects who have the capacity to partially *create*, rather than just passively apprehend, value and meaning in our lives.

Framed in valuational terms, this means that we regularly have an experience of valuing (and devaluing) the contents of our consciousness. We value and devalue material entities in the environment, such as objects, places, possessions, and events. We value and devalue *relational* processes, such as particular people, groups of people, qualities of others (e.g., attentiveness, attractiveness, confidence), and specific interpersonal patterns between ourselves and others (e.g., caretaking, professional achievement, social performance). We value and devalue dimensions of *ourselves*, such as certain personal qualities, internal factors (e.g., beliefs, emotions, desires, fantasies, memories, abstract concepts), and conscious views of identity, of ourselves "as people." We value and devalue *behaviors*, whether those be actions that we took in the past, that we are performing in the present, or that we are considering taking in the future. We also ascribe value to a range of moral and ethical phenomena—"right and wrong" actions; "good and bad" states of affairs; virtuous and wicked character traits; notions of human rights and social justice; general ethical principles and standards of conduct; and ideas about freedom and moral responsibility.

In everyday life, we are ascribing these values constantly and reflexively, so pervasively that it usually escapes our notice. In this way, value permeates and animates the fabric of our relational worlds. While many of our valuations are explicitly formulated (e.g., "It's so *horrible* that he did that," "I should really go clean out the garage"), most of our valuations are largely implicit in experience. For example, we judge someone for being unkind, without fully articulating this to ourselves, or we reflexively decide to get off the couch to get some ice cream (that is, we "ascribe value" to this particular action). Furthermore, while many of these valuations are moral in nature, most of our values have no specific moral valence, simply involving the internal and external minutiae of our intersubjective lives.

At the unconscious level, valuing always takes the shape of *relational configurations*, understood as our ascriptions of value to representations of ourselves, other people, and the interactional patterns between ourselves and others. On this model, unconscious process consists of multiple, often-contradictory relational configurations, some of which assume greater prominence within our psychic landscape at any given moment, influenced significantly by intrapsychic as well as intersubjective dynamics unfolding between ourselves and other subjects in the environment. Here, experience is multiply determined by a variety of factors simultaneously, including our conscious valuations, our unconscious ascriptions of value to Self-in-relation-to-Other, and our current intersubjective context. Even if we feel like we are issuing a valuation unrelated to another person (e.g., choosing to complete a household chore), we are implicitly valuing a certain way of being with others. This viewpoint is consistent with how we tend to think about patients' conscious choices, namely as representing some as-yet unformulated investment in different ways of being with others, which thus becomes the focus of analytic exploration.

Therefore, when working within a valuational frame, I am always listening for the patient's current subjective states (e.g., thoughts, desires, affects, fantasies), and considering the question—what do these states communicate to me about the person's conscious and unconscious ascriptions of value to Self and Other? In my experience, such subjective processes, in both the patient and myself, are likely the most direct route to the patient's valued and devalued relational configurations, and to the interpersonal configurations we are implicitly co-constructing with one another in the present moment.

It is important to note that, on this model, our relational configurations are not "more fundamental" than our conscious valuations. I suggest there is only *one valuing subject*, and she ascribes different (frequently contradictory) sorts of value simultaneously at varying degrees of awareness. This formulation highlights the dialectic between unity and multiplicity that is central to contemporary psychoanalysis—the notion that we are individual subjects with multiple identities, which continually shift and rise in prominence as we engage with other similarly unified, decentered subjects.

Value as a source of motivation

Within psychoanalysis, we tend to assume that the clinical pervasiveness of desires and affects somehow cements their status as a primary and irreducible source of motivation. However, ubiquity does not establish primacy. Value, too, saturates analytic process, but that fact does not settle the matter either. As Greenberg and Mitchell (1983) observed long ago, while all psychoanalytic theories encompass the exact same clinical data, different models assume distinctive "invisible, hypothetical processes and events which are not susceptible to observation or experience" (p. 104). Accordingly, there is no way to definitively "prove" this issue of motivational primacy—we can simply work to clarify a particular theory's basic motivational assumptions, and then consider the strengths and weaknesses of those assumptions in addressing the full range of intersubjective phenomena, both "inside" and "outside" of psychoanalysis.

Along these lines, I will now try to review some of the main benefits of conceptualizing value as a primary motivational source. For ease of reference, I will refer to such a model as a *valuational* theory of motivation, contrasting it with *derivative* notions of value, which tend to explain value in terms of other subjective states like drives, needs, or affects. Rather than try to establish value as *the* definitive form of motivation in psychoanalysis, I would simply like to argue for this as a defensible approach to psychoanalytic motivation, and to consider some of its therapeutic applications.

Reflexive ethical commitments

At the start of this book, I mentioned that psychoanalysis has perhaps been poorly equipped to explain and validate our reflexive ethical commitments, including our ordinary beliefs about altruistic motivation, human dignity, the importance of actions and their consequences, and freedom and responsibility. By embracing a valuational view of motivation, we can begin to "bridge the gap" between our psychoanalytic theories and these everyday ethical experiences.

First, as I suggested in Chapter 3, a valuational perspective is uniquely equipped to explain the possibility of altruistic or "intersubjective" motivation, understood as the ability to be genuinely motivated by the subjectivity of others. Even when formulated along relational lines, other constructs of motivation naturally signify the meaning that the subject *herself* supplies to the experience in question—she is motivated to satisfy some drive, to meet some need, or to generate some emotional state. In contrast, value is able to signify issues of importance and meaning without explicitly invoking internal processes unfolding in the motivated subject—we are able to talk about something being *valuable* or *worthwhile* without assuming this is "because" it facilitates some drive, need, or affect. Therefore, *valuing others* can stand as a motivational condition for intersubjective meaning—we are able to be motivated by another person's subjective meanings when we value the person in the same way that we value ourselves. In this way, value opens the door for a psychoanalytically grounded model of altruism that is highly consistent with how we normally think about altruistic motivation—and its siblings like compassion, empathy, and kindness—in everyday life.

Furthermore, as I discussed in Chapter 4, value is particularly adept at explaining our natural sense of human dignity, normally understood as the unconditional worth of human beings. Derivative formulations of value do not do justice to this dignity, since by definition they imply that the worth of human beings is necessarily contingent—we value others because they satisfy our drives, meet our needs, or make us feel good. Conversely, by conceptualizing value as a primary source of motivation, we make space for *intrinsic* value in psychoanalysis—we value other people for their own sake, because they are the sorts of beings who *are* worthwhile, not because of how they affect us subjectively. A valuational perspective thus allows us to embrace a psychoanalytically relevant concept of dignity that is highly consistent with our ordinary understanding of human value.

Moreover, a valuational approach is able to validate our basic conviction that our actions, as well as their consequences in the "real world," really matter. Historically, psychoanalytic theory has deemphasized these sorts of conscious and behavioral concerns, seeing them as more "superficial" compared to the unconscious processes that garner the majority of the attention in psychoanalysis (Wachtel, 2014). As Greenberg (2008) observes, "Psychoanalysts have been reluctant to theorize about choice" (p. 705), largely due to the tendency to emphasize unconscious motivation over patients' conscious choices. In contrast, by affirming the importance of *both* conscious and unconscious valuing, without placing either form of motivation in a position of priority over the other, I am embracing psychoanalysis' traditional emphasis on unconscious motivation, while also affirming the foundational role that our conscious valuations (e.g., of certain actions, of those actions' consequences) play in directing our lives. A valuational approach offers a genuinely psychoanalytic vision of motivation, without undermining our reflexive belief that our choices and behaviors constitute a deep and meaningful dimension of human experience.

Finally, a valuational perspective allows us to preserve our everyday sense of freedom and responsibility. In Chapter 4, I observed that all of us, even those who suffer from the most extreme forms of pathology, have at least intermittent access to an awareness of ourselves as *free agents*, who are able to serve as an essential source of meaning and value. Derivative notions of value necessarily undermine that awareness, since they imply that our conscious valuations are determined by whatever motivation is seen as "primary" or "fundamental"—we value something because it satisfies our drives, meets our needs, or generates positive feelings in us. On these views, agency becomes dissociated and concretized in the form of these other entities (e.g., drives, needs, affects) operating *within and on* the subject (Schafer, 1976).

On the contrary, a valuational theory preserves and validates our natural supposition of agentic freedom. Under such a model, when we consciously value something, it is entirely possible that we *as agents*—not other people, not past versions of ourselves, not our needs or emotions—are at least partially determining this valuation, and therefore are responsible for it. This formulation is highly consistent with the phenomenology of deliberation, in which it feels like we are engaged in a process whose outcome has not already been determined, and where we feel like *we* are determining the value of this action for us, *through the deliberation itself.*

Similarly, when thinking about the unconscious within this model, it is the subject *herself* who is unconsciously ascribing value to various modes of relatedness, and so we have no need to posit some additional factor (e.g., drives, needs, affects) that is somehow "acting" to determine our deliberations. While any stipulation of non-conscious motives partly undermines our sense of freedom, the present theory does so in a way that hopefully expands, rather than constricts, the agency of the analytic subject. Phenomenologically, it might *feel like* we are being controlled by forces inside of ourselves (e.g., overwhelming needs and desires, powerful emotional states), but there is a way in which we *ourselves* are somewhat responsible for that compulsion, namely by unconsciously valuing modes of relatedness that inadvertently constrict our experience of agency. This formulation is compatible with our everyday assumptions about freedom and responsibility, under which we feel like, regardless of what we consciously believe about the determinative power of development, genetics, and the unconscious, we are somehow irreducibly *responsible* for who we are and how we live.

As Mitchell (2002) observed, "All models of mind are based on metaphors; we can't really visualize mind without comparing it with something else" (p. 196). Within the history of psychoanalysis, theorists have traditionally enlisted *non-agentic entities* (e.g., needs, desires, emotions) as the primary metaphors for unconscious motivation. By employing our conscious awareness of agentic valuing as the primary metaphor for unconscious process, we arrive at a model of the mind that is more experience-near, and less likely to undermine our sense of ourselves as responsible agents.

Foundational nature of value

Further support for the valuational perspective comes from the fact that most of us already relate to value as if it is a foundational dimension of human experience. In our day-to-day lives, when we value something—a person, a relationship, an interpersonal approach, a project, a cause—we naturally assume that the thing can be motivating for us. We observe this in a range of situations, including those where we value something while also desiring it and having positive emotions about it (e.g., in the case of a new romantic relationship), where we value something but *lack* positive desires or emotions about it (e.g., following through on a promise primarily out of a feeling of obligation), or when our values *override* competing desires and emotions (e.g., when we want to say something hurtful but refrain from doing so in order to preserve the relationship). In all of these scenarios, we operate under the assumption that values themselves motivate us in a primary way—that is, if we take something to be worthwhile, meaningful, or good, we have a prima facie reason to actualize it, *in virtue of our valuing it.*

Interestingly, "alternative" types of motivation (e.g., desires, needs, affects) appear to be somewhat dependent on the idea of value. Without value, these conceptions would be empty, unable to explain motivation. For example, it is nearly impossible to even *think about* an affect without explicitly or implicitly invoking a notion of positive or negative value. This viewpoint has been developed extensively in the philosophy of the emotions, most notably in Martha Nussbaum's (2001) theory of emotions as *judgments of value*: "We cannot explain these emotions and the way they motivate us without thinking of them as value-laden intentional attitudes toward objects" (p. 79; see also Green, 1992; Roberts, 2003; Solomon, 1993). Ben-Ze'ev (2000) helpfully elaborates on this idea:

> Every emotion entails a certain evaluation. Hate implies the negative evaluation of a certain person, pridefulness indicates a positive evaluation of oneself, and regret involves evaluating what one has done as being wrong. Evaluating something to be dangerous underlies the emotion of fear; a highly positive evaluation of someone underlies the emotions of love and admiration. In a state devoid of an evaluative component, or one in which its weight is marginal, we are indifferent.
>
> (p. 56)

Considered from a psychoanalytic perspective, this philosophical formulation might appear overly simplistic, since it is framed primarily in conscious and cognitive terms. Nevertheless, when applied to unconscious process as well, the basic argument holds—if we were to subtract all conscious and unconscious notions of value from the aforementioned affects, it becomes virtually impossible to elaborate the content and meaning of the emotion in question.

A similar point can be made about needs and desires. When we talk about *needing* or *wanting* something, there is the implication that the focus of our desire has some sort of positive value for us (Oddie, 2005).

As the philosopher Sergio Tenenbaum (2007) explains, "A desire represents its object, perhaps implicitly, as good—that is, as something that is worth being pursued" (p. 21). In psychoanalysis, when our patients desire things that contradict their conscious beliefs and ideals, we end up assuming there are ways in which, outside of their awareness, the person is *unconsciously* valuing that thing, a possibility that thus becomes the focus of analytic exploration. Conversely, if we feel motivationally averse to some experience, we naturally assume that we ascribe negative value to that experience, either consciously or unconsciously. Like affects, needs and desires seem to rely on value in order to fully express their meaning.

Since we tend to relate to value as a foundational dimension of motivation, and since alternative models of motivation seem to be conceptually dependent on notions of value, then there is further reason to consider value as a primary source of motivation in psychoanalytic thought.

Neurobiological support

For many psychoanalytically oriented clinicians, one of the most compelling facets of affect as a motivational construct is that it appears to receive confirmation from neurobiology (Kaplan-Solms & Solms, 2000; Schore, 1994, 2003a, 2003b; Siegel, 1999; Solms & Turnbull, 2002), thus promising to fill the theoretical void left by drives as the central motivational unit in psychoanalysis. In this way, affects might seem to be the only candidate able to satisfy contemporary psychoanalysis' mandate for a source of motivation that is simultaneously embodied, empirically grounded, and relationally constituted (Anderson, 2008; Aron & Anderson, 1998; Sletvold, 2014).

However, there is also a substantial body of neurobiological research supporting the idea of *value* as a primary source of motivation. In recent years, neurobiologists have devoted extensive attention to our capacity to assess, predict, and determine the value of a wide variety of factors involved in the complex dimensions of human experience and decision-making (Glimcher & Fehr, 2014). There is now extensive evidence suggesting the existence of neural value signals corresponding to our subjectively constituted values, leading researchers to propose "a core network for subjective valuation" (Peters & Büchel, 2010), as well as "an automatic valuation system in the human brain" (Lebreton, Jorge, Michel, Thirion, & Pessiglione, 2009).

Researchers have also identified neuro-anatomical structures involved in the ascription of value, most notably the ventromedial prefrontal cortex/orbital frontal cortex and the ventral striatum (Levy & Glimcher, 2016). Interestingly, the ventromedial prefrontal cortex/orbital frontal cortex has been associated with other arenas relevant to psychoanalysis, including emotion, social behavior, learning and memory, various forms of psychopathology, and mentalization. Given the importance of value in all of these spheres, Levy and Glimcher (2016) "hypothesize that a unifying feature of this area might be the notion that this area is representing some kind of value-related signal in each of these contexts" (p. 107).

In addition to observing common neurobiological features of moral values (Moll, Oliveira-Souza, & Zahn, 2008), researchers have found that value impacts multiple non-moral forms of motivation, including instinctual activity, habitual patterns, and goal-directed behavior in general (Rangel, Camerer, & Montague, 2008). More recently, Ruff and Fehr (2014) have observed notable neurobiological commonalities between social *and* non-social experience, leading them to propose an overarching motivational system that ascribes value "to all stimuli and situations, irrespective of whether they relate to specific others, to abstract social principles or to material objects" (p. 1). Of particular relevance to psychoanalytic thinking, there is even evidence reinforcing the idea that value extends across conscious and unconscious dimensions, and that our conscious valuations can be significantly influenced by non-conscious valuational mechanisms (Uhlmann, Pizarro, & Bloom, 2008).

In all of this research, it is important to note that affects are not seen as "more fundamental" than value; rather, they are conceptualized as one of many neurobiological processes involved in "a common neural currency for value representations" in human life (Levy & Glimcher, 2012; see also Glimcher & Fehr, 2014). Taken together, all of these formulations affirm the perspective I have been developing here—that value constitutes a foundational source of motivation encompassing conscious and unconscious domains. This viewpoint has grounding in biology, neuroscience, philosophy, and clinical psychoanalysis.

Clinical utility

To many readers, the construct of value might seem poorly suited to analytic work. In everyday parlance, the term "values" evokes our conscious ideas about what is good, desirable, or worth pursuing—friendship, kindness, citizenship, and so on. Construed in this way, value presents an overly narrow, excessively conscious, and possibly superficial picture of human motivation. However, as I hope I have made clear over the past several chapters, I do not see value as a series of worthwhile entities populating the conscious mind. My notion of value concerns the *activity* of valuing, understood as a range of conscious and unconscious motivational operations continuously being enacted by the subject. I am thus slightly expanding the colloquial understanding of "values." For our present purposes, while we can consciously value practices or concepts, I am most interested in *our conscious and unconscious patterns of valuing Self and Other*. Framed in this manner, value is anything but superficial, since it encompasses not simply our idiosyncratic representations of Self and Other, but our unique motivational investment in those representations. From a valuational perspective, such processes form the motivational bedrock of our emotional and intersubjective lives.

To illustrate, I will return to my patient Fred. From an early age, given his father's absence and his mother's lack of emotional engagement, Fred never had an experience of being valued as a unique, specific person. The only potential source of his self-worth in his family lay in his technical performance, his ability to independently and effectively assist his father with household tasks. Since Fred was so rarely able to fulfill this role, and since his father so consistently *devalued* Fred in his failures, Fred gradually internalized a conception of himself as bad, worthless, and insufficient. This is the motivational category that I call unconditional badness—not simply the idea that we are doing something poorly, but that we *ourselves* are inherently flawed, unworthy of love and care from others. This impression only intensified as his siblings grew older, and he saw them effortlessly meeting his father's expectations in a way that he never could. There was something fundamentally and irrevocably defective about *him* as a person. These valuations manifested themselves in Fred's intense feelings of shame, deadness, and emptiness, emotions he was progressively able to access and express throughout the course of our work together.

Running parallel to this self-experience, Fred could not shake the conviction that value and connectedness were somehow tantalizingly within his reach. This is the motivational category I describe as conditional valuing, where we feel like there is something that we might "do" to earn our self-esteem, and (the mirror image of this) that our badness is only conditional. For Fred, this took the shape of the assumption that, if he could only "perform well" (e.g., by succeeding in school, by earning his own living, by winning the shooting contest), he could earn his parents' love and gain a sense of self-worth. Emotionally, these valuations presented themselves in Fred's desperate ambitions for success and accomplishment, as well as his deep feelings of insecurity and anxiety about his social and academic performance.

Fred's dilemma lay in the fact that his occasional successes, which offered him the hope of value and worth, were only met by his father's disdain, which further intensified his experience of worthlessness. This is what made his father's response to the shooting contest so traumatic. For the first time in his life, Fred had obtained concrete recognition of his talents from someone outside of the family—surely *this* would warrant his father's admiration. And yet, when he was forced to return the puppy, Fred took his father to be communicating to him—*there is no room for your value in this family. No matter how hard you work, I will not grant you approval and care. You will always be worthless, and forever on your own.* For Fred in this moment, even *conditional* self-worth was taken off the table; all that was left was separateness and shame. This situation ultimately crystallized as the symbol for Fred's tragic dilemma of self-worth: the people he most needed to endow him with value were unwilling to provide it, and so his only option was to *resist* them in order to escape from his sense of worthlessness.

These exigencies highlight the psychic interdependence between conditional goodness and unconditional badness—our need to escape from unconditional badness fuels our efforts to actualize a conditional sense of value, and yet our failures at meeting those conditions intensify our worthlessness. For Fred, all of his "failures" (e.g., his mechanical ineptitude, his poor academic performance, his parents' lack of responsiveness) served as the "evidence" for his defectiveness. This led to Fred's powerful feelings of shame, as well as a desperate need to distance himself from his own badness.

This is where the concept of dignity, explored in Chapter 4, becomes so clinically useful. While Fred never had an experience of being valued unconditionally by his parents, he began to develop the vague impression that he deserved more from the world than he was receiving. In valuational terms, he increasingly encountered an experiential tension between his natural dignity as a subject (*"I am worth something, I deserve to exist, I deserve love and care from others"*) and his value *as a Self*, which was always either conditional (*"I am only worthwhile if my father loves me, if I can perform well-enough to garner his approval"*) or absent (*"I am not good enough, I am worthless, I am a failure"*). To decrease this state of tension, Fred started to try to create something genuinely new for himself in his life and relationships, in which he might finally be able to achieve *a less conditional sense of worth and value*. In this mode, Fred stopped consciously trying to pursue his father's love and approval, instead attempting to shift the conditions for his worth to factors that felt more under his sphere of control—graduating from college, succeeding at work, fulfilling his role as a husband and father. As he was increasingly able to meet these conditions, he started to feel like he was finally able to *be* who he was meant to be—worthwhile, valuable, and deserving of care and attention from others. In these moments, Fred was able to temporarily inhabit a world where he had finally been able to earn his father's love.

And yet Fred's solution was destined for tragedy, since, from a valuational perspective, it failed to reflect the dignity of himself and others. While every new success temporarily endowed him with self-esteem, he never saw *himself* as intrinsically valuable; rather, to the degree that his actions generated positive consequences (e.g., increased income, recognition from colleagues, admiration from Betsy), those *actions* were valuable, and so he was temporarily permitted to partake in their worth. Fred thus lived with a perpetual experience of lack, and a constant pressure to prove his worth and value. While he encountered moments of excitement and pleasure, he could never access a durable sense of peace, fulfillment, and contentment.

In all of these pursuits, Fred was also unconsciously perpetuating the very problem he was attempting to solve. I have suggested that Fred's quest for conditional value can be seen as an effort to escape from his difficulties with self-hatred and self-loathing. However, as Fred desperately pursued these conditions for his self-esteem, he was unconsciously affirming his unconditional badness: *I am bad, unacceptable, and insufficient as I am—the only way that I can feel worthwhile is by arranging the world in a very specific way.* From this standpoint, Fred's narcissistic endeavors were animating and fueling his worthlessness, thus further subverting his dignity.

In a similar way, the above patterns contradicted the dignity of the other parties in Fred's life. The corollary to Fred valuing himself only conditionally is that he was only able to value other people under a narrow range of conditions, namely when they were helping him to maintain his self-esteem. This led to Fred's tendencies towards control, rigidity, impatience, and self-centeredness. When others failed to help Fred meet the conditions for his worth (e.g., Betsy asserting her independence, his colleagues disagreeing with him), they were threatening to *make him bad*. And so he was forced to devalue not simply their actions, but to devalue them *as people*, in order to distance himself from the sense of worthlessness they were evoking in him: *I am so bad, unacceptable, and insufficient—the only way that I can feel worthwhile is by making* you *bad, by focusing on your defects and inadequacies, by attempting to destroy you.* These processes led to Fred's susceptibility to criticism, combativeness, and extreme rage towards others.

From a valuational perspective, it is this proclivity—to undermine the dignity of other subjects—that led to Fred's relentless difficulties in interpersonal relationships. As others (e.g., Betsy, his adult children, his friends) recognized that Fred was primarily using them to buttress his self-esteem, with minimal responsiveness to their independent subjectivities, they began to withdraw from Fred—*I can only respect myself, and honor the value of my experiences, by distancing myself from you.* Furthermore, as other people increasingly saw Fred as devaluing them, they felt like they had to *resist* Fred, and to enforce their viewpoints onto him—*I can only respect myself, and honor the value of my experiences, by devaluing you and negating* your *experiences.* These forms of mutual devaluation led to Fred's pervasive conflicts with others, resulting in highly antagonistic dynamics that left him feeling increasingly separated from the world.

Perhaps the most dramatic example of these patterns came in Fred's relationship with Betsy. As we came to see throughout our work together, Fred ascribed largely conditional value to himself in this dynamic, contingent on him feeling strong and powerful, and on his ability to financially provide for Betsy and their children. In their early years together, as Fred was building their home and financially supporting her, he felt deeply nourished by this relationship, enjoying a burgeoning self-esteem and self-confidence. But in valuing himself only conditionally, Fred was trapped in valuing *Betsy* only conditionally, namely only when she was relying on him exclusively for all of her material and emotional needs. This meant that there were entire dimensions of her subjectivity (e.g., her professional ambitions, her joys and excitements unrelated to him, her own ideas about how to raise their children) to which he was unresponsive, since they had no direct bearing on the psychological function she was serving for him. I believe that, over time, Betsy came to understand this about Fred, and in an unconscious effort to maintain her dignity and value, she started to withdraw from him emotionally, and to invest in other relationships (e.g., with colleagues, with their children, with her family of origin) which offered her a more positive and less conditional sense of self-esteem.

These developments gradually threatened Fred's own experience of value, thus instigating a version of the conflictual interpersonal processes that had transpired elsewhere in Fred's life—Fred attempting to *force* Betsy to facilitate his self-worth (e.g., by refusing the divorce, by demanding they continue to live together); Fred denying her the right to have experiences (e.g., pursuing divorce, seeking shared custody) that evoked his worthlessness; and ultimately Fred devaluing Betsy *as a person*, in order to punish her for her transgressions and also to evacuate his badness onto her.

This brings us to Fred's memory of Betsy, near the end of their marriage, striking him repeatedly across the face. In recalling this incident, Fred was never able to elaborate on the context of this disagreement, aside from his impression that Betsy wanted him to "get angry" with her in some way, and that he was willfully withholding such a response. In my fantasy of this moment, I imagine there were a range of processes unfolding for Betsy—the desire to punish Fred for his obstinacy and self-centeredness, for his inability to help her feel worthwhile as a person; the urge to "get through to him," to transform him into someone who could value her and be motivated by her Otherness; and her need to reject the badness that he was constantly projecting onto her, to make *him* bad and thereby expunge this feeling out of herself.

Interestingly, Fred experienced this all in largely positive terms: the more that Betsy attacked him, the more powerful he felt, and the less willing he was to surrender. Unlike his father, who was never emotionally engaged enough to feel angry with Fred, Betsy was passionately and deeply invested in her attacks. Betsy cared enough about Fred *to try to change him*, to make him into the person that she needed him to be. In this way, through Betsy's devaluation of him, Fred felt deeply valued and cared for—he mattered to her, and so if he had acquiesced in any way, he would have been paradoxically relinquishing his value.

In this section, I have attempted to illustrate Fred's developmental trajectory in essentially valuational terms. Far from being superficial and overly cognitive, the valuational approach offers a vibrant and experience-near perspective on human motivation, reflecting processes that feel foundational and deeply meaningful to our patients' lives—their longings to feel unconditionally valuable, along with their fears that this will never be possible; their perception that there is something intrinsically wrong with them, which somehow makes them undeserving of love and connectedness with other people; their conviction that they are "only good if" they meet certain conditions; and their hatred towards (bad) others who have wronged them and abandoned them. As patients start to progressively represent these valuational modes, they are able to enter into a strange liminal dimension of intersubjective life where they can discover the ways in which they are both *choosing and not choosing* to value themselves and others in these ways, thus opening themselves up to new forms of experiencing Self and Other in the present moment. This brings us to considerations of therapeutic action.

Part 3

Clinical applications

At the start of this book, I suggested that psychoanalytic theory is poorly equipped to explain and validate our *reflexive ethical commitments*—our "everyday" assumptions about ethics that are inextricably bound up with our identities as human beings. I have proposed that, by more fully appreciating the role of value in human experience and analytic practice, we can begin to "bridge the gap" between our theories and these reflexive commitments, especially our ideas about altruism, dignity, freedom and responsibility, and the importance of actions and their consequences. This leaves one remaining commitment—our assumption that there is some basic connection between ethics and psychological health.

We thus arrive at the topic of *therapeutic action*. As Gabbard and Westen (2003) observe, therapeutic action involves two main components—the *aims* of treatment, and the question of *technique*. In Part 3, I will develop both of these dimensions along ethical lines, specifically conceptualizing psychoanalytic process as the co-creation of an intersubjective space that is progressively more consistent with the dignity and well-being of *both* patient and analyst, which is optimally facilitated by the analyst maintaining rather than collapsing certain generative dialectics that are fundamental to daily life. This ultimately leads to a reformulation of psychoanalysis itself, providing a new answer to the age-old question of "what makes it analytic?" that has dominated psychoanalysis throughout its history.

Chapter 6

Psychoanalysis as an ethical process[1]

In my first appointment with Fred, several years before I was overwhelmed by the desire to hit him, I inquired about what was bringing him to therapy. Discussing the range of interpersonal difficulties with which he was struggling, Fred answered quite plainly, "I want to find out why people have such a problem with me." At first, I was impressed with this response, naively assuming it implied a curiosity about himself and others that would serve Fred well in analytic work. I soon realized that Fred was not really *wondering* about this issue at all; rather, he was simply affirming his perspective: *People* should not *have a problem with me. I have done nothing wrong, and yet they insist on consistently mistreating me.*

Fred became quickly attached to me. He would arrive early to every session, waiting eagerly in the waiting room and smiling excitedly when I greeted him. He appeared to relish describing in painstaking detail the conflicts in which he would find himself, especially emphasizing the elaborate steps he took to seek revenge against the people who had wronged him. I worked to approach Fred's experience as closely as possible, articulating the various emotional states that continuously presented themselves in these situations—his rage towards authority figures who mindlessly enforced arbitrary rules; the pride he derived from his ability to forcefully articulate his position; his deep feelings of betrayal by Betsy; and his powerful conviction that he was destined for greatness, and that he could somehow achieve this if someone would finally recognize his natural potential.

As the treatment unfolded, Fred and I came to see how these emotions (which dominated his conscious life) constituted only a portion of his subjective world. Fred was gradually able to represent the ways in which his feelings of worthlessness and inadequacy were also operative in the above experiences, significantly fueling his attachment to these "less vulnerable" emotional states. To the degree that he was feeling rage, pride, betrayal, and a sense of superiority, he did not have to encounter another self-state consistently being activated when people failed to comply with his wishes—his belief that there was something essentially wrong with him, that he was unworthy of love and care from others, and that others were *right* to reject him, given his inherent badness.

As Fred came to appreciate this dimension of his subjectivity, he increasingly developed the capacity to simultaneously represent *both* his badness and the badness of others, in the same moment of intersubjective experience. So when he was kicked out of a restaurant for smoking cigarettes in it (he was personally opposed to public non-smoking laws), he continued to feel powerful rage towards the management for enforcing unfair and arbitrary rules, but he also spontaneously shared that he felt *humiliated* and *small*—staff would never treat him this way if they truly respected him, if they saw him as worthwhile and powerful.

I attempted to draw his attention to these shifts in his self-experience as they unfolded in our sessions: "Something different seemed to happen with you just now—when you started criticizing the management, your voice raised and your face hardened. Did you happen to notice that?" And then: "Could you try to put words on the difference between these moments—how you felt when you were talking about feeling 'humiliated and small,' and then when you started calling the management 'mindless assholes'?" Fred began to see that he felt so much more powerful when he was devaluing others, and how he was often *using* his rage to obliterate his feelings of worthlessness, and to quell his desires for people to appreciate and admire him.

In my view, throughout all of this work, Fred was becoming progressively desensitized to his own feelings of badness, coming to learn experientially that *he would not be destroyed by representing these more vulnerable parts of himself*. Fred's interpersonal difficulties gradually improved—as he gained the ability to access and represent the inferiority that was triggered in his interactions with others, he was less driven to constantly escape from that self-state, and so he felt less compelled to attack and devalue other individuals, at least at the level of behavior. Despite these improvements, Fred's experience remained quite constricted. Even though he was able to avoid entering into constant arguments with others, he still struggled with a powerful tendency to focus on their defects. Furthermore, he found it difficult to imaginatively consider, and to be motivated by, the perspectives of other people, especially when he felt disrespected or devalued by them.

I increasingly inquired about Fred's experience of the therapeutic process. Fred gave voice to the important meaning our relationship held for him, especially his sense of being connected to someone who truly *understood* him, and who was dedicated to his successes. He shared his longing that, as he recounted his various conflicts with other individuals, I would be impressed with his tenacity and intelligence, and that I would agree that *he was right* in these scenarios. Fred fantasized that I would criticize and look down on his enemies in the same way that he did, and that together (in sessions, even in our lives) we would align together against everyone who was undermining him—we could be closely connected together through our shared enmity towards others. In this, we began to see Fred's emerging wish that I could become the mother who would finally protect him against the harsh and uncaring fathers of his life.

We also explored Fred's yearning to be my "favorite patient," for me to be so enamored by his charm and complexity that I would devote long stretches of time thinking about him and how to best meet his needs. Fred shared his fantasy that I would one day write a book all about him, jokingly asking at the start of our appointments, "How's the book coming?" When we would arrive at something important in our work together, he would ask, "Is this one going in the book?" We came to understand these desires as expressions of Fred's powerful longing that he would become deeply important to me as a person. Where Fred's father was largely ashamed of him, I would feel so proud of him that I would want to "show him off" to the world. We could both become famous together, in a way that felt truly reciprocal to Fred. My book would help him finally receive recognition, and he would be helping me with a project that would make *my* life better—he could be useful to me in a way that he never could to his father.

Employing the theory I have been outlining here, I would suggest that Fred was ascribing unconditional value to certain *parts* of me (e.g., my intelligence, power, and success), while also ascribing unconditional value to particular *ways of being* that I actualized with him, such as my tendency to empathically validate him, to show him positive attention, and to admire his positive traits. In spite of this, Fred was still only able to value me *as a person* under a narrow range of conditions, namely when I was engaged in those very specific forms of relatedness with him, and there were significant dimensions of my subjectivity to which Fred was unresponsive, including my desire to consider Fred's role in his relational conflicts, my curiosity about the experiences of the people in his life, and my hope that Fred might gradually develop the ability to be motivated by the feelings of others.

In fact, when I displayed these non-contingent parts of myself, Fred could become quite impatient and frustrated with me, appearing uncomfortable and agitated until I got "back in line" and resumed attentively mirroring him. I soon discovered that, much like Fred's relationships with Betsy and the children, there was a powerful way in which he was primarily only *using* me—valuing me when I was helping him to feel worthwhile, devaluing me when I was interfering with his self-worth, and experiencing indifference to my qualities that he saw as irrelevant to his self-esteem. I saw this as a natural byproduct of Fred's tendency to value *himself* only conditionally—as long as he only took himself to be valuable under certain conditions (e.g., when people were complying with his wishes, when he was displaying his unique talents), he needed me to help him meet those conditions, and to subjugate the aspects of me that interfered with this.

Similarly, as I discussed in Chapter 2, there were important ways in which *I* was valuing Fred conditionally as well, namely to the degree that he engaged in the therapy in a way that I saw as "productive"—exhibiting an interest in his emotional states, displaying curiosity about his own patterns in relationships, and taking some degree of responsibility for these patterns. Like Fred, this conditional valuing was directly related to my tendency to value *myself* conditionally, for example when I felt like I was "performing well" as Fred's therapist, or helping him to implement genuine change in his life. When Fred enacted processes I saw as more detrimental (e.g., focusing exclusively on the defects of others, dissociating all vulnerability from his experience, exhibiting minimal curiosity or reflectiveness), I could start to devalue him *as a person*, encountering a desire to punish the pathological parts of him, and to make him into the "good patient" who would allow me to feel good about myself.[2]

For me, these processes manifested themselves most vividly when Fred would discuss his relationship with his ex-wife, Betsy. In a self-admitted act of defiance, Fred refused to refer to her by name, or even to describe her as his ex-wife; rather, decades after their divorce, he insisted on calling her "my wife." From Fred's perspective, Betsy never had the right to divorce him in the first place, so *they were still married*, "until death do us part." As I see it, since Fred's self-worth was so narrowly dependent on the compliance of others, he was psychically *unable* to acknowledge Betsy's right to leave their marriage—this would have been tantamount to Fred *making himself bad*, which meant complete emotional obliteration, the non-existence of the Self. While I understood this at both an intellectual and emotional level, at other moments, I became incensed at what felt like such a blatant disregard for Betsy's distinct subjectivity. *She fell out of love with you, Fred. She did not "choose" for this to happen—it was a natural response to feeling used and devalued by you for over a decade. Would you have preferred she stay with you even without loving you? Have you ever even considered what that would have been like for* her*?* Of course, there was a way in which I was identifying with Betsy, given my perception of Fred using *me* in our work together, with minimal regard for my independent subjectivity. Much like Betsy, I wanted to punish Fred, to transform him into the sort of person who could help me feel worthwhile, and to dissociate my own sense of worthlessness constantly being evoked in the dyad.

These dynamics, most of which were unfolding largely unconsciously at first, illustrate what I call the *intersubjective nexus of valuing*, which I see as a constant, if often unacknowledged, dimension of all clinical process. Fred and I each carried our characteristic patterns of valuing into the therapeutic relationship, and these patterns were further shaped, transformed, and mutually dissociated in response to our experience of the other person and the unique dynamic we were co-creating together. We each came to value and devalue each other under a specific and evolving array of conditions, such that both of us came to rely on the other for a feeling of self-esteem, and thereby to keep what Fairbairn (1952) calls the "burden of the badness" at bay. The problem is that, as the treatment progressed, it became clear that the respective conditions for our value placed us into natural opposition to each other—Fred had to cling to his rage and superiority in order to feel worthwhile, but his attachment to these patterns interfered with *my* self-worth, which substantially depended on Fred becoming more reflective about, and less exclusively attached to, his rage and superiority. In the same moment, the person we needed for a sense of value was simultaneously *depriving* us of that value. As I will later suggest, this dynamic is not unique to my interactions with Fred; it is a foundational feature of all human relationships, especially the connection between child and caregiver, and can be seen as the basis for the essentially ethical nature of analytic inquiry.

Ethics and therapeutic action

In Chapter 4, I argued that concerns about dignity and ethics played a pivotal role in inspiring the paradigm shift towards relational thinking in psychoanalysis. I would now like to extend this line of thinking one step further, suggesting that relational theory has been marked by a growing appreciation of the ethical dimensions of the psychoanalytic process itself. Here I am interested in the notion of *therapeutic action*—our theories about "how change happens" in clinical work. From Freud onward, analysts have long recognized the relevance of psychoanalysis to ethics (Hartmann, 1960; Meissner, 2003; Wallwork, 1991), as well as the importance of ethical conduct in professional practice (Celenza, 2007; Dewald & Clark, 2001; Gabbard & Lester, 1995). However, until relatively recently, psychoanalysts have shied away from conceptualizing therapeutic progress as essentially ethical in nature.

This likely stems from several factors, perhaps most notably our longstanding investment in viewing psychoanalysis as a natural science (Grünbaum, 1984; Holt, 1989; Mills, 2004; Wallerstein, 2006). Under the traditional conception, a scientifically oriented psychoanalysis is essentially "neutral" in nature, emphasizing *knowledge-based* elements (e.g., insight, understanding, analysis, interpretation), and eschewing the need to *change* our patients in specific ways (Aron & Starr, 2013; Mitchell, 1997). Freud (1917) proclaimed, "We are not reformers but merely observers" (p. 434), aligning behavioral techniques of "suggestion" with non-objectivity (p. 448). From this perspective, psychoanalysis has the ability to *describe and explain* ethics at the individual and cultural level, but it should never try to *promote* ethics by encouraging moral development or ethical behavior.

While the prominence of this scientific vision has decreased significantly in recent years, we observe its continued influence in our tendency to frame therapeutic action in more *value-neutral* terms, and in our implicit valorization of exploratory interventions (e.g., examination of past and present relationships, interpretation, validation of affect, self-disclosure) over more "change-oriented" interventions (e.g., advice-giving, psycho-education, behavioral strategies) (Aron & Starr, 2013). In all of this, I sense a lurking concern that introducing ethics into psychoanalysis risks overemphasizing the clinician's personal values in the analytic process—we start to sound like we are "converting our patients" to our own worldview, which feels ironically *unethical* and contrary to patients' autonomy.

Furthermore, I suspect that we have minimized ethics clinically due to our tendency to associate ethics with overly harsh cultural and religious practices (Fromm, 1950). Freud (1910b, 1917, 1918, 1923b, 1939) repeatedly aligned ethics with *asceticism*, implying a negation or denial of the self, stating emphatically, "We can present society with a blunt calculation that what is described as its morality calls for a bigger sacrifice than it is worth and that its proceedings are not based on honesty and do not display wisdom" (1917, p. 434). Even today, while psychoanalysis seems quite comfortable considering ethics at the social and cultural level (Layton, Hollander, & Gutwill, 2006; Samuels, 2016), many analytic practitioners see an ethical framework as oppressive, overly harsh, constrictive, and excessively focused on the needs of others, frequently at the expense of one's own well-being and fulfillment (Harlem, 2015; Teicholz, 2010).

Lastly, as I discussed extensively in Chapter 2, ethics can seem like a dramatically irrelevant frame for the clinical practice of psychoanalysis. In addition to feeling overly superficial and mainly oriented towards conscious concerns, ethics might appear to miss the most compelling aspects of analytic work, including issues of meaning, self-experience, and our sense of ourselves as subjects in collaborative, intimate contact with other meaning-making subjects.

In this chapter, I would like to suggest that the trajectory of theory development in psychoanalysis, which has largely been seen as evolving from a "one-person" to a "two-person" model of the mind (Greenberg & Mitchell, 1983), can also be mapped out along an ethical dimension—*the extent to which the theorist explicitly invokes ethics to explain "how change happens" in the analytic process.* I will offer a basic heuristic to organize theories along these lines, conceptualizing psychoanalytic models as ethically *neutral*, ethically *unilateral*, or ethically *intersubjective*. Without placing these approaches in a hierarchical relationship with each other, I am interested in shining a spotlight onto a relatively unexplored dimension of therapeutic process. My assumption is that, while we have come a long way towards recognizing the ethical dimensions of psychoanalysis, there is still an overall skittishness about theorizing along ethical lines, and greater attention to these matters might open up new possibilities for clinical experience.

Before I begin, a few disclaimers. First, like any heuristic, these categories are necessarily reductive, collapsing the messiness and complexity of our theories into an overly simplistic frame. There will be understandable disagreement about which models belong in which categories, and perhaps even about the validity of the categories themselves. Second, my treatment of these matters will be highly selective, focusing on the theories I personally see as most illustrative of these conceptual approaches, and admittedly ignoring other important perspectives that could have equal applicability here. And finally, in emphasizing the ethical neutrality of certain conceptions, I am doing so exclusively based on the theorist's *explicit language* in discussing therapeutic action. I do not mean to imply that the authors in question do not "care" about ethics, or even that their views have no ethical implications. On the contrary, I assume that *all* psychoanalytic models have ethical implications, and that all analysts, concerned with issues of human relationships and personal meaning, possess foundational ethical commitments that play a central role in how they conduct themselves in clinical practice.

For all of these reasons, I offer the following as a starting point for dialogue, not as a comprehensive or definitive statement.

Ethically neutral models of therapeutic action

By and large, most theories of therapeutic action in psychoanalysis are *ethically neutral*—that is, they explain the nature of analytic change without employing language or concepts related to ethical experience. The paradigmatic example of this is Freud's theory itself. It is widely understood that Freud's edifice underwent a gradual process of evolution, from the affect–trauma model to the topographical model and ultimately to the structural model (Fonagy & Target, 2003; Greenberg & Mitchell, 1983; Sandler, Holder, Dare, & Dreher, 1997). In the affect–trauma model, illustrated definitively in *Studies on Hysteria*, Freud conceptualizes therapeutic action namely in terms of *catharsis*, or abreaction of affect. Instigated by actual childhood sexual seductions, psychopathology is seen as the conscious ego repressing particular distressing ideas, wishes, or memories that are incompatible with the patient's conscious standards and ideals, with the "strangulated affect" finding subsequent, disguised expression in the patient's pathological symptoms (Breuer & Freud, 1893–1895, p. 7). By following the psychoanalytic "talking cure" based on free association, the patient can become conscious of the repressed ideas and affects, allowing for the cathartic release of these pathogenic affects and an integration of these ideas into the person's conscious personality. Breuer and Freud (1893–1895) describe their findings:

> Each individual hysterical symptom immediately and permanently disappeared when we had succeeded in bringing clearly to light the memory of the event by which it was provoked and in arousing its accompanying affect, and when the patient had described that event in the greatest possible detail and had put the affect into words.
>
> (p. 6)

With the introduction of the topographical frame of reference, Freud's theory of therapeutic action shifted to a focus on the analytic dyad itself, centering on *the interpretation and resolution of the transference* (Abend, 2009). At this point in Freud's (1915b) model, pathological symptoms essentially entail "the return of the repressed" (p. 154)—a substitutive satisfaction of repressed libidinal impulses fixated at earlier stages of development, in a way that circumvents the patient's ego-related prohibitions against these impulses (Freud, 1917). In the psychoanalytic situation, such psychic compromises manifest themselves in the patient's transferential attachment to the analyst, displaced from the aforementioned libidinal fixations, as well as the patient's resistance to the awareness of such processes, which reflect the repressive tendencies. By interpreting these impulses and resistances, the analyst assists the patient "in overcoming the resistances, lifting the repression and transforming the unconscious material into conscious" (Freud, 1917, p. 438). The patient's ego is thus both strengthened and expanded—she is able to consciously *own* her experience of conflict, which thus removes the repressive conditions necessary for the origination of symptoms: "We transform the pathogenic conflict into a normal one for which it must be possible somehow to find a solution" (p. 435).

In both the cathartic and transferential models, Freud frames therapeutic action in ethically neutral terms—"cathartic expression," "integration of repressed ideas," "lifting repressions," "interpretation and resolution of the transference." This is the language of psychology, not morality. As noted in Chapter 1, Freud takes great pains to highlight the ethical neutrality of psychoanalysis (1921), recommending that analysts remain impartial when faced with the conflict between patients' libidinal impulses and moral prohibitions (1917), and explicitly affirming that analysis does not result in moral outcomes: "The unworthiness of human beings, including the analysts, always has impressed me deeply, but why should analyzed men and women in fact be better. Analysis makes for integration but does not of itself make for goodness" (1915a, p. 188).

Despite Freud's emphasis on psychoanalysis' ethical neutrality, he regularly observes that the analytic process has ethical implications. When addressing the concern that analysis might lead to immoral behavior, Freud (1917) explains, "We tell ourselves that any one who has succeeded in educating himself to truth about himself is permanently defended against the danger of immorality" (p. 434). In granting the patient's ego increased autonomy over its libidinal and aggressive impulses, psychoanalysis sets the stage for sublimation, or the transformation of instinctual energies into socially valuable ends, such as morality, art, science, and intellectual and vocational pursuits (Freud, 1930). Freud (1911) writes along these lines:

> Our art consists in making it possible for people to be moral and to deal with their wishes philosophically. Sublimation, that is striving towards high goals, is of course one of the best means of overcoming

> the urgency of the drives. ... Whoever is capable of sublimation will turn to it inevitably as soon as he is free of his neurosis.
>
> (pp. 121–122)

For Freud (1910a), sublimation can be seen as the regular byproduct of the analytic resolution of repression: "Premature repression makes the sublimation of the repressed impulse impossible; when the repression is lifted, the path to sublimation becomes free once more" (p. 54).

While Freud never takes the leap of conceptualizing ethics as a central element of analytic change, the seeds of such a position are present in his formulations. As is widely known, Freud (1912) insists that all analysts should themselves receive psychoanalytic treatment prior to practicing psychoanalysis themselves:

> He should have undergone a psycho-analytic purification and have become aware of those complexes of his own which would be apt to interfere with his grasp of what the patient tells him. There can be no reasonable doubt about the disqualifying effect of such defects in the doctor; every unresolved repression in him constitutes what has been aptly described ... as a "blind spot" in his analytic perception.
>
> (p. 116)

According to Freud, an "analyzed" analyst is a *less-repressed* analyst, who, in light of the aforementioned points about the ethical consequences of psychoanalysis, possesses a greater capacity for sublimation. On this view, the analyst's ethical vulnerabilities could have a "disqualifying effect" on her ability to effectively implement analytic technique, and the therapeutic action of psychoanalysis would be predicated on the analyst's basic potential for ethical motivation. Due to Freud's attachment to a more scientific, ethically neutral vision of psychoanalysis, these elements of his theory were never fully explored or developed.

Freud's ethically neutral approach to analytic process has been largely preserved throughout the history of psychoanalysis thus far, as can be seen in our most prominent models of therapeutic action and therapeutic aims. Examples include Anna Freud's (1946) suggestion that the task of psychoanalysis is "to bring into consciousness that which is unconscious, no matter to which psychic institution it belongs" (p. 30); Hartmann's

(1958) assumption that psychoanalysis aims "to help men achieve a better functioning synthesis and relation to the environment" (p. 81); Strachey's (1934) influential theory of mutative interpretations and the analyst as auxiliary super-ego, resulting in the amelioration of the patient's super-ego and increased access to infantile id-impulses; Loewald's (1980) idea that psychoanalysis enables the patient to developmentally regress and simultaneously achieve "higher stages of ego reality organization" (p. 243); and Kleinian theory's notion of psychoanalysis as helping patients transition from paranoid-schizoid functioning to depressive functioning, such that they rely less on primitive splitting defenses (e.g., idealization, devaluation, projective identification) and have the capability for more balanced, integrated experiences in their relationships (Jacobsen, 1964; Kernberg, 1976; M. Klein, 1975).

But ethical neutrality is not unique to more classically oriented viewpoints. Many of our most important relational models of therapeutic action, regardless of specific theoretical orientation or how "progressive" they are along other dimensions (e.g., relationality/intersubjectivity, epistemology, technical approaches), have been framed in primarily non-ethical terms. This includes Fairbairn's (1958) conception that "*the chief aim of psycho-analytical treatment is to promote a maximum 'synthesis' of the structures into which the original ego has been split*" (p. 380); Sullivan's (1953, 1954) theory of the importance of the analyst's consensual validation of the patient's subjectivity, allowing the patient's parataxic distortions to transform into meaningful, reality-based syntactic experience (see Bromberg, 1980); Mitchell's (1988) position that the purpose of psychoanalysis is increased *flexibility*, "to broaden the analytic relationship, and by extension the analysand's other relationships as well, into richer, more dialectical exchanges" (p. 300); Bromberg's (1998, 2006) perspective that, through the joint processing of mutually dissociated experiences, the patient gains the ability to "stand in the spaces" between contradictory self-states, leading to an increased sense of wholeness and self-continuity; Ogden's (2005) view that the aim of psychoanalysis is "*the creation of conditions in which the analysand (with the analyst's participation) may become better able to dream his undreamt and interrupted dreams*" (p. 6); and the Boston Change Process Study Group's (2010) ideas about "moments of meeting" between analyst and patient, resulting in alterations of the patient's implicit relational knowledge, or fundamental "ways of being with" others.

I suggest that all of the above theories of therapeutic action are explicitly ethically neutral, that is, they can be fully elaborated without invoking ethical constructs. Interestingly, this is the case despite the fact that many of these models grew out of ethical concerns about classical thinking and practice (see Chapter 4), and despite the fact that these conceptions have profound implications for ethics, mutuality, and other-oriented experience at both the individual and cultural level. While relational thought is deeply focused on ethical matters, especially as they relate to issues of social justice, these concerns often remain separate from perspectives on therapeutic action.

Ethically unilateral models of therapeutic action

Expounded most comprehensively by Winnicott and Kohut, psychoanalytic authors also advocate what I call ethically *unilateral* models of therapeutic action, in which the ethical capacities of the analyst herself are seen as the central agent of analytic change. This approach is perhaps most common in theories where the adaptive development of the Self constitutes the primary achievement in both developmental process and in psychoanalysis. These theories usually entail some concept of the analyst's *optimal motivational responsiveness*, in which the analyst is able to recognize, empathically resonate with, and somehow respond to the needs and experiences of the patient. Examples of such concepts include Winnicott's (1958, 1965, 1971) notions of holding, attunement, identification, the "mirror-role," and the facilitating environment; Balint's (1968) idea of the analyst serving as a "primary object" for the patient, who unobtrusively facilitates the patient's regressive needs; Kohut's (1977, 1981, 1984) conception of empathic resonance and "vicarious introspection"; Bacal's (1998) theory of optimal responsiveness; Orange's (1995) vision of emotional understanding; Schwaber's (1981, 1983, 1992) formulation of analytic listening; Fosshage's (1995, 1997) construct of facilitating responsiveness; and Stolorow and colleagues' view of intersubjective empathic attunement (Stolorow & Atwood, 1992; Stolorow, Brandchaft, & Atwood, 1995).

While these concepts differ in significant ways, all of them constitute some notion of ethical capability, in which the agent is motivationally and behaviorally responsive to the well-being, dignity, or subjective meanings of the Other. From an ethical perspective, these approaches constitute a momentous advance from the aforementioned ethically neutral models. They imply that analytic work constitutes ethical work in and of itself, such that the clinician must possess some basic capacity for ethical motivation in order for therapy to be effective, and that she must remain continuously receptive to the patient, perhaps even bracketing her own subjectivity (Slochower, 2014), in order for the treatment to progress on a moment-to-moment basis. Consistent with an ethical frame of reference, such models shift the clinical focus from the analyst's "knowledge" and "analysis" (e.g., about repressed impulses, resistances, internalized object relationships) to the analyst's *empathy* and *care*, an evolution that partially fueled the "insight versus experience" debate that has long dominated psychoanalytic discussions about therapeutic action (Gabbard & Westen, 2003).

While these theories conceptualize the practitioner's involvement along ethical lines, they tend to maintain ethical neutrality when it comes to the patient, for example by framing pathology in terms of the patient's stalled developmental needs, or by conceiving therapeutic progress in terms of the healthy maturation of the Self. In ethically unilateral models, the clinician is the ethical agent in the psychoanalytic equation, and the patient is the beneficiary of the clinician's ethical endeavors—therapeutic action relies on the ethics of the analyst, not the patient.

I am not suggesting that ethically unilateral theories ignore the patient's own ethical faculties. In contrast, many of these theories portray these faculties as the ideal outcome of clinical work. For example, Kohut (1984) suggests that "a successful analysis is one in which the analysand's formerly archaic needs for the responses of archaic selfobjects are superseded by the experience of the availability of empathic resonance, the major constituent of the sense of security in adult life" (p. 77). Similarly, Winnicott (1971) defines health in terms of the potential for identification and empathy (chapter 10), positing this ability as developmentally *more advanced* than the capacity for object-usage that has received so much attention in contemporary psychoanalysis (p. 118; see also Winnicott, 1965, pp. 83–84, 90–91).

However, positioning ethics as an "outcome" of psychoanalysis is not the same as endorsing a fundamentally ethical vision of psychoanalysis. Just as successful development depends on the caregiver's tendency towards other-oriented motivation, the patient's ethical maturity can be seen largely as a consequence of the analyst's successful ethical responsiveness. Since the patient's ethical capabilities are a *byproduct* of analytic change, they cannot be an antecedent of that change. Consider Winnicott's (1971) language when he describes the evolution of what he calls "cross-identification," or the ability to empathize and identify with another person:

> In this case, and in similar cases, I have found that the patient has needed phases of regression to dependence in the transference, these giving experience of the full effect of adaptation to need that is in fact based on the analyst's (mother's) ability to identify with the patient (her baby). In the course of this kind of *experience* there is a sufficient quantity of being merged in with the analyst (mother) to enable the patient to live and to relate without the need for projective and introjective identificatory mechanisms. Then comes the painful process whereby the object is separated out from the subject, and the analyst becomes separated off and is placed outside the omnipotent control of the patient. The analyst's survival of the destructiveness that belongs to and follows this change enables a new thing to happen, which is the patient's *use* of the analyst, and the initiation of a new relationship based on cross-identifications. The patient can now begin to stand imaginatively in the analyst's shoes, and (at the same time) it is possible and good for the analyst to stand in the patient's shoes from a position, that is, of having his own feet on the ground.
>
> (pp. 184–185)

In this passage, all of the ethical "work" (e.g., adaptation, identification, survival) is being performed by the analyst, while the patient's work is to regress, depend, merge, and attack, processes that largely involve indifference to, and even violation of, the analyst's rights as an independent subject. In such a model, we could not even speak about the patient's "ethical obligations" to the analyst, since such obligations are predicated on a capacity the patient has not yet developed.

These observations highlight an interesting implication of conceptions of therapeutic action that frame ethics as a "capacity" someone does or does not possess. In such theories, ethics only becomes clinically meaningful for the patient when she acquires the capability for ethical functioning. This leads to what might be called "mixed model" theories of ethical development (Greenberg & Mitchell, 1983), where one set of intersubjective and motivational processes dominates pre-ethical functioning (e.g., needs for attunement, mirroring, omnipotent control), and another set of processes (e.g., empathic resonance, identification) emerge in ethical life.

These models define ethics in terms of *content*, specifying actions, capacities, and experiences that have ethical value. As I suggested in Chapter 2, this approach has the effect of limiting the applicability of ethics in clinical practice—it implies that, for patients who do not yet possess the ability for "fully ethical relatedness," ethics is not particularly relevant, and a whole different conception of psychoanalysis is needed to explain and address the experiences of these patients. An alternative approach is to envision ethics not in terms of definite motivational or behavioral content, but as a co-constructed *process* unfolding in the therapeutic dyad. This perspective dramatically expands the utility of ethics in psychoanalytic practice.

Ethically intersubjective models of therapeutic action

With the advent of relational thinking in psychoanalysis, we have seen the emergence of a genuinely innovative model of therapeutic action, in which the ethical development of *both therapist and patient* is seen as the active ingredient in analytic change. While these theories differ considerably in their focus and specific conceptualizations, most of these models entail some (more or less elaborated) view of pathology that is either implicitly or explicitly ethical in nature. As the therapy unfolds, the participants end up mutually enacting some version of this pathological/ethical process, consistent with their individual personalities and the unique dynamic they are co-creating together. This leads to some form of "impasse" or disruption, such that, in order for the work to proceed, both parties must consciously or unconsciously move towards a *more ethically responsive* approach to the therapeutic relationship, which somehow enables them to work through the intersubjective disturbance in question. This reciprocal "ethical development" within the dyad serves as the basis for the patient's own psychological maturation, helping her to move towards a healthier, more adaptive experience of Self-in-relation-to-Other that can be seen as the fundamental aim of psychoanalysis.[3]

The first ethically intersubjective theory can be found in the writings of Harold Searles. In "The Patient as Therapist to His Analyst," a paper which I see as one of the most groundbreaking and unique contributions to the analytic literature, Searles (1979) outlines a model in which the ethical potentials of both analyst and patient stand at the center of therapeutic change. In Searles' view, psychopathology in general, and especially psychotic illness, involves the failure of the person to undergo "the firm establishment of an individual human self" (p. 384), due developmentally to the person's caregiver rigidly engaging him in a symbiotic merger in order to meet the caregiver's own unmet and repressed dependency needs (pp. 436–437). The person ultimately blames *himself* for the caregiver's psychological vulnerabilities, internalizing an "unconscious, lifelong guilt at his own failure in his therapeutic effort" (p. 385).

In the clinical situation, the patient seeks to recreate with the analyst those early merger experiences, displaying altruistic tendencies Searles identifies as *therapeutic strivings*: "He is endeavoring to contribute to the analyst's emotional growth, integration, maturation. He is endeavoring to help the analyst to fulfill the latter's emotional potentialities and healthy ego ideals" (p. 427). From the perspective of intersubjectivity, the crucial point is that the analyst "inevitably and necessarily" starts to symbiotically merge with the patient (p. 444), becoming emotionally dependent on the patient for a degree of his psychological functioning.

> The therapist comes to feel that he *really* is, to a significant degree, at one with the patient, and to experience it as becoming a *real* issue whether he, the therapist, can bear the loss, to his own ego functioning, of the individuation toward which the therapeutic endeavor is directed.
>
> (p. 444)

This establishes the analyst's central ethical dilemma, the resolution of which is essential for therapeutic action—the analyst must essentially "choose" between continued satisfaction of his symbiotic dependency needs and the patient's own need for individuation. Under optimal circumstances, as the analyst becomes aware of his dependency on the patient, he increasingly comes to integrate these dependency needs into his broader personality, and (implicitly or explicitly) to *communicate* this awareness to the patient (p. 428). The patient is thus able to see himself as genuinely helping and healing the analyst, resuming the process of individuation never fully possible in his early relationship with his caregiver: "The patient can become sufficiently free from such guilt, sufficiently sure, as it were, of his symbiotic worth, so that he can now become more deeply a full human individual" (p. 385).

In contemporary psychoanalysis, the theorist who has articulated the most purely ethical model of therapeutic action is Jessica Benjamin. As I explored in Chapter 3, Benjamin's (1988, 1995) notion of mutual recognition is a fundamentally ethical construct, implying the capacity of two people (e.g., child and caregiver, patient and analyst) to respect and value each other as essentially distinct but similar independent subjects. In her more recent clinical formulations, Benjamin (2004) conceptualizes pathology in terms of "doer and done to" experiences that derive historically from early developmental processes in which the child feels like her perspective is "denied and supplanted by the parent's reality" (p. 30). In the therapeutic relationship, such dynamics are unconsciously re-created between patient and analyst, such that:

> Each person feels *done to*, and not like an agent helping to shape a co-created reality. ... In such interactions, we can see the underlying symmetry that characterizes the apparent opposition of power relations: each feels unable to gain the other's recognition, and each feels in the other's power.
>
> (pp. 9–10)

Interestingly, Benjamin employs intersubjectivity theory to arrive at an ethical solution to these ruptures. If we accept the idea that all relational contexts necessarily involve bidirectional patterns of mutual influence, then the analyst herself is always partially responsible for the impasses and sufferings inherent to the analytic process: "If involvement in the interaction cannot be avoided, then it is all the more necessary that we be oriented to certain principles of responsibility" (pp. 40–41). To formalize these considerations, Benjamin (2009) introduces her concept of the *moral third*, understood as "those values, rules, and principles of interaction that we rely upon in our efforts to create and restore the space for each partner in the dyad to engage in thinking, feeling, acting or responding rather than merely reacting" (p. 442). This third involves a deep acceptance of the inevitability of co-created enactment, a faith that both parties can survive such enactments, and perhaps most importantly, a willingness to assume responsibility for our role in perpetuating our patients' sufferings. Benjamin (2004) explains:

> In taking such responsibility, the analyst is putting an end to the buck passing the patient has always experienced—that is, to the game of ping-pong wherein each member of the dyad tries to put the bad into the other. The analyst says, in effect, "I'll go first." In orienting to the moral third of responsibility, the analyst is also demonstrating the route out of helplessness.
>
> (p. 33)

By assuming responsibility for her own contribution to the patient's sufferings, the analyst is able to work with the patient to collaboratively co-create what Benjamin calls a *shared third*, understood as "a dyadic system that contains by virtue of mutual reflection on the interaction" (p. 35), in which both individuals are able "to recognize that the object of [their] feelings, needs, actions, and thoughts is actually another subject, an equivalent center of being" (p. 6; my brackets). With these ideas, Benjamin is clearly positioning the ethical development of analyst and patient at the center of therapeutic action—when the analyst "goes first" in assuming responsibility for clinical ruptures, she helps to open up space so that the patient can achieve increased ethical responsiveness towards herself and others, which in turn leads to "more emotionally authentic, more spontaneous and inventive, more compassionate and liberating" modes of affect and experience (p. 42).

Several other relational authors have further elaborated ethical intersubjectivity along different lines. Influenced by their psychoanalytic approach to evolutionary biology (Slavin & Kriegman, 1992), Slavin and Kriegman (1998) draw attention to the inherently conflictual nature of the therapeutic relationship, due primarily to each party operating from a standpoint of *self-interest.* For Slavin and Kriegman (1998), self-interest encompasses much more than just hedonism or "selfishness;" it comprises the innate human tendency to structure experience in terms of our personal subjective worlds, and to "create and maintain a sense of self" in a fundamentally biased way that reflects primarily our own needs and identities (p. 251). Slavin and Kriegman posit that this self-interest, combined with the naturally asymmetrical nature of the analytic dyad (Aron, 1996a), leads to what might be called an *ethical imbalance* in therapeutic work. The patient is forced to adapt herself to the specific person of the analyst, while the analyst, despite her best intentions, is not proportionately invested in the specific person of the patient: "The therapeutic relationship does not carry with it the inherent investment in the patient's interests that kin and other natural, reciprocal relationships regularly entail" (p. 261).

According to Slavin and Kriegman (1998), analytic process involves the analyst personally recognizing and explicitly acknowledging to the patient the ways in which their interests diverge, while progressively opening herself up to be changed by the patient, such that her "core self-interests" come to encompass the identity and needs of the unique patient in question (p. 261).

> Because the relationship between analyst and patient entails real conflicts between their identities, the negotiation process, ultimately involving real changes in the analyst, provides the crucial experience for the patient to reopen and rework old conclusions about his or her self and the potential for effective negotiations with the relational world.
>
> (p. 280)

With these formulations, Slavin and Kriegman are essentially placing the dialectic between self-interest and altruism at the heart of the therapeutic project. As the analyst comes to revise her identity along more "patient-centered" lines, the patient is able to feel safe enough to allow herself to change. This leads to a more reciprocal ethical dynamic in the dyad, in which each person's identity comes to reflect an optimal balance between her own self-interest and the needs and interests of the other party (p. 259).

Irwin Hoffman offers yet another example of ethical intersubjectivity. Hoffman's (1998) model of therapeutic action is predicated on what he calls the analyst's *moral authority*, understood as the power to influence (through her actions and inaction) the patient's experiences, self-worth, and life directions, in a way that significantly reflects the analyst's idiosyncratic personality, subjectivity, and values (pp. xx, 8–10, 26, 82–88, 95). This authority derives from the analyst's attachment to "the book" of psychoanalysis, which encompasses the ritualized asymmetry of the treatment frame, the principles of analytic technique, the content of psychoanalytic theory, and the analyst's personal identification with the larger analytic community (Hoffman, 1998, chapter 3).

In Hoffman's (1998) vision of analytic work, the analyst is continuously faced with a tension between responding to the patient's "immediately expressed desires" (pp. 215–216), and honoring "other narcissistic and object-related investments" in her own life (p. 216), including attachments to her own authority and to psychoanalytic theory itself. Trouble arises when the analyst collapses this dialectic, for example by embracing pure spontaneous responsiveness to the patient (which undermines her responsibility to herself), or by rigidly adhering to arbitrary standards of technique (which undermines her commitment to the specific patient with whom she is connected). In contrast, under optimal circumstances, the analyst is able to maintain rather than collapse the tension between her own personal investments and the patient's desires:

> When the patient senses that the analyst, in becoming more personally expressive and involved, is departing from an internalized convention of some kind, the patient has reason to feel recognized in a special way. The deviation, whatever its content and whatever the nature of the pressure from the patient, may reflect an emotional engagement on the analyst's part that is responsive in a unique way to this particular patient.
>
> (p. 195)

As the analyst finds a way to simultaneously respect herself *and* the patient, the patient starts to feel truly valued as a unique, agentic subject who is "ultimately deserving of love" (p. 95; see also Hoffman, 2009b).

But the patient is not simply an ethical bystander in this process. In his more recent writings, Hoffman (2000, 2006, 2016) explores the patient's ethical obligations to the analyst herself, emphasizing the clinical importance of the patient *forgiving* the analyst for her unavoidable limitations and vulnerability:

> If there is to be any therapeutic benefit, in the end the patient must *forgive* the analyst for the reality that he or she is indeed simply a person like the patient. The patient must choose *to forgive* in order to choose *to take* whatever good the analyst has to offer.
>
> (Hoffman, 2000, p. 845)

With these ideas, Hoffman is conceptualizing therapeutic action in terms of the mutual ethical development of analyst and patient. Just as the analyst must partly sacrifice her authority in order for the patient to feel truly valued, the patient must "see through" that authority in order to value *the analyst* as a fellow human being, with limitations and vulnerabilities like herself. This mutual valuing of Self and Other enables the patient to surrender her attachments to constrictive forms of interaction, helping her to cultivate "an enhanced capacity for responsive and creative living" in her life and relationships (p. 845).

A final important model of ethical intersubjectivity is Peter Fonagy and Anthony Bateman's theory of *mentalization*, defined formally as "the mental process by which an individual implicitly and explicitly interprets the actions of himself and others as meaningful on the basis of intentional mental states such as personal desires, needs, feelings, beliefs, and reasons" (Bateman & Fonagy, 2004, p. xxi; see also Bateman & Fonagy, 2012, 2016). As Allen (2013) has recently highlighted, this vision of mentalization is central to ethics, since it implies the potential to *perceive, understand, and reflect on* subjective experiences in oneself and others, which can be seen as a necessary condition for ethical motivation and behavior. Fonagy, Gergely, Jurist, and Target (2002) conceptualize pathology in terms of context-dependent deficits in mentalization—if the child receives persistently non-contingent forms of mirroring from the caregiver, she internalizes representations of the *caregiver's* subjectivity rather than her own. The child thus never acquires the basic capacity to represent her own internal world, resulting in "the poor establishment of agentive self-structure" (p. 250). In contemporary life, when the person's needs for attachment and closeness are intensified, primitive forms of psychic experience begin to emerge—characterized by rigidity, disconnection from emotions, concreteness, and "splitting" mechanisms—and the person struggles to maintain contact with subjective states in herself and others. This basic deficit helps to explain the characteristic functional impairments we tend to see in patients suffering from severe developmental trauma and neglect (Fonagy et al., 2002, chapters 9–11).

On this conception, effective psychotherapy strengthens the patient's ability to represent psychological processes in herself and others, starting in the relationship with the therapist and ultimately generalizing to the patient's close relationships outside of the therapy. The therapist is consistently at risk of losing her own ability to mentalize in emotionally charged interactions with the patient (e.g., by falling into rigidity and concreteness, by becoming disconnected from authentic emotionality in herself and the patient), and so she must actively work to "maintain and regain" mentalization when it is lost (Bateman & Fonagy, 2016, pp. 206–207). Over time, the patient "is able to find himself in the mind of the therapist as a thinking and feeling being—the representation that never fully developed and was probably further undermined by subsequent painful interpersonal experience" (Fonagy et al., 2002, p. 433). As the therapist cultivates a representation of the patient that is contingently related to the patient's subjectivity, the patient reintrojects these representations and uses them as a representation of her own thinking, resulting in improvements in her ability to mentalize *herself.*

But this process is not one-directional. From the standpoint of technique, the mentalizing therapist "openly communicates what is in his/her mind when it is relevant to the patient–clinician interaction" (Bateman & Fonagy, 2016, p. 282). The patient thus internalizes an image of the therapist as a person with whom she is related, laying the foundation for a more robust sense of agency and self-coherence.

> Over a long period, frequent and diverse interpretations about the patient's perception of himself, the analyst, and their analytic relationship may enable him to attempt to create a mental representation both of himself and of his analyst, as thinking and feeling, together

> and independently. This can then form the core of a sense of himself with a capacity to represent ideas and meanings and create the basis for the bond that ultimately permits new possibilities of separation and intimacy.
>
> (Fonagy et al., 2002, p. 480).

Like the other theories we have considered, this model frames therapeutic action in terms of the patient and therapist's ethical achievements—as the therapist continuously accesses and represents subjective processes in herself and the patient, the patient increasingly feels "recognized" and "seen," allowing her to risk representing mental states in herself *and* the therapist, which gradually facilitates an experience of agency and self-coherence that was not possible in her earliest relational contexts.

As is widely known, the above ideas have been formalized in mentalization-based treatment (MBT), which has emerged as a leading empirically validated therapy for borderline personality disorder (Choi-Kain, Albert, & Gunderson, 2016). While psychoanalysis has had an admittedly rocky relationship with evidence-based practice (Hoffman, 2009a), I suggest that these findings have important implications for the theories we have considered in this section. Employing their own idiosyncratic language and concepts, all of these theories maintain that *enhanced, bi-directional ethical responsiveness between therapist and patient lies at the heart of therapeutic action.* MBT essentially systematizes this perspective. Its substantial empirical validation suggests that this approach has the potential to extend beyond the confines of psychoanalysis proper into the more "mainstream" practice of psychotherapy (Aron & Starr, 2013), opening the door to settings, populations, and diagnostic presentations not typically associated with traditional psychoanalytic work (Bateman & Fonagy, 2012).

It is important to note that, in affirming that the clinician necessarily becomes ethically implicated in the patient's pathology, none of the theories considered in this section construe the clinician's ethical culpability as simply the patient's projection, or even as the clinician's own unresolved countertransference. Rather, these models of ethical intersubjectivity are suggesting that, in order for progress to occur in psychoanalysis, the analyst must *actually* ethically violate the patient (e.g., by becoming too dependent on the patient, by inadvertently victimizing her, by insufficiently investing in the patient, by prioritizing theory and authority over the patient's needs, by failing to mentalize the patient), and the analyst must *actually* repair that transgression by advancing more fully along ethical lines (e.g., by prioritizing the patient's individuation over her own dependency needs, by assuming responsibility for the impasse, by revising her identity to encompass the patient's interests, by surrendering her attachment to theory and authority, by persistently seeking to mentalize the patient).

Compared to other models of therapeutic action that have dominated psychoanalysis throughout its history, this is an admittedly strange vision of psychoanalytic change. It amounts to the suggestion not simply that we must "become better people" in order to help the patient, but we must be continuously in the process of *harming* the patient, and of *becoming* better people, for the sake of the particular patient with whom we are working, and for our sake as well. This is a daunting proposition, one that demolishes any ceiling of ethical evolution for us. If we fully accept this idea, we are no longer permitted to comfortably sit back and say "I'm all set" from the perspective of ethical capabilities, or to blame the patient for the deficiencies or pathology in the relationship. Given the relative extremity of this approach, it is reasonable to ask why so much should be required of us as clinicians, and specifically why our own *ethical* development might be such a necessary condition for our patients' *psychological* change.

Psychoanalysis as an ethical process

Throughout this book, as well as in several previously published papers now synthesized into Chapters 3 and 4 of this volume (Drozek, 2010a, 2010b, 2015a, 2015b), I have sketched out my own conception of ethical intersubjectivity, in which psychoanalysis involves the co-creation of an intersubjective space that is progressively more consistent with the unconditional worth of both therapist and patient. On this view, psychopathology entails an experience of Self and Other as *only* conditionally valuable, or as *only* unconditionally bad, without a simultaneous recognition of dignity and worth. As the analytic process unfolds, therapist and patient naturally co-create intersubjective patterns that, to a greater or lesser degree, fail to sufficiently express the intrinsic worth of Self and Other, and in many cases functionally undermine that worth. This inevitably leads to moments of disruption and impasse, in which each party comes to feel like she can only possess value if the other individual changes in some way, usually by actualizing some state of being that she (consciously or unconsciously) sees as more desirable, valuable, adaptive, or healthy.

At such moments, if we were to press "pause" on these treatments and attempt something of an "ethical X-ray" of the dyad, we would find that each person is selling *herself, the other subject, and the relationship* short—that she is unconsciously insisting that she is only valuable under a very specific (and usually unformulated) range of conditions, that the other person is only valuable under certain (similarly unformulated) conditions, and perhaps most importantly, *that she herself can only achieve a sense of value if the other individual meets the conditions in question.* Or, framed in more experience-near terms: each participant comes to rely on the other for self-esteem, which inevitably leads to significant constrictions in her ability to experience Self *and* Other as worthwhile in this particular relationship.

These processes of conditional valuing serve as the fuel for our tendencies to ascribe conscious and unconscious badness to others, as if we are essentially saying, at a brute level—*You are bad because you are keeping me from having value. I want to make you into the sort of person who can make me feel worthwhile, or at least to punish you for refusing to give me what I need.* On this view, every treatment, if it is to generate what might be seen as more "fundamental" personality change, must reach a point in which both parties become the ethical *victims and violators* of Self and Other. As all of the ethical intersubjectivists have suggested, it is the responsibility of the clinician to arrive at some degree of reflection about these dynamics, and somehow to "own" her role as violator of the patient. In the terms of my theory, I suggest that, in order for the treatment to move forward, the therapist must begin to recognize, represent, and take responsibility for her own valuational patterns, and ultimately to find a way to value herself and the patient under a greater diversity of conditions, which in turn liberates the patient to start valuing herself and the therapist more expansively as well. This is the basic source of therapeutic progress, enabling the patient to access a more durable sense of dignity and worth that can co-exist with her tendency to ascribe conditional value, or unconditional badness, to Self and Other.

Therapeutic action can thus be seen as a progressive, iterative process in which the analytic relationship *itself* comes to increasingly reflect the unconditional worth of both participants, allowing for experiences of increased intimacy, connectedness, and mutuality in the dyad, and eventually in the participants' lives outside of the therapy.[4]

To illustrate these conceptions, I will return to my work with Fred. In hindsight, the session where I felt compelled to hit Fred served as a defining moment in the therapy. Personally, it alerted me to the foundational importance of my desire to punish Fred, to force him to see that *he* was in the wrong in many of these situations where he was exclusively blaming others. Consciously, my punishing desires were related to my belief that Fred was insufficiently motivated by the needs, desires, and interests of other people, and that he was regularly violating the rights of others, especially when they failed to comply with his demands.

In my experience, this sort of belief state is quite common during periods of impasse or disruption, as Benjamin (2004) has illustrated with her model of "doer versus done to" processes. Both parties are ascribing some form of badness to the other, and they (often unconsciously) justify that ascription by invoking some idea that is explicitly ethical in nature, that is, involving the negative value of specific actions, subjective states, character traits, and interpersonal approaches that undermine the dignity and well-being of Self or Other. For the clinician, common examples of such formulations are our belief that our patients should somehow "be" different (e.g., more compassionate, flexible, motivated, or reflective; less aggressive, stubborn, self-centered, or concrete); that they should "do" something differently (e.g., taking particular actions, refraining from others); or that they are somehow responsible or "at fault" for certain difficulties in the therapeutic relationship and beyond. Especially once we become rigidly attached to such formulations, they constitute crucial analytic data, signaling that some *mutually dissociated form of badness* has started to grip the dyad. At such moments, there is usually a way in which *I* am unconsciously insisting on my own worthlessness; the patient is unconsciously insisting on her defectiveness; and *both of us* are reflexively devaluing the other in order to escape from our shared sense of insufficiency.

I came to realize how I was *using* my belief about Fred's selfishness to serve a psychological function for myself—namely, to justify my ascription of badness to him, and thereby to diminish my feelings of worthlessness perpetually being evoked in our work together. As long as Fred was "in the wrong," I did not have to experience *myself* as being wrong, bad, and incapable as Fred continued to struggle with these difficulties. While I still believed Fred was violating the rights of others, my emotional relationship to that belief began to shift. I was aware of myself "holding" rather than *gripping* this belief, while simultaneously accessing my more vulnerable emotions and desires with Fred —my fears that I was somehow responsible for his ongoing difficulties, my feelings of insecurity and worthlessness, and my desire to escape from those feelings, to shift the blame onto Fred.

As I increasingly accessed these parts of myself, I felt freer to communicate them to Fred, explicitly and implicitly. So, when I encountered that familiar frustration as Fred itemized Betsy's negative qualities, I was able to share with him, "I am feeling a strong desire to punish you right now, to convince you that you are 'in the wrong' for failing to see things from Betsy's perspective. I think I am afraid that, if I am unable to change you in this way, you will continue to suffer along these lines, and I will be somehow failing you." These sorts of disclosures—of my aggression, and of the insecurities fueling it—deepened my relationship with Fred. Fred shared that he saw me as a more "three-dimensional" person in these moments, which gradually laid the foundation for Fred bringing a broader array of his own emotions into the process. We also discovered how my subjective states provided us with a direct window into the experiences of the other characters in his conflicts—while Fred only *saw* other people's aggression towards him, he started to consider the possibility that he was triggering their insecurities as he was attempting to control and demean them, which in turn helped him to approach these interactions in a less aggressive, more vulnerable manner.

By increasingly accessing and "owning" these subjective processes in my work with Fred, I believe that I was coming to value myself and Fred under a wider range of conditions—to value myself even if I was unable to help Fred alter these patterns, and to value Fred even if he continued denying others' viewpoints and reality. It is important to note that, in making this shift, I was not *discontinuing* my pattern of devaluing myself for failing Fred, or of devaluing Fred for failing me. Rather, at least at first, I was valuing myself and Fred "in the same breath" as the devaluing. This is an ethical version of Bromberg's (1998) seminal notion of "standing in the spaces"—keeping one foot in our shared sense of badness and another foot in our shared sense of dignity, in "what we deserve" from ourselves and each other. I see this directionality—moving from a place of *exclusive* worthlessness ("I am a piece of shit, and you are bad for not rescuing me from that feeling") to *inclusive* worthlessness ("We are both pieces of shit, but we also might have value and worth anyway")—as the optimal therapeutic stance, which is most likely to facilitate patients taking the risk of accessing previously unformulated dimensions of their subjectivity, and of experiencing the current relationship in a new and generative way.

As I made these alterations, Fred gradually shifted in his interactions with me. Fred seemed to be listening to me more, to be "taking in" my point of view as I shared it—his verbal responses seemed less like tangentially related monologues and more like actual responses to me and what I was saying. When Fred would describe incidents in his life from outside of the treatment, he included comments like, "Well, I was thinking about what you had told me . . ." and "I really wanted to tell her off, but I knew that you wouldn't like that, and that I would just have to come back in here and talk about it, so I decided to hold myself back." I began to feel like Fred was seeing and relating to *me*, the person that I actually was in this particular relationship, rather than just my behaviors and tendencies (e.g., listening, mirroring, admiring) that he saw as facilitating his self-esteem.

I started to feel less pressured by Fred, also encountering a growing freedom to relate to him in a way that felt authentic to my natural inclinations in the moment—sometimes mirroring and validating his emotional states, sometimes pursuing avenues he saw as less interesting or relevant, and at other moments, actively challenging him by offering a perspective that departed from his own understanding of his experiences. Fred seemed to "roll with" these shifts in my approach, with minimal disruption to our relationship—he would not tacitly pursue mirroring from me if my mind happened to be focused on some other topic, nor would he attack me for enacting these more flexible relational patterns. I became increasingly comfortable with Fred. I found myself genuinely enjoying our sessions, even looking forward to them. I was not fully aware of how much I had been "holding back" with Fred, until I had the unexpected experience of reflexively bringing a fuller sense of myself to the work.

Fred's narratives of his relationships outside of treatment also evolved. Rather than focusing primarily on other people's wrongs and deficiencies, Fred progressively came to access his longings for closeness with others, most notably with his children, whom he had long kept at bay because they had not exclusively "taken his side" in the divorce. Fred began to spend much more time with them, actively attempting to remain present and engaged in their lives. While past memories of the divorce still evoked strong feelings of anger and humiliation for Fred, he was able to brave such feelings without allowing them to completely overtake these interactions. Where formerly he would regularly enumerate Betsy's negative qualities with his children, in the hopes that they would align and agree with him, Fred sought to ask about his children's experiences (e.g., their relationships, emotions, plans for the future), remaining present with them in a way that formerly had been impossible for him. These relationships improved dramatically. Fred developed a close and mutually supportive bond with his son, and he began repairing his connection with his daughter, from whom he had long been estranged. As his children achieved various milestones (e.g., getting married, having children themselves), they sought to include Fred in these events, and Fred peacefully engaged with them in a way that felt meaningful and touching to his children and to him, especially given their long and unstable history with each other.

In this case, I see therapeutic action as involving an expansion of the conditions under which Fred and I were able to value ourselves and each other in the analytic process. As I became able to value myself and Fred under a wider range of conditions, Fred was able to take the risk of valuing himself and me under a wider range of conditions—valuing himself even when he was not directing aggression towards others, when he was experiencing his insecurities, and when he was accessing his longings for closeness with others; and valuing me even when I was not directly facilitating his self-esteem, and when I displayed behaviors and qualities (e.g., challenging him, offering my divergent perspective) that evoked his inadequacy. Consistent with the theories of ethical intersubjectivity reviewed earlier, these evolutions were fundamentally ethical in nature, since they embodied modes of relatedness more consistent with our unconditional worth as human beings, ultimately resulting in a relationship that *itself* was more expressive of our shared sense of dignity and well-being. As Fred internalized these experiences, I believe they were able to "carry over" into his relationships outside of therapy—he began to value himself even when he was representing his more vulnerable subjective states (e.g., his desire for closeness with others, his feelings of smallness and inadequacy), and to value other people even when they were not perfectly responsive to him, or when they took actions he continued to see as "insensitive" or "disrespectful." I see these evolutions as indicative of the progressively expansive nature of therapeutic change—as we come to value ourselves and our patients less conditionally, our patients come to value themselves and us less conditionally, resulting in centrifugal repercussions of valuing that extend beyond the dyad into the broader relational world.

The intersubjective nexus of valuing

How then do we explain the dramatic correspondence between my aggressive fantasy—me hitting Fred repeatedly with an open hand while he remained seated—and important elements from Fred's experience which he had never before disclosed to me? These include Fred feeling neglected by his father's disciplinary practices, the nun publicly slapping and humiliating him, Fred's longstanding conscious aversion to being slapped, and perhaps most remarkably, his memory of Betsy striking him repeatedly across the face while he remained seated. Of course we have a variety of analytic constructs well-suited to explain this sort of phenomenon, including mirror neurons (D. N. Stern, 2004), projective identification, and Ogden's (1994) analytic third. In their idiosyncratic ways, all of these models blur any clear boundary between Self and Other, thus affirming an intersubjective permeability that would help to explain the sort of "telepathic interchange" that unfolded between Fred and me.

In Chapter 3, I developed the idea of intersubjective motivation, understood as the capacity to be motivated by the meanings of another. This ability is clearly relevant to my experience with Fred—had I not been capable of some basic form of intersubjective motivation (e.g., had I been narcissistically organized in a more fundamental way), I probably would not have been sitting in that office trying to help Fred in the first place, and I likely would not have been unconsciously receptive to Fred's subjective processes and fantasies. Nevertheless, I do not think that intersubjective motivation is able to fully explain the phenomenon in question. This concept concerns *my* motivational potentials, but it does not address the fundamental "us-ness" of the encounter that feels essential to that moment and its sequelae.

I thus return to my notion of the *intersubjective nexus of valuing*, introduced earlier in this chapter. This nexus involves not simply each participant's typical valuational tendencies (e.g., to value oneself or others in certain ways), but it constitutes *the dyad's* unique and perpetually evolving bi-directional patterns of valuing, including the ways in which each participant's valuations (of herself, of the other party, of the relationship) become inextricably dependent on *the relationship itself*. On this view, much like Mitchell's (1988) relational matrix and Ogden's (1994) analytic third, the intersubjective nexus of valuing transcends any one person's psychology, instead encompassing *both parties'* psychologies while also functioning as something of a hypothetical "agent" in the treatment, continually shaping, constraining, and expanding the unique conditions under which each individual experiences Self and Other as valuable and worthwhile in this dynamic, at this specific moment in time.

As I mentioned earlier, of particular relevance here is the way in which each subject comes to rely on the other for a sense of value, while simultaneously relating to the other person as a primary obstruction to that value, affirming at an unconscious level—*you are both the source of and the impediment to my self-worth*. In moments of impasse, this problem becomes more acute and seemingly intractable, since the conditions for each person's worth are often respectively the conditions for the other's badness—*the thing that I most need from you is the thing you believe will destroy you*. The therapeutic relationship thus comes to mirror the early relationship between caregiver and child. Given the extended period of childhood dependency, as well as the comparatively unstructured nature of the child's psyche, the caregiver's valuations of the child play an inordinately influential role in shaping the child's subjectivity. At the level of behavioral and affective process, caregiver and child both contribute equally to the bidirectional patterns of mutual influence that govern the dyad (Beebe & Lachmann, 2002). However, at the level of the child's relatively undifferentiated internal world, while the child might cognitively recognize her "separateness" from the caregiver (D. N. Stern, 1985), the boundary between Self and Other is significantly blurred, such that, in an important respect, the caregiver's valuations largely *constitute* the child's developing subjectivity. In this way, the caregiver is able to serve as both *the source and the depriver* of the child's value (Chapter 4).

In more pathological developmental scenarios, the caregiver sees the child as *only* conditionally valuable, or as *only* bad, without a capacity to simultaneously relate to the child as good, worthwhile, and deserving of love and care. Due to the caregiver's vulnerabilities in such cases, it is essentially impossible for her to value the child under a wider range of conditions, since doing so would necessarily evoke her own sense of unconditional badness, thus equaling a complete obliteration of the Self. Like the analytic dyad at times of impasse, the intersubjective nexus of valuing in such cases becomes rigid and calcified—each person experiences the other party as the source *and* the impediment to her value, and the conditions for one party's worth are the same conditions for the other's badness.[5]

Once the therapeutic relationship has reached such a point, both subjects occupy a position of increased sensitivity and receptivity to the other. This is how I understand the dramatic overlap between my aggressive fantasy and Fred's history—since we had reached a point in our work where we both felt deeply dependent on *and* victimized by the other, we had entered an intersubjective space in which, much like the dynamic between caregiver and child, the boundary between Self and Other was powerfully weakened, such that our subjectivities were especially receptive to being shaped and structured by the other person's internal world. This included my unconsciously "receiving," and actualizing in the form of my own aggressive fantasy, Fred's complex memories, longings, and fears about being slapped in the face. In the intersubjective nexus of valuing, "my" fantasy belonged to Fred, me, and our relationship all at the same time.

Not surprisingly, this particular therapeutic climate is especially conducive to fundamental psychic transformation for both parties. I needed to "try everything," and to feel like I had no further options with Fred, in order to be willing to make a more radical shift in my approach to our dynamic—that is, I needed to genuinely rely on Fred for self-esteem, and to feel consistently deprived by him, in order to become desperate enough to face my own worthlessness in our work together. This is the point at which most of Fred's previous relationships had collapsed. Due to their understandable limitations and Fred's maddening tendencies, his loved ones had all either devalued him or abandoned him. Experientially, Fred thus became unconsciously convinced of his own badness, and the only way for him to alleviate this was through attention-seeking, retaliation, and devaluing others. I suggest that, as I became able to access, own, and metabolize my sense of worthlessness in the therapeutic process, and to value both myself and Fred even in the face of that self-state, Fred was able to finally trust that we could inhabit a genuinely new intersubjective world together, one where he could take the risk of accessing his feelings of badness as well, while finally coming to value himself and me under a broader domain of conditions than had previously been possible for him.

This formulation offers one explanation for the essentially ethical nature of analytic change. In so many cases, patients have never had the experience of a caregiver fully valuing them as people, since doing so would have evoked the caregiver's intolerable, dissociated sense of badness. In every treatment, we thus need to repeat this fundamental ethical failure—to rely on the patient for self-esteem, to encounter our own worthlessness, and to become similarly unable to value the patient in the way she most deserves—and ultimately to repair that failure by developing the capacity to brave that worthlessness *for the sake of the patient.* I suggest it is *this* experience—the experience of being in a relationship with another subject who is willing and able to sacrifice her self-esteem in order to "put the other person first"—that helps the patient finally feel safe enough to access her sense of insufficiency, and to begin valuing herself and us in a manner more consistent with our intrinsic worth as human beings.

Conclusion: Ethical intersubjectivity in contemporary psychoanalysis

In this chapter, I have explored ethically intersubjective theories of therapeutic action, proposing my own vision of analytic process as the co-creation of an intersubjective space that progressively reflects the dignity of both analyst and patient. I have suggested that, by historically conceptualizing ethics primarily in terms of *content* (e.g., specific motives, capabilities, or behavior patterns), we have limited the relevance of ethics to psychoanalysis, since ethics is thus only analytically relevant when the patient or analyst possesses the ethical quality in question. The conceptions of ethical intersubjectivity considered here are able to circumvent this problem, since they construe ethics as an intersubjective *process* unfolding between two individuals who—while constantly shifting between forms of ethical, non-ethical, and unethical experiencing—can never fully "arrive" and remain at some fixed state of ethical enlightenment.

Put somewhat differently, these models emphasize ethical *directionality* rather than ethical achievement. Accordingly, in keeping with relational thought's tendency to eschew universal motivational formulations (see Chapters 1 and 5), the ethical constructs these theories employ (e.g., therapeutic strivings, mutual recognition, moral thirdness, moral authority, mentalization, my own unconditional valuing) only minimally specify the particular motivational content involved in ethics, instead exploring evolutions in the participants' *ethical stance* towards themselves and others. In my view, these "low content" theories dramatically expand the relevance of ethical thinking to psychoanalysis—they are better equipped to explain a fuller range of pathological experiences, and to represent progress in treatments that do not initially seem to involve ethics or morality.

While these theories' key conceptions differ considerably from one another, they share a fundamental set of humanistic convictions about psychoanalytic work—the belief that analyst and patient possess a basic value and agency as human beings, that pathology involves some form of impairment in that experience of value and agency, and that therapeutic improvement involves a fundamental restoration of this capacity for *both* patient and analyst. In this way, I believe these approaches remain fundamentally ethical while also addressing what feels most essential to clinical process—namely, the strengthening of patients' sense of meaning, selfhood, and agency (Harlem, 2015; Mitchell, 1993).

Some readers may take issue with my proposed distinction between ethical and non-ethical psychoanalytic visions. As other authors have highlighted with the notion of the "ethical turn" (Goodman & Severson,

2016; Orange, 2016; Shane & Brothers, 2017), contemporary psychoanalysis is deeply concerned with matters of ethics, and so it might appear unnecessarily divisive to divide our theories into different camps of *ethically neutral, ethically unilateral*, and *ethically intersubjective*.[6] While I agree that contemporary psychoanalysis is devoting increased attention to ethical matters, it is still quite uncommon for theorists to conceptualize therapeutic change *as* ethical change, and to construe the *mutual ethical development* of analyst and patient as the source of therapeutic action. While ethically intersubjective concepts—such as mutual recognition, mentalization, and "why the analyst needs to change"—have become highly influential within mainstream psychoanalysis, they are often subtly stripped of their original ethical valence, as they become repurposed by models that employ more ethically neutral ideas, such as creativity, play, "flexibility," and the spontaneous gesture.

As I see it, there is significant value in maintaining the distinction between ethical and non-ethical psychoanalytic perspectives. As Stephen Mitchell (1988, 1993) regularly argued, by blurring the distinction between classical and relational paradigms in psychoanalysis, we masked important differences between these approaches and hindered our recognition of new advances in theory. Similarly, by blurring the distinction between ethical and non-ethical conceptions, we risk obscuring genuine innovations that have been unfolding in analytic theorizing, while also impeding the further development of an ethical psychoanalysis, which requires directly wrestling with a myriad of questions involving the thorny intersection between psychoanalysis and ethical experience. *What does it mean to conceptualize pathology along ethical lines? What is the basis for the connection between ethical health and psychological well-being? How do we understand the relationship between ethical content and ethical process in clinical work? Specifically, can we say anything general about the "ethical outcomes" of analytic inquiry? What are the technical implications of envisioning psychoanalysis as a fundamentally ethical endeavor?* By maintaining the distinction between ethical and non-ethical approaches, we will create the imaginative space to begin tackling these sorts of questions in both the theoretical and clinical spheres.

Broadly speaking, I suggest that the central innovation of ethical intersubjectivity involves the *expanded responsibility of the analytic dyad*. The patient's focus can no longer remain simply on herself; rather, self-actualization is *constituted by* enhanced responsiveness to others, from the analyst to other important people in her life. This forecloses the possibility of an insular psychoanalytic climate in which the patient lies passively on the couch exclusively focused on her own emotions, desires, fantasies. It forces us to look outward as well, inquiring—to what extent do those emotions, desires, and fantasies reflect the patient's motivational responsiveness to herself and others? How might the patient remain lying "on the couch" while simultaneously *standing up* to look out at the world, and the needs of the people in it?

Ethical intersubjectivity enhances the analyst's responsibility as well. As we have seen, ethically intersubjective models imply that we are always *morally implicated* in the patient's suffering, and that we ourselves must be ethically transformed by clinical work—assuming a greater sense of responsibility about our role in this process, and evolving in a way that is more responsive to the patient and to ourselves. *Since our hands are never clean, we are always obligated to assume a deeper level of responsibility and accountability in the therapeutic relationship.* This is what Benjamin (2004) is getting at when she stresses the importance of "orienting to the moral third of responsibility," and of "going first" in acknowledging our role in the impasse that has disrupted the treatment (p. 33). This imperative to "go first" does not imply a proportionally greater contribution to the difficulties, but it does mean that, given our formal role as clinicians, we are professionally and ethically obligated to shepherd this relationship in accordance with the patient's long-term interests and needs.

This ethical vision is uniquely well-suited to promoting a more "egalitarian" approach to psychoanalysis (Benjamin, 1997; Renik, 1996; D. B. Stern, 1992; Wachtel, 1986). Traditional concepts like countertransference, participant-observation, co-construction, and the analyst's irreducible subjectivity all emphasize the *bi-directionality* of analytic interaction, implying that we are always causally or behaviorally implicated in the interpersonal dynamic at play in the dyad. However, we can cognitively "believe" that we are behaviorally embroiled in a problematic relational pattern without necessarily feeling *ethically responsible* for that pattern, or ethically obligated to change ourselves in order to alter it.

Especially in moments of disruption and impasse, when we are most unconsciously invested in keeping our sense of badness at bay, we are more at risk of seeing the patient as primarily responsible for the present dynamic—*well, of course I have co-created this impasse with the patient, and of course this dynamic is as much a reflection of my own subjectivity as the patient's, but it is really the patient's pathology that has led us to this difficult spot. If I could just help the patient recognize the role that her [distortion/enactment/transference/dissociated self-state/repressed impulse or affect] is playing in this disruption, then we could finally get out of this mess.* By blaming the patient for our shared challenges, this attitude implicitly situates the patient in an inferior position in the dyad, also placing an inordinate burden on the *patient* to change, largely by subordinating herself to our point of view. This dynamic can problematically parallel the patient's early experiences of intersubjective imbalance—*the only way this relationship can survive is if I subjugate my perspective to the viewpoint of the Other.*

In contrast, by affirming the analyst's irreducible culpability in the analytic process, ethical intersubjectivity never allows us to "blame the patient" for the disruption, or to adopt a comfortable stance of superiority over the patient. And by emphasizing the clinical necessity of the analyst's continuous ethical development, this approach enjoins us to doggedly search out the ways in which we are insufficiently valuing the patient, and to implement relational modifications more consistent with the patient's intrinsic worth. Taken together, these principles serve as a great equalizer in the therapeutic relationship, affirming the fundamental ethical equality of analyst and patient (see Aron, 1996a, appendix), along with the responsibility of both parties to move towards a position of deepening care and respect for the other.

Personally, these formulations play a powerful role in my experience of psychoanalytic work. At the start of every treatment, I feel a strange mixture of exhilaration and dread—I know that I am going to violate this patient, and ultimately to fail her in a very real way. There is no way for me to entirely predict what shape this will take, and I will likely be unaware of this for quite some time. I simply know that, if I am able to recognize and *own* that violation, I will somehow become a better person for this particular patient, in a way that is expressive of something that both of us need from each other. And perhaps most strangely: in becoming better for *this* patient, I will somehow "become better" for myself as well, and for the people in my life outside of the therapy—more respectful of them and their experiences, and more respectful of myself in relation to them.

Notes

1 Chapters 1 and 6 contain material from the following paper, reused here by permission of Taylor & Francis, LLC: Drozek, R. P. (2018). Psychoanalysis as an ethical process: Ethical intersubjectivity and therapeutic action. *Psychoanalytic Dialogues, 28*, 538–556.

2 For an illuminating recent monograph examining common transference/countertransference dynamics in the treatment of narcissistic patients, along with particularly useful technical guidelines, see Gabbard and Crisp (2018).

3 The earliest forerunner of the ethically intersubjective approach can be found in the work of Erich Fromm. In his landmark work *Man for Himself*, Fromm (1947) developed what still stands as the most fully elaborated psychoanalytic model of ethical character. Fromm conceptualizes pathology in terms of characterological configurations in which Self and Other are either negated or insufficiently recognized (pp. 62–82), alternatively envisioning health as *productiveness*, or the capacity to actualize one's own agency and potential while simultaneously displaying responsibility, care, and respect for other human beings (pp. 82–107). With these formulations, Fromm was anticipating the contemporary relational tendency to associate self-development with the ability to recognize other subjects: "Respect for one's own integrity and uniqueness, love for and understanding of one's own self, can not be separated from respect for and love and understanding of another individual" (p. 129).

However, when reflecting on the mechanisms of change in psychoanalysis, Fromm (1991) continues to advocate an ethically neutral conception, involving an awareness of the archaic unconscious and the concomitant activation of "a striving for health" (p. 591), rather than a vision in which the patient experiences increased ethical responsiveness to the particular person of the analyst herself. Similarly, while Fromm (1994) proposes that the effective analyst must possess a basic level of ethical capacity—the ability to love, empathize, and identify with the patient (pp. 192–193)—he never conceptualizes the activation and resolution of the analyst's ethical vulnerabilities as an essential element in the patient's own therapeutic change. This likely stems from Fromm operating within a largely humanistic/interpersonal, rather than fundamentally intersubjective, framework—to borrow Greenberg's (1981) language, Fromm views the analyst as participating *with* the patient, but not as fully participating *in* the patient's psychological/ethical illness. See Bacciagaluppi (1989) for a helpful discussion of this distinction and its utility in positioning Fromm in relation to other interpersonal and intersubjective psychoanalytic theorists.

4 I see my theory as selectively integrating aspects of the various models of ethical intersubjectivity reviewed in this chapter. Searles' (1979) notion of the therapist's "symbiotic dependency on the patient" overlaps with my suggestion that we come to rely on the patient for a sense of self-worth and self-esteem. Slavin and Kriegman's (1998) conception of "self-interest," as well as Hoffman's (1998) view of the "analyst's narcissistic and object-related investments," corresponds to my emphasis on the analyst's idiosyncratic patterns of valuing Self and Other. Benjamin's (2004)

theory of the "doer and done to" dynamic, as well as Bateman and Fonagy's (2016) illustrations of how rigid, non-mentalizing interactions can overtake the dyad, dovetails with my model of therapist and patient enacting patterns of mutual devaluation of Self and Other. Furthermore, in emphasizing how the therapeutic relationship comes to progressively reflect the unconditional worth of therapist and patient, I am incorporating Benjamin's (1995, 2018) seminal notions of mutual recognition and shared thirdness. Finally, by suggesting that therapist and patient both come to value Self *and* Other under a wider range of conditions, I am attempting to synthesize the four poles of change that characterize models of ethical intersubjectivity, each of which is emphasized to a greater or lesser degree by the different theorists—the patient's increased valuing of herself (consistent with Searles' idea of the patient's evolving "symbiotic worth," and with Hoffman's observations about the patient feeling more "deserving of love"); the patient's increased valuing of the therapist (correlating to Searles' therapeutic strivings, Hoffman's forgiveness, and Fonagy and Bateman's ideas about the patient mentalizing the therapist); the therapist's increased valuing of the patient (mirroring Searles' vision of the therapist encouraging the patient's individuation, Slavin and Kriegman's ideas about the therapist revising her identity to further reflect the patient's interests, and Hoffman's illustration of the therapist "throwing away the book" of psychoanalysis in order to better meet the patient's needs); and perhaps the least explored pole, the therapist's increased valuing of *herself* in the relationship, articulated most directly in Searles' (1979) observation that the therapist actually receives "emotional growth, integration, and maturation" from the patient through the therapeutic process (p. 427).

5 The reader might understandably wonder why impasses tend to characteristically take this particular shape, which Benjamin (2004) describes as the "doer and done to" dynamic. In my view, this stems directly from the multiplicity of human experience. As I suggested in Chapter 4, all of us come to value Self and Other in a range of different, often contradictory ways—positively, negatively, conditionally, unconditionally. In the analytic relationship, these multiple forms of valuing gradually emerge in the transference–countertransference matrix, such that each party comes to value the other in ways that, at the experiential level, interfere with her sense of self-esteem and self-worth (e.g., by only conditionally valuing the other person, or by devaluing the other person). Over time, this process evokes each person's sense of badness, which inevitably we try to escape by ascribing badness to the other person—in other words, each person's worth is dependent on the other party's badness. I see these processes as not unique to psychoanalytic process, but as a fundamental dimension of all intimate relationships (e.g., with romantic partners, with children, with caregivers) that allow multiple valued and devalued configurations of Self and Other to emerge over the course of the relationship. On this view, it is interpersonal relationships *themselves*, their intimacies and exigencies, that continuously nudge us towards ways of being that are progressively more consistent with the dignity of Self and Other.

6 As Goodman and Severson (2016) observe, the ethical turn consists of a range of related lines of theorizing, including psychoanalytic applications of neuroscience, attachment theory, and mentalization; examinations of the relevance of psychoanalysis to issues of culture, social justice, and human rights; and explorations of the convergence between psychoanalysis and philosophical phenomenology and hermeneutics (see pp. 4–9). Goodman and Severson (2016) suggest that the ethical turn can be seen as a further development of the relational turn, specifically emphasizing "moral considerations in human identity, development, and relationships" in psychoanalytic thinking (p. 4). They elaborate further: "This movement is about the primacy of the suffering other. It is a turn

toward the one who suffers, along with the awareness that this suffering calls into question any philosophical framework that might make sense of it" (p. 2). In light of these specifications, I suggest that the ethical turn can be understood as a broad movement within psychoanalysis, encompassing a diverse group of theories that affirm the foundational importance of ethics in psychoanalytic thought, while ethical intersubjectivity might constitute a specific development *of* the ethical turn, consisting of those theories that frame analytic change in terms of the mutual ethical development of analyst and patient.

Chapter 7

The ethical dialectics of technique

It was 6:52 AM on a Tuesday morning, in the heart of winter. I was driving down the road on the way to my first appointment of the day, past a golf course that serves as the regular backdrop for my morning commute. It had just snowed the night before, and white, rolling hills stretched before me on either side. The sky was dark and overcast; the sun was just starting to rise. Approaching on my left, I was surprised to notice something I had never seen before on this drive: two deer standing on a patch of flat ground—one small fawn with its head down, flanked by a much larger one (I assumed this was the mother), looking directly at me. I found myself smiling, feeling a sense of gratitude that I live and work in a place where, while so close to the city, I still occasionally encounter this guileless tranquility of nature. I was reminded of my childhood, when we would stay for a time in the country with my grandmother, and we would regularly see deer like this in her backyard, unselfconsciously living their lives in a space that somehow felt more theirs than ours.

And then, out of nowhere, I felt the hard *thud* of my car hitting a body. Slamming the brakes hard, the car slid twenty feet to a halt. Looking in my rear-view mirror, I saw the two deer scampering up a hill, followed by a third—another fawn, this one stunned and dragging its leg from the collision. The deer looked injured, but was able to stagger up the hill and disappear behind the others.

When I arrived at my office, my heart was still racing, and my head felt like it was floating above my body. I surveyed the damage to my car: the right headlight had shattered, and the bumper was hanging off, with deer hair in its creases—the evidence of the crime. I had come very close to killing something; it was out there right now, severely injured and perhaps dying, confused and in pain. It was strange and disorienting to think that I was about to head into a session. The time was 7:03 AM, and my 7 AM patient, Jonathan, was sitting right next to my office door.

Jonathan was born and raised in upstate New York, to parents who divorced when he was quite young, leaving him and his younger sister in the care of their mother. He describes an enmeshed relationship with his mother, who was controlling, self-focused, and "needy" for Jonathan's constant attentiveness. His father was a prominent banker in their hometown—high achieving, critical, emotionally cold, and attached to "success" as a measure of one's worth. Now in his 40s and single, Jonathan was a visual artist, a painter—moderately successful and able to support himself through his craft, but deeply insecure about his talents and abilities, and envious about other artists whom he saw as more accomplished than him. He spent much of his time fantasizing about the fame and glory that he felt lay tantalizingly just out of reach. Jonathan was also desperately indecisive, relying on his friends and family to provide him with what he called "reassurance" about feared negative consequences in his life.

Jonathan struggled with several concerns, varying in their levels of abstraction. He worried a certain person did not like him, or was upset with him in some way. He felt afraid that something he had done in the past was bad or problematic (e.g., starting or ending a specific romantic relationship, taking or not taking a job), and that thing was somehow responsible for his failure to achieve at life. He feared that various valued positive outcomes would never transpire for him, such as getting a girlfriend or obtaining an exhibition that would help him to finally become "famous" in the art world. He struggled with deep uncertainty about some inherently ambiguous life direction—should he continue dating this particular individual? Should he quit painting and return to graduate school in another field? Perhaps most essentially, he worried there was something fundamentally wrong with him, which also meant that he was unfit for relatedness with other human beings. Most of Jonathan's discrete fears could be traced back to this more basic fear. *"If this person doesn't like me, then there is something wrong with me, and I will never have a relationship." "If I never land a big exhibition, then no woman will ever want to be with me, which proves there is something wrong with me, and I will never have a relationship."*

Jonathan would initiate extreme interpersonal measures to obtain validation that the feared scenario would not transpire. This came out most prominently in his relationship with his long-term psychoanalyst, whom he had seen on the couch for sixteen years of four-sessions-weekly analysis. Jonathan would frantically seek his analyst's opinion that the feared situation "was going to be OK." This reassurance often came in the form of cognitive restructuring interventions, where the analyst would highlight some form of negative bias in Jonathan's thinking, which would temporarily assuage Jonathan's anxiety. "Maybe I *will* get a girlfriend." "Maybe I *did* pick the right career path." But if the analyst was not inclined to provide such reassurance, Jonathan would start to experience extreme emotional dysregulation—despair, sobbing, and rage towards the analyst, threatening suicide if the analyst refused to console him. This resulted in multiple inpatient admissions, suicide attempts, and severe functional impairment, as Jonathan became so overwhelmed with anxiety and despair that he was unable to continue painting. Understandably frustrated and concerned by Jonathan's deterioration, the analyst ultimately recommended their termination, which only intensified Jonathan's depression and suicidality.

I was asked to consult for Jonathan while he was hospitalized on an inpatient unit for the third time in one year, after fantasizing extensively about killing himself with a kitchen knife. After hearing Jonathan's story, I was concerned there was something about the structure, nature, and dynamic of the analysis that had contributed to Jonathan's regressive tendencies in the transference, resulting in his instability and suicidality. In an effort to *not* replicate this pattern, I agreed to see Jonathan for only once-weekly psychotherapy, with the focus of attempting to understand what might be responsible for Jonathan's severe decompensation, and helping him to start rebuilding his life.

As I will explore more fully in this chapter, Jonathan had been able to make miraculous strides in our first two years of working together. No longer suicidal, he described significant improvements in his emotional stability, as well as an overall experience of well-being, fulfillment, and hope in his life. He began dating again, was able to successfully reengage with his creative work, and had not required hospitalization in the past two years. Perhaps most notably, Jonathan was finally starting to feel a sense of peace and contentment, in which he felt free to enjoy himself, pursue his interests, and to engage more fully in his close relationships with friends, who were very important to him.

As I walked down the hallway on that morning at 7:03 AM, Jonathan looked at me sternly. Shaken and vulnerable, I felt a strong desire to share my experience with him: "I'm so sorry that I'm late. You won't believe what happened—I just hit a deer!" With most of my patients, I would have said just that, naturally and without even thinking about it. But walking towards Jonathan, in the face of my desire to share myself with him, I found myself feeling strangely humiliated and ashamed. For some reason I did not understand, there was no way that I could disclose what had just happened to me. I simply apologized for my lateness, and I opened the door.

The perils of technique in contemporary psychoanalysis

Throughout this book, I have attempted to highlight what I call the *anti-theoretical slide* in psychoanalysis, understood as an aversion to explicitly articulating the general assumptions and principles that shape (and are shaped by) our experiences in the clinical encounter. Not surprisingly, these tendencies have found their way into the ever murky and contentious topic of *technique*—"what we do" in the analytic process to facilitate the changes espoused in our models of therapeutic action. As other authors have observed (Foehl, 2010; Mitchell, 1993, 1997; Tublin, 2011), under the influence of postmodernism and constructivism, contemporary psychoanalysis is marked by a notable antipathy towards formulating the general principles that might guide the clinical practice of psychoanalysis.

From one perspective, the anti-theoretical slide can be seen as a reaction against the unrestrained objectivism of classical thought. Traditional classical technique—involving neutrality, abstinence, anonymity, free association, and interpretation as the analyst's primary technical tool—is predicated on the supposition that the analyst is able to operate at least partially *outside* the analytic field, allowing for an authoritative knowledge about the contents of the patient's mind, and a therapeutic relationship that ideally remains uncontaminated by the analyst's subjective involvement. In contrast, relational theorists have argued persuasively that the subjectivity of the analyst plays an irreducible role in structuring analytic experience (Aron, 1996a; Hoffman, 1998; Mitchell, 1993; Renik, 1993). If we can never access a purely objective standpoint on clinical process, then we have no basis for proposing an objectively valid theory of technique, or even for authoritatively endorsing specific decisions or general technical approaches. On these views, neutrality is an impossible fiction, and the classical emphasis on free association and interpretation is unnecessarily constrictive and limiting. As Gabbard and Westen (2003) observe, this has led to a sea change in prevailing psychoanalytic conceptions of technique: "We no longer practice in an era in which interpretation is viewed as the exclusive therapeutic arrow in the analyst's quiver" (p. 823).

Contemporary relational thinkers have largely advocated what might be called an *atheoretical* or deconstructionist approach to technique—eschewing general principles of technique, in favor of emphasizing the uniqueness and specificity of each patient, clinician, and therapeutic dyad. This has led to a dramatic increase in case examples and clinical illustrations in the psychoanalytic literature, as if to say—*I may not be able to tell you what you "should" do in general, but I can tell you what I* did *in this particular case.* As Jay Greenberg (2001) observes, such tendencies have led to a valorization of spontaneity and authenticity in the relational literature, where analysts privilege interventions that violate or transgress the more traditional analytic stance. While relational authors clearly advocate certain technical *approaches* (e.g., empathic resonance, judicious self-disclosure, taking responsibility for therapeutic ruptures), most stop short of articulating general theories of what to *actually do* in everyday practice. Ironically, this has created a subtle pressure towards conformity in relational psychoanalysis, in which we are culturally rewarded for framing our ideas in terms of the professionally sanctioned notions of "uniqueness," "specificity," "spontaneity," and "improvisation," while our *objectively* framed assumptions are seen as naive and unsophisticated, as if the practitioner is unable to tolerate the inherent ambiguity of clinical experience. Such assumptions can thus get driven underground—hidden, unformulated, and even dissociated from our conscious awareness as the forbidden "not-me" of contemporary psychoanalysis.

While classical thought constitutes a problematically objectivist, overly narrow vision of analytic inquiry, relational thought is perhaps overly *subjectivist*—attending so much to uniqueness and phenomenology that it fails to articulate the basic principles operative in analytic work. There are several limitations involved in such a subjectivist method. First, it fails to appreciate, as I have argued throughout this book, that we *necessarily* objectivize in our practice —that is, we naturally operate based on more general or universal notions about how we "should" engage in the analytic process. While we may avoid articulating such principles, and while we might consciously believe in tailoring all of our interventions to the uniqueness of the clinical moment, if another party were to observe all of our sessions with our various patients over the course of any given week, this observer would likely be able to outline some of the operative principles that govern our approach to the therapeutic hour, across patients and across diverse scenarios. Whether we like it or not, we necessarily view the clinical encounter from simultaneously subjective *and* objective perspectives (Nagel, 1986)—that is, we respond to the uniqueness of the current intersubjective situation, but in a way that is informed by all of our past experiences with patients, and our more general ideas about how to best facilitate a productive and useful analytic dialogue.

If we fail to appreciate this point, then we can remain problematically disconnected from certain parts of ourselves that play a foundational role in the unique shape, texture, and focus of the therapeutic relationship. This is particularly relevant in the arena of technique, which includes our explicit and implicit assumptions about how to best interact with our patients (and how to *not* interact with them); our optimal levels of activity and engagement; what we should prioritize in any given moment; our ideal forms of transparency, self-disclosure, and personal expressiveness; how validating or supportive we think we should be with our patients; and the extent to which we should focus on the past versus the present, transferential versus countertransferential dynamics, fantasy versus reality, cognition versus affect, subjectivity versus behavior, and so on. To the degree that we remain detached from our operative technical principles, we remain less aware of our contributions to the therapeutic process, and less able to intentionally shift our approaches to better meet the needs of our patients.

These anti-theoretical tendencies also impact psychoanalytic discourse more generally. As Tublin (2011) points out, "The failure to render explicit various assumptions and norms limits the community's capacity for self-reflection" (p. 536). When we avoid articulating our implicit technical principles, such principles remain less shareable with our colleagues—in the best case, tacitly embedded in our case examples and clinical discussions, and in the worst case, unacknowledged and dissociated within the broader psychoanalytic culture. In addition to limiting our access to technical innovations unfolding in everyday therapeutic practice, this means that there exists a large body of technical assumptions that remain simply presupposed. Left in the forgotten "back closet" of psychoanalysis, these assumptions can become stagnant, stale, and problematically unresponsive to questions about what *actually works* in helping our patients.

The anti-theoretical slide can also have a deleterious impact on our ability to disseminate psychoanalytic knowledge. In my experience, new clinicians wanting to learn analytic and exploratory psychotherapy are most interested in highly practical questions—*what do I actually say to my patients? How do I structure my sessions? When do I decide to interpret, or empathize, or ask for further clarification, or self-disclose?* Our responsibility to answer such questions is not simply pedagogical—it is *ethical*. When clinicians wrestle with such matters, they are usually not doing so in order to cognitively learn a particular technique for its own sake. They are asking because they want to know how to best help their patients—real human beings presenting to treatment under the expectation that analytic work can actually help them to decrease their suffering, and to improve the quality of their lives. As Stephen Mitchell (1997) observed, we cannot evade that responsibility by simply responding, "It depends." Of course it depends, but it is incumbent upon us to explain what such decisions depend *on* (see Mitchell, 1997, pp. x–xi).

This failure to clearly outline our technical principles has likely contributed to the marginalization of psychoanalysis as a discipline. In contemporary clinical training programs, beginning therapists are exposed to a wide range of therapeutic modalities, many of which clearly specify how to intervene when working with patients. In my experience, only a small minority of clinicians are naturally drawn to psychoanalytic models, usually because they feel like *something is missing* in more manualized, behaviorally oriented modalities. For most other practitioners, psychoanalysis comes across as an abstruse relic—possibly useful in understanding patients, but generally unconcerned about *what to do* in order to help them improve their lives. Such clinicians selectively borrow those psychoanalytic constructs that seem useful (e.g., the dynamic unconscious, defense mechanisms, transference and countertransference), but they ultimately gravitate to more fully articulated technical methods (e.g., CBT, DBT, ACT) for the scaffolding that directs their daily practice.

While many analysts might not be bothered by this marginalization of psychoanalysis, if we believe strongly in the ability of psychoanalysis to generate deep and lasting transformation in patients' lives, I suggest that we have an ethical obligation to frame analytic ideas and principles in a manner that is accessible and digestible to people who want to learn the technique. We now have some recent examples of more "manualized" and empirically supported formulations of analytic technique—including mentalization-based treatment (Bateman & Fonagy, 2016), transference-focused psychotherapy (Yeomans, Clarkin, & Kernberg, 2015), and brief dynamic interpersonal therapy (Lemma, Target, & Fonagy, 2011)—which have the benefit of specifying broad technical principles while leaving considerable room for clinician creativity and the uniqueness of each therapeutic situation. However, aside from a handful of exceptions (Atlas & Aron, 2017; Barsness, 2018), this approach to technical theorizing has not made its way into psychoanalytic discourse more generally. By failing to articulate our technical principles, we are inadvertently farming out the practice of psychotherapy to more superficial models, in this way depriving a whole generation of patients the life-changing benefits of an analytic process.

In light of the above, it appears there exists an inherent tension between psychoanalysis' constructivist epistemological commitments, which discourage universal and objective technical prescriptions, and the practical and ethical imperative to articulate our basic principles of technique (Tublin, 2011). One possible way to navigate this tension is to attempt to formulate our principles in a *descriptive* rather than *prescriptive* fashion—that is, specifying the behavioral ideas that *do* govern our practice, in specific clinical moments and in general, without implying that such ideas are objectively correct, or that they should apply categorically to diverse therapeutic scenarios. We would thus maintain rather than collapse the dialectic between subjectivity and objectivity around our theories of technique—articulating the subjective *and* objective assumptions we bring to psychoanalysis, without losing sight of the fact that all of these suppositions are distilled representations of our subjective worlds. We can have specificity without constriction, generality without naive objectivity. Our task would thus be to outline our general technical assumptions; to illustrate in some detail what it looks like to implement such principles; to explicitly consider the benefits and disadvantages of employing the strategies in question; and to consider this pesky but crucial notion of *efficacy*—how helpful is this particular method in helping to improve patients' lives? And how do we even go about evaluating such a thing?

By taking such an approach, we would be better situated to avoid the various pitfalls associated with the anti-theoretical slide. We would have greater access to our operative technical principles, and thus be better able to tailor our interventions to the unique needs of our patients. Our psychoanalytic communities might also become more cognizant of such principles, allowing for an open dialogue about what we *actually do* in clinical practice, and for the constructive development of techniques that are more responsive to the diverse challenges we face in our consulting rooms. We would also be better equipped to teach psychoanalytic technique, in specific rather than vague terms. Over time, this could make analytic work accessible to a wider range of clinicians and patients, helping to transition psychoanalysis from a state of ostracization to a position of what Aron and Starr (2013) call *optimal marginality* within the larger world of psychotherapy and mental health.

The ethical dialectics of technique

I will not attempt anything like a comprehensive theory of technique here—such a project would require an entire volume of its own. I will simply attempt to illustrate, without sufficiently defending, some of the technical implications of the ethical model of psychoanalysis I have been advancing in this book. In Chapter 2, I proposed that, in order to allow for the harmonious integration of psychoanalysis and our reflexive ethical commitments, we need to maintain rather than collapse certain fundamental paradoxes in human experience, including the dialectic between behavior and motivation, between consciousness and unconsciousness, between Self and Other, between freedom and determinism, between subjectivity and objectivity, between content and process, and between individuality and multiplicity. It is important to note that such dialectics are what we might call *conceptual* dialectics, that is, they represent tensions between different theoretical constructs and perspectives. I suggest that, to uphold such dialectics in everyday therapeutic practice, we need to preserve several *behavioral* dialectics, understood as inherent tensions between techniques employed to facilitate various dimensions of an analytic process (Hoffman, 1998). By upholding these technical dialectics, we will be able to simultaneously integrate our psychoanalytic assumptions with our reflexive ethical commitments as human beings—maintaining a closer contact with foundational dimensions of our patients' experiences, while continuing to implement the analytic principles essential for more fundamental alterations in our patients' templates for relatedness. Such dialectics include:

- The dialectic between subjectivity and behavior
- The dialectic between consciousness and unconsciousness
- The dialectic between exploration and change
- The dialectic between Self and Other.

The distinctions between these dialectics are admittedly somewhat arbitrary, since they overlap and mutually enrich each other in diverse and complex ways. I offer them here simply to articulate my own principles of practice, recognizing that other clinicians could propose different dialectical formulations to express similar views.[1] I am also aware that, for some readers, these methods might seem to extend beyond the boundaries of appropriate psychoanalytic technique, into more "non-analytic" domains. Accordingly, I will weigh in on the perennial question about "what makes it analytic" in the conclusion of this book.

To illustrate these ideas, I will return to my work with Jonathan, considering some of the broad technical approaches I have employed in this case.

The dialectic between subjectivity and behavior

In Chapter 2, I argued for the importance of preserving rather than collapsing the tension between motivation and behavior. In order to sustain that tension in everyday clinical practice, I attempt to explore the various aspects of patients' conscious subjective worlds, while concurrently expressing an interest in their behavioral experiences—"who they are" and how they behave in their relationships with themselves and other people. This dialectical stance enables me to obtain a basic "lay of the land" for the work, an experience-near sense of what it feels like to be in the person's skin, while also providing a broader context for understanding the diverse mechanisms by which unconscious processes are maintained and reinforced behaviorally. As Wachtel (2014) has compellingly observed:

> Just as the shaping and maintenance of the inner world by daily experience is complemented by the simultaneous shaping of daily experience by the expectancies and schemas of the inner world, so too are the dynamics of the psyche and the dynamics of overt behavior bidirectional, reciprocal, and mutually contextually embedded. . . . We cannot adequately know ourselves from the inside out without knowing ourselves from the outside in, and we cannot adequately know ourselves from the outside in without knowing ourselves from the inside out.
>
> (p. 39)

In my sessions with Jonathan, this took the shape of listening for (and often actively inquiring about) his expressed affects, longings, fears, and emotionally salient beliefs about himself and others. Jonathan shared extensively about his powerful desires for others to admire him, to see him as brilliant, talented, funny, and insightful. He fantasized about painting the next great work of art, of rocketing the medium into unexplored dimensions through his innovative command of the craft. Once he achieved that, he would become much more attractive to women, and he would finally be able to have a relationship with someone to whom *he* was attracted—someone much younger than him, successful but not too successful, intelligent, playful, witty, highly sexual, and in possession of certain physical characteristics he saw as essential in a partner. They would become enamored with each other, living truly as companions—spending extended periods of time together; sharing all of their interests; having non-stop, passionate sex; and remaining instinctively attuned to each other's aspirations and desires.

This is what would finally satisfy him, endowing him with the peace and fulfillment for which he had long been yearning.

And yet Jonathan also struggled with intense fears that these fantasies would never be realized—that he would never create a great work of art, or achieve true fame within the art community; that he would just keep scraping by financially, without achieving wealth or even stability; and that he would continue to get older and remain alone forever, becoming progressively less attractive and ultimately losing his ability to attract a compelling romantic partner. It was at these moments—when he faced rejection in his profession, romantic relationships, and friendships, or even when he contemplated how he did not yet "measure up" in such areas—that Jonathan would become overwhelmed with a violent and all-consuming sense of badness. He was worthless, a failure at his own life, and the only thing that could assuage this feeling was some form of reassurance, whether that came from some form of tangible success (e.g., finishing or selling a painting, going on a date with an attractive woman), or from someone he trusted informing him that he *was* good, he *was* worthwhile, he *was* deserving of those positive things he desperately longed for.

In addition to exploring with Jonathan these aspects of his subjective world, I actively inquired about the behavioral dimensions of these same processes. Jonathan devoted extensive time and energy "performing" his way towards self-worth and self-esteem—when he was alone, pursuing endeavors (e.g., painting, attending exhibitions and gallery openings, researching others' work, applying for grants and art contests) that offered the hope of external validation of his talents and desirability; and in his interactions with his friends and colleagues, engaging in relational patterns (e.g., making jokes, crafting insightful social and political commentary, sharing about his successes, serving as a "counselor" for his friends' difficulties) that could secure people's admiration and dependency upon him.

We saw how Jonathan appeared to regularly "alternate" between relational dynamics in which he was the *provider* of care to others, and then in which he was the recipient of such care. Jonathan could be highly concerned, supportive, and empathetic to others—ministrating to his friends, complimenting them and highlighting their positive qualities, explicitly validating their perspectives and viewpoints, and "taking their side" when they discussed interpersonal conflicts. On the other hand, Jonathan was deeply concerned with issues of reciprocity—if he provided support and guidance to a friend, then he emphatically expected similar things in return, and he would maintain a mental balance sheet about what was owed to him along these lines.

This presented itself most prominently in Jonathan's fierce desires for reassurance from others. Jonathan would seek out reassurance in a range of overt and subtle ways—expressing his fears about the future, in order to elicit feedback that the feared scenario would not occur; criticizing himself to his friends and his analyst, in the hopes that the other party would respond by emphasizing his positive qualities; and explicitly asking others to tell him very specific things that would alleviate his particular anxiety in the moment: he *would* someday have a romantic relationship, he *had* interpreted some social scenario in a reasonable way, he *did* respond appropriately in some situation, his new painting *was* impressive, he was *not* at fault for his difficulties—they were clearly the result of historical factors beyond his control (e.g., his mother's neediness, his father's emotional coldness). While Jonathan pursued such reassurances explicitly and tenaciously, he was also continuously vigilant for implicit affirmations (and negations) in others' experiences. The slightest look of unhappiness from another person could send him into a state of panic—had he done something wrong? Was the individual unhappy with him? This would set off chains of behaviors to reassure Jonathan about others' mood states—obsessively monitoring their subsequent interactions, behaving generously (to make up for any possible infractions), asking people if they were upset with him, and apologizing for any possible harms.

Jonathan also regularly struggled with the concern that he could not manage his life, and so he persistently needed the guidance and direction of others to feel confident that he was making the "right" decisions that would help him to achieve the highest level of happiness and success. Along these lines, Jonathan would share about some uncertainty causing him emotional distress (e.g., whether to return to graduate school, whether to continue dating someone), and once he was able to apprehend the other's outlook on the matter, that perspective would assume a powerful position of prominence in his experience, such that it would become nearly impossible for him to access his own feelings about the situation—the person was clearly right, and he needed to do everything in his power to incorporate and implement the other's viewpoint.

Jonathan and I discovered how such processes of reassurance played out internally for him as well. Jonathan did not simply seek out reassurances—he *hoarded* them. He carried his sketchpad with him everywhere, dutifully recording people's statements that alleviated his anxiety about various topics. When such concerns arose for Jonathan throughout the day, if he could not receive such reassurances "from the source," he would replay such statements in his mind to obtain the needed relief. *"It is not your fault." "It is healthy for a man to have intense emotions—this does not make you weak." "You will get a girlfriend one day." "That person was probably just having a bad day. It has nothing to do with you."* Long after the analysis ended, in moments of despair and sadness, Jonathan would evoke a fantasy he had constructed, in which his analyst was holding him as he sobbed uncontrollably. In these moments, in addition to feeling deeply comforted by this image, Jonathan could finally feel like he had permission to inhabit strong emotions without this being a sign of his weakness. And yet this was still *his analyst's* permission—even in fantasy, Jonathan was unable to personally affirm his right to experience an emotion, relying exclusively on the reassurance of an imagined Other in order to access and validate his subjective states.

The dialectic between conscious experience and unconscious process

I have also argued for the importance of maintaining the polarity between consciousness and unconsciousness (Chapter 2). When employing such an approach technically, I attempt to maintain contact with the practical and phenomenological dimensions of my patients' everyday lives—their conscious beliefs, emotional states, and longings; their own formulations of their sufferings and interpersonal challenges; and their behavioral patterns in their social environments, including the impact these behaviors have on themselves and others. Rather than regarding such processes as superficial derivatives of unconscious dynamics that are comparatively more meaningful, I see them as having an important phenomenological value of their own, offering an essential window into patients' lived experiences while simultaneously serving as a reflection and expression of their unconscious worlds. Accordingly, I also attempt to articulate my evolving understanding of the patient's foundational relational templates. While the shape this takes varies depending on the particular patient, I often start by exploring relational configurations related to processes that are most accessible in patients' conscious awareness, and most relevant to the emotions, desires, and interpersonal patterns that patients see as central to their difficulties. As the treatment unfolds, usually through working transferentially and countertransferentially, we progress to exploring and elaborating configurations that are more dissociated, unformulated, or repressed within patients' subjectivity.

Early on in my therapy with Jonathan, we began to articulate several relational configurations that seemed to be central to his challenges. On the most basic level, we identified a configuration in which Jonathan took himself to be bad, worthless, intrinsically defective, and irrevocably alone. In this state, Jonathan saw other people as angry, critical, and disappointed with him, so disgusted by his badness that they had no desire to engage with him; or else they were simply *unmotivated* by him, so narcissistically organized that they were uninterested in investing in his experience. Here we saw the echoes of Jonathan's relationships with both of his parents. While his mother appeared to have the capacity to provide him with care and attention, he felt like she was primarily focused on how he could meet her emotional needs—he never felt *seen* by her, and there were fundamental dimensions of his personhood that simply did not exist for her, leading him to feel a powerful sense of separateness, disconnection, and isolation. If he ever attempted to actualize those parts of himself that felt threatening to her (e.g., his desires for separateness and autonomy, emotional states that were not *about* her), she could respond critically and aggressively, withdrawing her nurturance and attacking him for his selfishness. These critical tendencies were even more pervasive in his dynamic with his father, whom he experienced as perpetually disappointed in him for his emotionality, liberal political leanings, and overall "weakness" as a person. While Jonathan's sister—whom he saw as sarcastic, stoic, emotionally cold, and academically high achieving—naturally and easily connected with his father, he felt like his father only tolerated him, without ever appreciating him for who he was. He was left with the deep conviction that there was something fundamentally wrong with him. It was his badness, his insufficiency, that kept his parents from wanting to truly know and engage with him; this sense now carried over into his contemporary life, in his belief that it was his badness that was keeping him fundamentally alone, and that if others were to truly know him, they would be disgusted and repulsed by him.

In order to keep this feeling of badness at bay, Jonathan became highly reliant on an experience of himself as conditionally valuable. Derived significantly from his interactions with his father, Jonathan became attached to the idea that he could *earn his worth* by performing well academically and professionally, a relational template he transferred to aesthetic contexts as well—if he could earn the respect and admiration of his fellow artists, if he could create a genuinely new contribution to the medium, if he could sell one of his works for an exorbitant amount of money, then people would value and admire him, and he could finally attain peace and fulfillment. And influenced largely by his history with his mother, Jonathan was drawn to dynamics in which his self-worth was contingent on him remaining in a highly enmeshed, dependent relationship with his caregivers. His role was to remain weak, dependent, and idealizing of others, and to surrender his agency to their judgment; as long as he "stayed in line" and fulfilled that role, people would provide support, nurturance, guidance, and of course, reassurance that he was the good child who had not done, and *could not do*, anything wrong. But if he ever failed to perfectly tailor himself to the needs and preferences of his caretakers, he became overwhelmed with a panic that others would reject and abandon him. *His only sources of worth were achievement and abject dependency—without such things, he would be left worthless, deficient, and horribly alone, devoid of the care that he desperately needed in order to survive.*

As I came to understand it, Jonathan's behavioral and interpersonal patterns reviewed earlier (e.g., excessive dependency on others, social perfectionism, pursuing professional and aesthetic achievement, reassurance-seeking) were not simply "byproducts" or "derivatives" of these unconscious processes. Rather, these behaviors were the overt, conscious mechanisms by which his unconscious relational configurations were perpetuated and maintained. For example, when he furiously pursued his aesthetic ambitions, he was unconsciously affirming that he could only possess value if such ambitions were fully realized. By persistently seeking reassurance and dependency upon others, he was unconsciously avowing that he only possessed worth if people were ministrating to him. And simultaneously, since all of these behaviors were predicated on the idea that he needed to distance himself from his badness and worthlessness, whenever he engaged in them, he was insisting on his insufficiency. On this view, Jonathan's conscious efforts to escape from his sense of worthlessness were the exact mechanisms by which that sense was maintained and exacerbated. As I increasingly came to recognize this, I began to realize that "something more than interpretation" was going to be needed to alter these mutually reinforcing conscious and unconscious patterns (D. N. Stern et al., 1998).

The dialectic between exploration and change

I have also emphasized the advantages of upholding the contradiction between determinism and freedom (Chapter 2), a construct that might be expressed technically as the polarity between *exploration and change*. While exploration tends to concern *what is or what has been* for patients (the past and the present), change-oriented interventions involve possibility and potentiality—*what could or will be* in patients' lives (the future). Framed in this way, exploration focuses on what D. B. Stern (1997) refers to as the "given" dimensions of human life—the experiential processes that often feel beyond our conscious volitional control, including family and developmental history, past events, dispositions, and "unbidden" subjective states and personality traits. Perhaps paradoxically, exploration is also closely aligned with patients' awareness of agency. It involves helping patients understand how and why they have come to experience the world (and to choose) in the particular way that they do, thereby serving as an essential vehicle for expanding their sense of freedom in their lives, as Freud (1933) famously expressed in his dictum "Where id was, there ego shall be" (p. 80).

While exploration is clearly a staple of analytic technique, it is strangely difficult to define. Personally, I conceptualize exploration as *a collaborative endeavor in which I work with patients to access, represent, and validate a progressively broader range of their conscious and unconscious subjective processes, including emotions, longings, fantasies, beliefs about Self and Other, and (usually unconscious) foundational templates for interpersonal relationships.* This approach encompasses a relatively expansive set of interventions, ranging from more "basic" exploratory techniques (e.g., reflections, summary statements, identifying and labeling emotions and desires, empathic validation) to more complex exploratory modes, such as highlighting broader patterns of cognition, emotion, and desire; elaboration and contextualization of emotions; consideration of defensive and dissociative mechanisms; and more formal "interpretation" of the deeper historical and motivational meaning of manifest subjective phenomena.

On this view, exploration is geared towards deepening our *understanding* and *affective experience* of ourselves, from the perspective of the present—"who we are"—as well as the past—"who we have been, and what happened to us to make us that way." When working from an exploratory frame, I variously devote myself to the patient's past, to aspects of the patient's life outside of the therapy, and of course to the therapeutic relationship itself, ultimately considering how all of these dimensions mutually influence and constitute each other in complex and bidirectional ways.

At the same time, I explicitly attempt to explore and promote the possibility of "change" in patients' lives. At the start of every treatment, I try to be actively curious about the patient's conscious goals for her life, allowing these goals to play a foundational role in influencing (although not fully determining) the directionality of the treatment. I am regularly interested in the question of whether or not the therapy is actually *helping* the person, from the patient's perspective but also from my own, and from the viewpoint of other important people in the patient's life. As I discussed in Chapter 2, such assessments are inextricably value-laden and subjectively constituted, and so there is no objective method of answering these questions. However, I believe that the fact that I am asking that question, to myself and with the patient, plays a crucial role in the shape and texture of the therapeutic relationship. To the extent that I am explicitly wrestling with such matters, I communicate that the patient's growth and flourishing should serve as a primary barometer of the value of our work together, an orientation that is consistent with the American Psychoanalytic Association's position that the goal of psychoanalysis is not insight for its own sake, but "to reduce suffering and disability and enhance growth and autonomy." This also has the effect of setting limits on other factors that, in my opinion, can attain inordinate power in clinical process, such as our theories, technical stance, or professional authority. If every treatment is accountable to the notion of progress, then we are not permitted to sit back and assume that *anything* about our approach is beyond reproach.

Other "change-oriented" interventions I employ include inviting reflection on psychological and behavioral potentials not yet fully realized for the patient (*"I notice that it didn't seem to occur to you to share what you were actually feeling with her. Any sense on why that might be?"*) (Cooper, 2000); imagining the possible actualization of such potentials (*"What do you think it would feel like if you were able to finally set a boundary with him?"*); and sharing my own fantasies and desires about the patient's latent capacities (*"I am realizing there is a part of me that wants you to actively commit to experiencing your more vulnerable emotions here"*). As other authors have increasingly advocated in different ways (Hoffman, 1998, 2009b; Mitchell, 2001; Safran, 2016; Wachtel, 1997, 2014; Wheelis, 2010), I am also comfortable at times taking a more strictly behavioral approach to patients' challenges, including everyday "advice giving"; consideration of strategies patients might employ to address problems and pursue certain goals; role-playing; actively working with patients to eliminate behaviors (e.g., suicide or self-injury, violence or aggression, specific maladaptive or self-sabotaging interpersonal patterns) that undermine the dignity and well-being of themselves or others; and collaborating with patients to promote other behaviors (e.g., self-care and self-compassion, empathic responsiveness to others, interpersonal tendencies that are able to balance responsiveness to Self and Other) that patients regard as more consistent with the dignity and well-being of themselves and other people.

I see this dialectic between exploration and change as an essential element of effective analytic work. While exploration helps patients to deepen and expand their experiential access to their subjective worlds, change-oriented interventions affirm patients' agency to actively revise and transform those worlds, through both internal and behavioral means. In my view, many impasses and "stalled treatments" stem from the collapse of this tension between exploration and change. Without exploration, change-oriented interventions risk becoming superficial, judgmental, controlling, and insufficiently tailored to the needs of each patient. Patients begin to feel invalidated by the therapist, and unseen in a manner that frequently parallels their early patterns in neglectful and traumatic contexts. And without a change-orientation, exploration can become self-indulgent, stagnant, insular, and problematically divorced from patients' actual functioning and circumstances, failing to appreciate things they can *do* to alter their unconscious dynamics and improve their lives. Here, patients can start to feel passive in relation to their lives, and excessively dependent on the analysis in order to function and manage their emotions.

Seen in this light, these dialectically constituted approaches mutually define and enrich each other, each approach requiring the other for its fullest expression. Exploration helps to develop the psychological infrastructure for change, creating a shared sense of the contextual meaning of patients' past and present experiences, including the natural limitations and tensions involved in these experiences that provide the personal impetus for progress and growth. Change-oriented interventions similarly facilitate exploration, helping to construct the broader rationale and purpose for a deeper connection with Self and Other, while strengthening patients' motivation and agency in the exploratory process.[2]

Throughout my treatment with Jonathan, I have worked to maintain this balance between exploration and change. Our earliest sessions all took a similar shape. Jonathan would arrive reporting that he was "not doing well," describing some topic that had taken hold of his mind that week—he was worried he would never get a girlfriend, that he had chosen the wrong career, that he would never get another exhibition, that he was inherently weak due to his emotionality. He would begin crying, elaborating on his reasons for the concern, and then, usually about halfway through the session, he would commence asking me for reassurance about the matter in question. *I feel like I need you to tell me that I am not weak, that it is OK for me to be vulnerable. If I don't hear that from you, I'm not sure if I am going to be able to be safe tonight.*

I could see quite clearly I was being invited into the same dynamic that had gripped his analysis for sixteen years. Rather than focus on the content of Jonathan's specific requests and their historical, familial, and developmental antecedents (an approach Jonathan and his analyst had pursued extensively), I invited him to express what such reassurances would mean to him, and about our relationship together. He shared that this would show that I cared about him, and that I wanted to alleviate his suffering. Jonathan was able to both express and inhabit these longings, which were often so powerful in his experience that they verged on desperation. We saw how Jonathan's desires and requests affirmed an image of himself as weak, dependent, and unable to effectively manage his life without the intervention of others, while also expressing an image of me as powerful, omniscient, and able to almost magically bestow comfort onto Jonathan with a single word or gesture. When I inquired about the exact mechanism of such reassurances, Jonathan explained he would need me to say the thing in question about three times—that would show I really believed it, and it would allow him to finally have a moment of peace, such that the corrosive thought would no longer torment him. He had no clear sense of how long that feeling would last (a few hours, a few days), and he admitted sheepishly that he would likely require further reassurance again sometime soon, either about this same issue or whatever new concern gripped his mind at that moment.

I empathized with Jonathan's desire for me to reassure him—such an action would require such little effort from me, and it could have such a powerful impact on Jonathan's suffering in the moment. However, in addition to being potentially dishonest on my part (I actually had *no idea* if he would someday get a girlfriend or sell a painting for an exorbitant sum of money), I shared my perspective that, if I were to provide him with what he was requesting, I would be contributing to a futile dynamic that could continue this way indefinitely. The more that I reassured him, the more he would need me to keep reassuring him, such that these processes could threaten to overtake our relationship and ultimately his entire life. I also observed that so many of these requests for reassurance were saturated with a self-state in which Jonathan only had conditional worth—*"I am only valuable if I [succeed in art/get a girlfriend/become wealthy/receive my therapist's care]."* I raised the possibility that, by incessantly pursuing reassurances, he was unconsciously *creating* an experience of himself as only conditionally valuable, and thereby behaviorally preventing the emergence of a self-state in which he saw himself as worthwhile and valuable exactly as he was, without having to "earn" love or care from others.

This is where the "change" part of the dialectic came in. Jonathan and I discussed the basic principles of exposure-based interventions to address obsessions and compulsions (Foa, Yadin, & Lichner, 2012), whereby the patient is progressively exposed to the feared scenario (e.g., Jonathan's thought that he might be fundamentally weak) while refraining from engaging in the compulsive behavior (e.g., requesting reassurance about his strength), which over time desensitizes the person to the triggering circumstance, resulting in decreased anxiety symptoms and compulsivity. I hypothesized that, if Jonathan were to "lean into" and embrace his anxiety about these matters, while voluntarily refraining from pursuing reassurance from myself and others, he might actually begin to feel better, while moving towards a less dependent and more agentic stance in his life and relationships.

To my surprise, Jonathan was highly interested in pursuing this course in therapy. We embarked on the process of developing a written hierarchy of Jonathan's feared scenarios, as well as a comprehensive list of Jonathan's diverse avoidance strategies. We completed a handful of exposures in session at first, in which Jonathan would focus on one of his fears (e.g., "I might not be spending enough time painting each day"), intentionally emphasizing his uncertainty about such matters (e.g., "I really don't know the answer to this—it is highly possible that I am not spending enough time, and I could be unaware of this fact"), all the while monitoring his anxiety levels and avoiding seeking clarity and comfort about the topic, whether through behavioral means (e.g., by asking me how long he should be painting each day) or through ideation and cognition (e.g., by reminding himself what friends and mentors have recommended to him in the past). Over the course of each of these sessions, Jonathan's anxiety would gradually decrease, and he started implementing these exposures independently outside of appointments, such that soon we were soon able to resume our more exploratory approach to our sessions.

The results of these efforts were remarkable. Jonathan described a notable decrease in his anxiety symptoms, ruminations, and compulsiveness. He began to encounter moments of relative peace and contentment, when his mind was not completely captured by an obsessive concern, and he was able to feel comfortably "present" in his day-to-day circumstances. Jonathan was perhaps most struck by a shift in his experience of interacting with others. Whereas formerly he had to be perpetually working in order to secure reassurances from other people (and to stave off potential criticism), now he felt like he could emotionally engage in the interaction—when he was talking about art with his friends, his mind was *on the art*; when his friends were sharing about some life situation, his focus was on the situation itself. Jonathan felt like a momentous weight had been lifted from him, as if he had finally been given permission to become a participant in his own life.

As I see it, these changes were not simply related to "symptom reduction" for Jonathan. By intentionally refraining from certain behaviors (e.g., reassurance-seeking, obsessively seeking guidance from others) that were fueling his unconscious sense of himself as only conditionally worthwhile (and as intrinsically bad), he was unconsciously affirming the possibility that he might *not* have only conditional worth, that he might *not* be fundamentally bad as a person. This brought with it a tremendous feeling of relief and hope, opening up a psychic space where Jonathan could potentially begin to recognize himself as naturally and fundamentally worthwhile, regardless of whether or not he could attain all of those markers of extrinsic success (e.g., wealth, fame, admiration), or whether or not others were constantly tending to his emotional needs. The work then became cultivating and strengthening Jonathan's growing appreciation of himself as *actually mattering*, intrinsically and unconditionally, in his own life.

The dialectic between Self and Other

The final dialectic I will consider is the one between *Self* and *Other* (see Chapter 2). This concerns the verbal and internal focus of analytic practice—the extent to which I direct attention to the experiences of the patient, and the extent to which I attend to the experiences of *other subjects* in the patient's life, including myself. If I collapse this dialectic in my therapeutic stance, then I risk contributing to a relational dynamic that subtly reinforces a fundamental imbalance at the level of the patient's subjectivity—the patient can remain excessively self-focused, continuing to see other people as existing primarily to facilitate her needs and desires; or she can remain overly focused on others, seeing herself as existing largely to satisfy *their* needs and desires. Conversely, by maintaining the dialectic between Self and Other, I am affirming the unconditional value of both the patient and other subjects, while attempting to cultivate an ethical and intersubjective balance in *this* relationship, in which both of us are able to be simultaneously receptive and responsive to our own subjectivities and to the subjectivity of the Other —in the same moment, in the same breath.

From a technical orientation, the dialectic between Self and Other essentially contains all of the polarities already reviewed in this chapter. That is, I work actively to explore patients' subjective worlds *and* their behavioral patterns, their conscious experiences *and* unconscious processes, while also considering their goals, potentials, progress, and the steps they might take to advance these domains (e.g., subjectivity, behavior, conscious patterns, unconscious relational configurations) in a manner consistent with their visions for themselves and their lives. This involves considering patients' experiences of these domains, as well as me sharing my own constructions (e.g., observations, impressions, interpretations, suggestions) about these topics.

I also direct attention to *other subjects* in patients' lives (Bateman & Fonagy, 2016)—their subjective states (*"What do you think she was feeling when she said that to you?"*) and behaviors (*"It sounds like she is starting to withdraw from you a bit"*), their conscious experiences (*"I wonder what she would say about why she is so angry at you . . . "*) and their unconscious mechanisms (*"Where do you think all of her anger is coming from? What might be fueling it?"*). These "impressions of others" are of course significantly shaped by patients' subjective processes, and so they can provide us with an invaluable window into patients' conscious and unconscious worlds. However, I also assume that, to a greater or lesser degree, it is possible for patients to have genuine contact with the subjective meanings of others (see Chapter 3), and that there is value in deepening patients' experiences of other people's subjectivity, especially as a vehicle for strengthening their capacity for enhanced intimacy and mutuality in their relationships.

This area of inquiry has particular relevance when it comes to transferential dynamics, as we see from Aron's (1996a) groundbreaking work on the analyst's subjectivity: "An important aspect of making the unconscious conscious is to bring into awareness and articulate the patient's denied observations, repressed fantasies, and unformulated experiences of the analyst" (p. 79). While we possess no unmediated access to the experiences of other subjects in our patients' lives, we can access and understand *our own* subjectivity in this specific relationship with the patient, which provides us with crucial information about patients' unconscious processes (Ogden, 1994; Sandler, 1976; Racker, 1968), as well as our personal psychologies and the dynamic we are co-creating in the dyad. Accordingly, in addition to internally "attending to" the aspects of myself under discussion here (e.g., subjectivity, behavior, consciousness, unconsciousness), I am prepared to direct explicit therapeutic attention to these domains, whether by asking open-ended questions about these topics (*"What is your sense about how I felt about you reaching out to me between sessions?"*); expressing a subjective state without drawing any conclusions about it, for the purposes of encouraging the patient's associations (*"I'm not sure what this means, but as you were speaking just now, I felt a vague but powerful feeling of dread"*); or sharing about an aspect of my subjectivity that seems to have direct relevance to the patient's relational patterns that have been the focus of analytic inquiry (*"I notice myself feeling a bit protective of you lately—wanting to comfort you when you feel angry, and maybe even to criticize your wife when you describe how she has been treating you"*).

I also consider my participation in the therapeutic process from the perspective of *change*. What shifts in my approach would better serve this patient, helping her to achieve a greater sense of meaning, fulfillment, and mutuality in her life? What am I not doing that I could try? What *am* I doing that might not be helpful to her? Through reflecting on such questions, I might decide to attempt a broader shift in my clinical stance (e.g., being more validating or nurturing to the patient, perhaps challenging or confronting her more); to discontinue techniques that have not been helpful (e.g., particular interpretations, types of self-disclosure); or to attempt some new intervention or strategy—pursuing questions or lines of inquiry I have thus far neglected; observing aspects of our interactions that have remained largely implicit or unformulated; offering a new interpretation or formulation of the patient's challenges; or disclosing potentially relevant aspects of my subjectivity I have not yet brought into our work together.

I also wrestle with such questions from a more imaginative and affective perspective, a process akin to what Cooper (2010) evocatively calls the analyst's *ethical imagination*. What might it look like for me to value myself and the patient more expansively in this relationship? How would this change how I feel about the patient, how I see her, how I treat her, what interventions I use? How might it impact how I feel about *myself*, how I see myself when I am with her? How could such changes affect her experience of being with me in sessions? What repercussions could this have on the patient's perceptions of her challenges, and on her relational circumstances outside of therapy? While such reflections sometimes result in direct and clear-cut technical modifications, usually their impact is more subtle and difficult to define—a slight shift in my emotional experience of being with the patient, an increased receptivity to certain aspects of the patient, a sudden inspiration to "try something new," or even to say something to the patient in a way that *feels* strangely new, with a tone or emotional resonance that is somehow more authentic, impactful, vulnerable, or *real*.

I have already discussed at length what I could call "self"-oriented techniques in my therapy with Jonathan—examining Jonathan's conscious and unconscious patterns, considering his subjective and behavioral worlds, and working to explore and deepen Jonathan's sense of himself while also attempting to promote change and progress across all of these domains. I will conclude by saying a bit about ways in which I began to introduce my *own* feelings into my interactions with Jonathan, in order to help him cultivate a stronger capacity for agency and mutuality in his life and relationships.

This approach became perhaps most relevant in addressing Jonathan's challenges with aggression, envy, and self-centeredness. When I first started meeting with Jonathan, despite my trepidation that our treatment would inevitably become a problematic repetition of his analysis, I found him interesting, intelligent, and engaging. I could identify with his insecurities and ambitions, with his powerful drive to make a meaningful contribution to his field, which others would hopefully admire. I also felt important in our relationship. Jonathan took what I said extremely seriously, gratefully absorbing my observations and interpretations and deftly applying them to his experiences in a way that felt sophisticated and emotionally nuanced. He would dutifully "take notes" in our sessions, spontaneously bringing up comments I had made in passing several sessions previously, which made me feel like I was offering him something that was genuinely helping him. As the process evolved and Jonathan's life substantially improved, this feeling only intensified. While I did not fully recognize it at the time, I think that I was reflexively and favorably comparing myself to Jonathan's analyst—while that treatment had resulted in Jonathan's dependency, suicidality, and psychological deterioration, I was helping to free Jonathan from such patterns, into a position of greater agency, self-esteem, and improved psychological and interpersonal functioning.

At the outset of therapy, Jonathan tended to present himself as primarily needy, dependent, and emotionally vulnerable—in his words, he was the "baby bird" in the nest with his neck outstretched, waiting desperately for the mother bird to give him a worm. As I have already mentioned, we came to understand these processes in terms of Jonathan's tendency to ascribe unconditional badness to himself—by himself, he was nothing, completely devoid of any internal resources—and so he was forced to seek *conditional* self-esteem—if only he could be the perfect patient (e.g., taking notes, applying my insights, even "getting better"), then he could feel good about himself, partaking in the value and worth residing perpetually outside of himself, just beyond his reach. Of course I was the mother bird in this scenario, since all of the goodness and value lay in *me*, hence his fierce hunger to incorporate my thoughts, interpretations, and attentiveness, which had the power to endow him with worth temporarily, until their effect maddeningly subsided. While I explicitly highlighted and challenged Jonathan's idealization of me and devaluation of himself, he would continually gravitate back to this familiar relational posture.

At this early phase of the process, I think that I was reflexively taking a highly nurturing and attentive therapeutic stance with Jonathan—likely due to my anxiety about triggering his severe suicidality and instability, but also as something of a compensation for my guilt for depriving Jonathan of what he saw as the optimal therapeutic dynamic. *I may not be willing to see you four times weekly and explicitly reassure your every conscious concern, but at least I can be as attentive and nurturing to you as possible.* While I was consciously dedicated to not explicitly reassuring Jonathan, I suspect that I was unwittingly *relationally* reassuring Jonathan through my especially kind and supportive clinical approach. In hindsight, I believe there was an important way in which I was valuing

Jonathan and myself largely conditionally here—valuing myself to the degree that I was able to nurture and rescue Jonathan, and valuing him to the degree that he appreciated me, admired me, and continued getting better. I was thus more naturally attentive to the "baby bird" dimensions of Jonathan (e.g., his neediness, desperation, and dependency) and the "mother bird" dimensions of myself (e.g., my attentiveness, nurturance, and capacity to soothe him)—these were the self-states that most directly facilitated our shared sense of worth and value. But lurking in all of this was also our mutually dissociated sense of deficiency—the idea that I would be bad if I failed to help Jonathan (or if he failed to appreciate me), and that Jonathan would be bad if he were ever something other than a vulnerable supplicant (or if I ever had anything other than mothering feelings towards him).

Over time, I started to notice the aspects of Jonathan's subjectivity not simply related to neediness and vulnerability. As I mentioned earlier, Jonathan agreed to forgo reassurance-seeking in his daily life, and to expose himself to the anxiety generated by this alteration. While he enthusiastically threw himself into these exposures outside of therapy, Jonathan was far less drawn to shifting the dynamic in our relationship. Several months after initiating the exposures, he began arriving to our appointments appearing visibly perturbed, and this attitude seemed only to intensify throughout the course of each session. While he verbally attributed such emotions to whatever specific concern he was discussing at the moment, his distress seemed more like frustration and anger, particularly directed towards *me*. I inquired about this possibility, and Jonathan confirmed a powerful feeling of anger and even rage at me for refusing to give him the reassurance that he needed in order to survive. He shared his impression of me as cold, uncaring, and indifferent to his suffering, possibly even taking pleasure in the pain that I was causing him. I was now clearly in the role of his disconnected father, but with one simple comment, I could easily become the warm, nurturing, enmeshed mother who was happy to regulate all of Jonathan's emotional states. "I'm getting by on scraps here!," he would say in anguish, in reference to both the frequency of our sessions and my refusal to console him. I validated these experiences, affirming that I understood how my boundaries could seem so cruel and cold, especially given his history of receiving so much reassurance in analysis. I also shared my conscious belief that I was not trying to cause Jonathan pain. In contrast, while I knew it did not feel that way to Jonathan, my hope was that this approach might serve as the most expedient route out of the obsessions and suffering that had dominated so much of his life.

While these discussions relieved Jonathan somewhat, he continued to perceive me as quite withholding, and to regularly return to this mode where he was demanding that I comfort him about some specific conscious concern (e.g., that he was fundamentally weak, that he would never get a girlfriend, that he held the incorrect political views). My empathy towards Jonathan gradually shifted to frustration and irritation —despite my repeated explanations of why I saw this stance as most facilitative of Jonathan's long-term well-being, he ceaselessly pressured me and became angry with me for withholding from him. A pivotal moment in the treatment came when I began not simply to explore and validate Jonathan's sense of longing and rage (the self-oriented dimension of the dialectic under discussion), but to articulate how *absent* I appeared to be in Jonathan's experience of these feelings. "Obviously you are quite upset with me right now, since you feel like I am depriving you of something you desperately need. But I am also struck by the fact that you don't seem to care that *I* actually would not feel comfortable giving you what you think you need. It's almost as if you are trying to bully me into reassuring you, the way that you did with your analyst, regardless of how I might feel about it, or whether or not this is causing *me* discomfort and distress." Jonathan was visibly shocked by these comments, but surprisingly, he did not get angry with me; instead he became sheepish and embarrassed, as well as a bit surprised with himself that, while he had been consciously experiencing himself as a victim in our relationship, he had never considered the possibility that, by attempting to wear me down and force me to reassure him, he might be victimizing me as well.

Over the next several months, we started to progressively consider a range of other interpersonal patterns between us—Jonathan consistently delaying paying his monthly bill; his reluctance to change our appointment time, whenever the change was initiated by me; his strong desire to talk extensively without being interrupted in our sessions, such that he could become impatient and irritated when I wanted to ask a question or make an observation about something he was saying. In exploring these matters, Jonathan recognized there was a part of him that really did *not* want to pay me, that perhaps even felt entitled to care from me without payment. And for reasons he could not fully explain, Jonathan did not like the idea that I might need to reschedule our appointment. Even if doing so was not an inconvenience for him, he felt a compelling desire to *not* gratify my wish. He was also able to own his frustration with me for interrupting his monologues with questions and observations. While he cognitively understood that my interruptions were about him, and purportedly for his benefit, on another level, he saw them as intrusive and selfish. *My job is to talk, and your job is to listen to me—this is not all about you here.*

For Jonathan, all of the above scenarios were examples of me betraying that *I* had needs and desires, whether those be for money, flexibility, or even to speak. This generated a profound, existential panic in Jonathan. If I had needs and desires, then there was no space for *him* to have needs and desires—there was really only room for one "needer" in any relationship. Jonathan saw how these experiences derived significantly from his experiences with his mother, where so much of his emotional energy was devoted to satisfying her demands for comfort and self-esteem, and he felt like there was such minimal space for him to explore and develop his emotional world apart from her. This led to a worldview where there was only a finite amount of emotional resources to go around. While he knew he had to acquiesce to others in order for them to like him, he felt like he did this only begrudgingly, always anxiously awaiting the moment when it would be "his turn" to be tended to. This is part of what made the therapeutic situation so powerful for Jonathan—it was the one dynamic that was allowed to be *all about him, all the time*. In this way, the seemingly "one-sided" nature of the dyad had perpetuated the idealized fiction that it was both possible and preferable to have a relationship that was oriented primarily towards satisfying one person's longings and demands. There could be *successive* needers in any given interaction, where each individual alternates between giving and receiving care, but not *mutual* needers, where both parties are simultaneously and joyfully responsive to the experiences of Self and Other.

This is where Jonathan and I found ourselves on the morning when I hit the deer. As I noted earlier, I did not mention the incident to Jonathan at the time. Several months later, as we were exploring one of Jonathan's romantic relationships in which he felt afraid that the woman's desires would overwhelm and consume him, I felt moved to try to articulate my experience of that morning—me hitting the deer, realizing I was late for our appointment, and feeling that vague but powerful aversion to sharing about the event with Jonathan. I explained further: "While I didn't fully formulate this to myself at the time, I think I recognized that, if I had told you about what happened to me, you would have listened politely and even sympathized with me, but inside you would have just been feeling like I was stealing your time. I think that I assumed you wouldn't genuinely care about what had happened to me, so I couldn't allow myself to be vulnerable to you in that way. So I just sort of shut that part of myself down, and I went back to listening to you talk about yourself." As I spoke these words, for reasons I did not understand, my voice began to crack, and I found myself starting to cry.

Jonathan identified with my fantasies of him in this hypothetical scenario. "It's true. I would have been very nice about it, sympathizing with you and showing you empathy, but I don't think I would have really cared. And really I would have just been waiting for this discussion to be over so that I could get to the stuff I had to talk about that day."

I reflected, "Even now, I have this sense that you might even be wanting *this* discussion to be over, so that we can get to the stuff that you have to talk about today."

"It's true, I am starting to get a little bit antsy—sort of like, let's stop talking about Bob, and let's get back to me."

This interchange opened up a period of exploration in which Jonathan began to access and communicate, in many ways for the first time, the powerful aggressive and destructive dimensions of his subjectivity—fantasizing about planes exploding as they flew across the sky, and everyone inside being burned alive; feeling deeply threatened by his friends' and family members' happiness and successes, such that he secretly longed for their pain and suffering, and actually took steps to make them feel bad about themselves (e.g., bragging about his achievements, making hurtful comments he knew would trigger their insecurities); and even experiencing pleasure at the idea of other people's deaths, for example wishing that a family member would not recover from a medical illness, or even feeling satisfaction when he imagined *me* dying, and the pain this would cause for my family. For Jonathan, this was a deeply challenging period in the therapy, evoking his intense emotions of shame and self-loathing. Jonathan expressed a strong desire to change these things about himself, to develop a capacity to care more fully about others, but he also articulated his fear that he was beyond help, that there was something intrinsically wrong with him that could never be altered or redeemed. While I felt heartened and hopeful that Jonathan was finally owning these dimensions of his personhood, these discussions were sad and chilling for me as well—to be approaching so closely Jonathan's sense of essential separateness and isolation from the rest of humanity. In longing to destroy humanity, there was a way in which he *was* destroying humanity in his own psychic landscape, thus leaving himself utterly alone and afraid. I was also filled with dread and hopelessness at this stage. While I was deeply committed to helping him, like Jonathan, I was not entirely sure of the extent to which he could be helped, or even if he authentically wanted to alter and evolve these foundational dimensions of his psyche.

As the treatment has continued to unfold, Jonathan has gradually but noticeably shifted his manner of participating in our relationship. He has begun paying his bills on time, the week after I provide him with the invoice. If I ever need to reschedule our appointment, he does so graciously and without hesitation—I no longer experience him as resentful or begrudging about having to accommodate me. Similarly, Jonathan does not appear impatient or frustrated with me when I want to speak in our appointments—he seems to be listening to me and what I am saying, to be "taking me in" without feeling like I am intruding on him and his process. Perhaps most notably, Jonathan has generally stopped asking for reassurances from me. This is particularly striking, given how significantly this pattern dominated our early work together, as well as Jonathan's entire psychoanalysis. Whereas Jonathan would formerly arrive to sessions in states of extreme emotional distress, with highly specific ideas about what he needed to hear from me to avoid descending into despair and suicidality, Jonathan now simply *arrives to sessions*. He often smiles, giving some report about how he has been doing since our last meeting, and then we begin to talk about whatever is on his mind, which is usually some relationship or life situation that is emotionally meaningful to him, and that is causing him some degree of confusion or unrest. Interestingly, it no longer seems as if Jonathan is seeking something predetermined from me in such discussions; rather, he is simply *sharing* about them, and we are able to engage with one another in whatever way feels natural and compelling as the interaction unfolds.

Jonathan himself does not see these changes as incidental byproducts of the therapy. Rather, as we have come to understand the aforementioned selfish and aggressive dimensions of his relational world, he has been actively taking steps to continue accessing and representing his emotions and desires along these lines (e.g., his tendency to use people for a sense of self-esteem, his murderous and aggressive impulses towards others), *while simultaneously working to cultivate a more mutual and benevolent approach to his interpersonal relationships, including his relationship with me.* In Jonathan's own words: "I am embarrassed to say it, but before I think I saw you as something of a servant to me—you were just there to give me what I thought I needed at the time. I have been trying to care about you as a person, as a human being with a life of your own, with needs and feelings that have nothing to do with me. You have a family, you have projects, you have things that you want for your life just like I do. When I am able to experience you in this way, I feel much better, much more peaceful in myself. I'm not really sure why. This feeling doesn't really last long, and if I start to get afraid again, I can lose it very quickly and feel like you and other people are going to harm me and start taking things from me. But I am able to get back to it, and then I feel connected to you as a person, and safe again."

These developments have had a powerful impact on my experience of working with Jonathan. When we first began meeting together, I felt a strong sense of pressure, as if only a very narrow window of possibilities was open to me—either I satisfy Jonathan's demands and temporarily appease him, or I resist these demands and fuel his perception of me as depriving and victimizing him. Now I am aware of a relative comfort and flexibility in our interactions, where I have the freedom to respond more naturally to what he brings to sessions, in a way that is somehow responsive to what *I* am experiencing in the moment, as well as to my perception of what Jonathan might need from me. I also feel much more emotionally safe with Jonathan, less worried he is going to pressure and coerce me in some way. Perhaps most fundamentally, I have come to trust that Jonathan is going to respect my rights as a person who is independent from him (e.g., to speak, to respond authentically, to decline his requests), and that he might even be able to be responsive to my needs and perspective in our relationship. This has led me to feel much more connected to Jonathan, more comfortable with myself when I am with him, and a greater enjoyment of our time together in sessions.

Jonathan's progress has extended beyond the therapeutic situation as well. Given his increased awareness of his tendencies towards attention-seeking and aggressiveness, Jonathan has begun to refrain from many of the behavioral approaches (e.g., bragging about himself, making obliquely hurtful comments to friends) that have alienated people from him and increased his emotional isolation from others. In an effort to cultivate greater mutuality in his relationships, Jonathan has also been working to imaginatively consider the needs and desires of his friends, family members, and dating interests, and to take active steps to try to meet those needs and desires—for example, by asking people questions about themselves, by trying to listen to others as if from their own point of view (D. N. Stern, 2004), and by taking actions that have the potential to contribute to others' lives and experiences (e.g., bringing a friend struggling with depression out to dinner, calling and visiting his socially isolated mother more frequently). Especially in moments of emotional unrest, Jonathan has discovered that this process of "shifting the focus" from himself onto others' needs has, perhaps paradoxically, led to a significant decrease in his feelings of anxiety and despair.[3] While he continues to struggle with insecurities, Jonathan now encounters periods of time during which he feels like he "might be OK" even if he does not attain the objects of his longing (e.g., fame, wealth, a long-term romantic partner), and that he might possess a natural worth and value as a person, without having to do anything to "earn" or actualize that. In such moments, Jonathan experiences a sense of freedom and hope that is almost disorienting in its unfamiliarity, as if he is discovering that the world he has been inhabiting his entire life is far more welcoming than he ever could have imagined, and that *he* is far more valuable than he ever thought possible.

In keeping with the ethical vision of psychoanalysis I have outlined here, I see Jonathan's improvements as involving an expansion of the conditions under which Jonathan and I came to value each other in the therapeutic relationship. As I increasingly noticed, represented, and highlighted the selfish and aggressive dimensions of Jonathan's subjectivity, I believe that I was starting to value Jonathan under a wider range of conditions (e.g., when he was not admiring me, when he was blaming me and devaluing me, when I feared he was incapable of genuine psychological change), while valuing myself under additional conditions as well (e.g., when I could not comfort and appease Jonathan, when I felt insufficiently able to help him, when I was "standing up for myself" rather than being solely nurturing). Along these lines, a key moment came when I finally felt able to communicate my experience of hitting the deer—in that moment, I believe that I was able to begin valuing myself as a vulnerable child who felt neglected and unloved by a narcissistic parent, and to value Jonathan even in the face of all of his self-centeredness and lack of concern for me as a person. These evolutions gradually enabled Jonathan to value *himself* under a broader array of conditions (e.g., when he was experiencing aggression and murderous rage, when he asserted himself rather than "performing well" as the perfect patient, when he felt afraid that he was unable to progress in the treatment), and to value me under expanded conditions as well (e.g., when I failed to reassure him, when I expressed my own needs and desires, when I highlighted non-vulnerable dimensions of his subjectivity). I suggest that, as Jonathan began to take the risk of valuing us under these expanded conditions, he became more able to value himself and others more expansively outside of the therapy as well—to value other people not simply as providers of admiration and care, but as complex, multidimensional subjects who can attend to him while also having needs of their own; and to value himself not simply as a damaged supplicant, but as a vulnerable *and* agentic subject who can gratefully receive care from others while also graciously providing that care as well.

These changes have led to a dramatic shift in Jonathan's experience of his life. With an enhanced awareness of himself as unconditionally valuable, Jonathan relies less compulsively on all of these strategies (e.g., reassurance-seeking; pursuing one-directional caretaking; seeking wealth, fame, and professional recognition) to supply him with a temporary feeling of conditional worth, and he has begun to enjoy a growing peace, comfort, and emotional stability. And with a burgeoning appreciation of others as unconditionally valuable, Jonathan has discovered a source of motivation outside of himself, endowing him with a more durable sense of meaning and purpose that does not have to be continuously "achieved" through behavioral strategies, but that can be naturally *discovered* through engaged connectedness with other people. Jonathan's existential "center of gravity" has thus started to shift towards a position of greater balance *between* himself and others, allowing him to cultivate an emergent capacity for progressively mutual responsiveness to his own internal world, and to the internal world of other subjects.

Conclusion: Dialectical pragmatism in psychoanalytic technique

In this chapter, I have explored four technical dialectics that I see as consistent with the ethical vision of psychoanalysis I have proposed in this book—the tensions between unconsciousness and consciousness, subjectivity and behavior, exploration and change, and Self and Other. In my view, psychoanalysis as traditionally practiced tends to emphasize the "first terms" in each of these polarities (i.e., unconscious process, subjectivity, exploration, the Self), while the "second terms" in these polarities (i.e., consciousness, behavior, change, and other people) are often associated with more practically oriented, "non-psychoanalytic" approaches to human life, such as cognitive behavioral therapy, morality, and religion. In conclusion, I would like to suggest that there is significant therapeutic value in maintaining rather than collapsing these dialectics in the clinical practice of psychoanalysis, namely since doing so might further enable us to "bridge the gap between theory and life" discussed throughout this book (Chapter 1). By bringing our technical constructs into closer contact with our everyday experiences as human beings, we might cultivate a more accessible, pragmatic, and hopefully *effective* model of analytic work.

In our daily lives, we tend to relate to our conscious experiences in a foundational way, naturally investing significant energy into our beliefs, perceptions, emotions, desires, and values *as we experience them* in conscious awareness. Even when reflecting on the unconscious meaning of such processes, we regard our conscious states as having a status and meaning that is primary and irreducible, independent of any relationship with non-conscious factors. Of course, our patients ascribe significant meaning to these areas as well, basing much of their lives (e.g., careers, parenting styles, choice of partners and friendships) on their conscious formulations about these topics. While I suspect that all psychoanalytic clinicians spend a significant amount of time considering the conscious dimensions of patients' lives, most analytic perspectives still frame these dimensions as *deriving* from unconscious mechanisms, and few theories of technique explain how to explore and elaborate consciousness in a primary way. This approach to consciousness has reinforced the "tell me about your mother" caricature of psychoanalytic technique—that is, focusing predominantly on fantasy, unconscious dynamics, and historical factors and remaining generally unconcerned with patients' functioning and symptomatology in the "real world"—which I believe has contributed unfortunately to the widespread marginalization of psychoanalysis as a discipline.

In contrast, by upholding the dialectic between consciousness and unconsciousness, we would be maintaining our fundamental commitment to unconscious dynamics, while preserving and reflecting the importance we naturally ascribe to our conscious experiences. This might lead to a more relevant and accessible technical posture, one that places the unconscious on an equal footing with patients' phenomenology, or what Foehl (2014) calls "the immediacy of the immersive perceptive moment" (p. 289), in therapeutic process and in patients' daily lives.

Along similar lines, in everyday life, we care deeply about the issue of *actions and behavior*—"what we do" and how we conduct ourselves in the world. We see this in ethical matters—for example when we consider if we are morally permitted to take certain actions, what political positions we ought to endorse, whether we should donate to charity—but perhaps most commonly in our practical and self-interested concerns—which job to take, where to live, how to spend our money, and how to engage in our specific relationships. Our patients care about these topics as well, presenting to treatment with definite questions about what they should *do* to improve their mood, self-esteem, relationships, and sense of meaning and personal fulfillment. However, apart from some notable exceptions (Hoffman, 1998, 2009b; Mitchell, 2001; Safran, 2016; Wachtel, 1997, 2014; Wheelis, 2010), psychoanalytic theories of technique have largely ignored the topic of behavior, leading analytic practitioners to devote insufficient clinical attention to behavioral matters and sometimes even to dismiss this arena as unimportant and superficial compared to the examination of subjectivity.

Conversely, by sustaining the dialectic between subjectivity and behavior, we would be supporting our fundamental goal of expanding patients' access to their subjective worlds, while honoring patients' behavioral concerns as valid and foundational dimensions of human experience. This would constitute a more experience-near technical approach, one that accords with patients' phenomenology while also allowing us to bring a fuller range of our own subjective states—including our natural interest in actions and their consequences—to the clinical interaction. Furthermore, by drawing attention to the role that patients' behavioral patterns might be playing in perpetuating their conscious and unconscious challenges, this dialectical stance could begin to "set the stage" for more change-oriented interventions at later stages of the analytic process.

We also care about the issue of *progress* in our daily lives. We have hopes, dreams, and aspirations for ourselves and our loved ones, regularly reflecting on such matters and taking active steps to actualize these goals in a real way. When internal and external barriers prevent us from achieving our goals, we can get frustrated, disappointed, and even impatient about the situation, modifying our behaviors and interpersonal approaches to increase the possibility that we will get what we want. Our patients care about these matters as well, presenting to treatment because they feel "stuck" in some way that has been difficult to resolve, and because they want to *get better*, for their sake and for the benefit of the people closest to them. When our friends and family members are struggling in similar ways, in addition to empathizing with them and discussing the possible meaning of their difficulties, we reflexively give advice about what actions they might take to address the situation in question, and we are usually curious about whether or not this advice was *effective* at generating the desired outcome in their lives.

While I believe that all analytic practitioners care about their patients' well-being and therapeutic progress, I am concerned that, in our discussions of technique, we tend to idealize exploratory interventions while ignoring and implicitly devaluing more "change-oriented" therapeutic strategies (see Crumbley, 2011), including perhaps most importantly how to consider, explore, and collaboratively evaluate the efficacy of our treatments. As Hoffman (1998) observes in his influential work on the myth of analytic neutrality:

> A common illusion that I think we try to maintain is that analysis is a kind of *sanctuary* from the world of choice. . . . But a person's lifetime keeps on going relentlessly through every analytic hour, week, and year. The clock keeps running, and more or less agonizing choices are being made continually, with the analyst's witting or unwitting participation, right under his or her nose.
>
> (pp. 73–74)

This relative neglect of change-oriented interventions risks creating something of a double-standard around clinical practice—we care about progress in our personal lives, and in the lives of our loved ones, but we often overlook the things that our patients can *actually do*—cognitively, behaviorally, imaginatively—to address the challenges that led them to seek treatment. This can lead us to minimize our own agency in helping patients to improve their lives, and to inadvertently disregard whole categories of interventions that might be helpful for our patients.

By maintaining the technical dialectic between exploration and change, we would be affirming our fundamental commitment to deepening patients' experiences, while simultaneously attending to the steps that we and our patients might take in order to enhance the efficacy of the therapeutic process. This could lead to a more pragmatic vision of psychoanalysis, one that is more consistent with our own natural interest in behaviors and their consequences, as well as our patients' desire for treatment that is genuinely effective at helping them generate deep and lasting transformation in their lives.

Finally, in our personal experiences outside of analytic work, we expect ourselves to actually *care about* other human beings—to be cognizant of (and motivationally responsive to) their needs, desires, interests, and rights; to treat them with a basic level of respect and dignity; and to take steps to contribute to their well-being and flourishing. If we fall short in these areas, we hold ourselves accountable for that, feeling emotions of guilt, embarrassment, and shame, and attempting to "make things right" by apologizing and making reparations to the other party. We tend to hold others to similar standards as well. We expect other individuals, especially those with whom we are close, to actually care about us—to "keep us in mind," to want good things for us, and to actively invest in making our lives better. We also want others to care about us *for our own sake*, not simply because we are doing something for them. If we discover that people are merely using us, or that they do not truly value us as persons, we naturally start to withdraw from them emotionally, stopping ourselves from being vulnerable with them and avoiding investing in those relationships in the future.

Given the foundational importance of these matters in everyday human life, it is remarkable that such considerations have not fully made their way into the heart of psychoanalytic theory and technique. While the relational turn has expanded the scope of analytic inquiry to include the actual experiences of other subjects (Chapter 6; see Aron, 1996a), our approaches to technique, including case discussions in the analytic literature, tend to focus on exploring and elaborating the "self-oriented" dimensions of patients' experiences, while devoting far less attention to cultivating patients' capacity to be motivationally responsive to others' subjectivity.

This imbalance can negatively impact clinical practice in subtle but important ways. Perhaps most crucially, we end up holding ourselves to a different moral standard than we apply to our patients, which essentially positions them in a separate moral universe from ourselves. There is something patronizing and even demeaning about this—*of course* I *need to care about other people, and my loved ones do as well, but you are a patient, so we do not expect such things of you.* This can lead to a self-indulgent vision of psychoanalysis, inadvertently promoting a "one-sided" picture of human intimacy that contributes to psychologically destructive tendencies towards self-centeredness, entitlement, and perpetual deprivation in our patients. And yet we still *do* expect some degree of mutuality and care from our patients, and so we feel victimized and unfairly treated when they fail to meet these standards. Without a model of technique that identifies and validates *our right* to expect some degree of altruism from our patients, these standards (and their associated affects) can become problematically split off and dissociated in clinical practice, resulting in countertransference enactments that are never fully appreciated as being "about" our recognition of ethical imbalance in the dyad.

In contrast, by preserving the dialectic between Self and Other in psychoanalytic technique, we would be better situated to co-construct a therapeutic relationship involving genuine mutuality with our patients, thus helping to lay the groundwork for more intimate, authentic, and durable forms of connectedness in patients' relationships outside of treatment. Under these conditions, analytic work is able to cultivate and strengthen patients' ability to be motivated both by their own experiences *and* the experiences of others, while at the same time affording the various psychological benefits—for example, an increased sense of agency, self-esteem, purpose, and personal fulfillment—associated with having a source of meaning that does not reside solely within the Self.

My patient Jonathan's history in psychoanalysis illustrates some of the dangers of collapsing the technical dialectics considered in this chapter. Admittedly, I cannot consider that analysis from any objective standpoint, since so much of my understanding has been filtered through Jonathan's narratives, his analyst's reports, and my own individual biases. However, my tentative impression is that, while Jonathan's analyst likely devoted ample attention to Jonathan's unconscious *and* conscious processes, the analyst likely overemphasized exploration, subjectivity, and Self in his technical approach. In prioritizing Jonathan's subjectivity, he likely minimized the role that Jonathan's specific behaviors were playing in perpetuating his challenges with emotional dysregulation, low self-esteem, and excessive dependency upon others. In employing a primarily exploratory technique, the analyst possibly overlooked the things that he and Jonathan could *do* to shift Jonathan's maladaptive interpersonal patterns, especially his tendencies towards reassurance-seeking in the analysis and beyond. And by attending predominantly to the self-oriented dimensions of Jonathan's life, the analyst likely missed the ways in which Jonathan's aggression and self-centeredness might have been fueling his suffering, contributing to relational dynamics that left him devoid of a genuine connection to himself and others.

In the latter case, based on my own relationship with Jonathan, I fantasize that there was a powerful way in which his analyst felt devalued and selfishly used by Jonathan, and that this experience might have played a role in why he terminated the analysis in the way that he did. Without a theory that validated the analyst's rights to expect care from Jonathan, and without a technical model that explained how to bring such concerns into their work together, these emotions were sadly wasted, unable to be used for Jonathan's ultimate therapeutic benefit. This scenario feels deeply tragic to me—Jonathan's analyst left essentially isolated with his feelings, and Jonathan continuing to perpetuate these same patterns inside and outside of the treatment, both of them suffering alone in the presence of the Other. I suggest that, by bringing our theories into closer contact with the more "practical" dimensions of human experience (e.g., consciousness, behavior, progress, and other subjects), we will hopefully be "bridging the gap" not just between theory and life, but between ourselves and our patients *as people*, with equivalent rights, needs, and vulnerabilities in a shared relational world.

While I suspect that some readers will identify with the technical principles I have outlined here, others could take issue with them as a representation of psychoanalytic practice. "Sure, this approach might have been effective in this particular case, as certain patients do require more conscious, behavioral, and change-oriented interventions. *But that's not psychoanalysis*." We thus arrive at the perennial controversy of how to conceptualize and define psychoanalysis *itself*, a concern I will attempt to address in our conclusion.

Notes

1 Other technical dialectics, which I will not consider here but which serve a central role in my clinical approach, include the dialectics between content and process, between presence and absence, and between treatment and life.

2 In my view, the dialectic between exploration and change mirrors the central ethical dialectic that I have been exploring in this book—the polarity between dignity and well-being. Exploration seems to be clearly aligned with the patient's own intrinsic worth as a person—in attempting to deepen patients' own understanding and affective experience of themselves, it affirms the idea that patients have an inherent value as they are, a value that can be most fully realized by helping them to know and experience themselves in more complex and elaborated ways. *"You are worthwhile as you are. It is not your fault—there are reasons why you developed in the way that you did, and there are reasons why you*

are still drawn to this way of being. We need to invite all of these parts of yourself into this space, so that you can come to value yourself more expansively." And change-oriented interventions seem closely aligned with patients' well-being—in helping patients to reflect on their goals and potentials, as well as the steps they might take to actualize these things, we are working to increase their sense of well-being and flourishing in their lives. *"You deserve to actually get better, to feel better, in a manner consistent with your goals for yourself. Our relationship is fundamentally answerable to the question of whether or not we are helping you. You can do things to make your life better, to evolve yourself as a person, and I want to do anything that I can to help you achieve that."*

3 Interestingly, Jonathan's approach here is reflected in substantial empirical research correlating negative affect with self-focused attentional processes (Aldao, Nolen-Hoeksema, & Schweizer, 2010; Mor & Winquist, 2002).

Chapter 8

Conclusion

The dialectical method of psychoanalysis

In this book, I have developed a vision of psychoanalysis as an essentially ethical process—answering potential objections to such a model (Chapter 2), outlining motivational propositions that might ground an ethical psychoanalysis (Chapters 3–5), and exploring the clinical applications of these ideas, from the perspective of therapeutic action as well as technique (Chapters 6–7). Throughout, I have argued that, by bringing our theoretical constructs into closer communication with our reflexive ethical commitments, we can cultivate a more pragmatic and accessible psychoanalytic approach, one that is able to uphold the fundamental tenets of psychoanalysis while also reflecting our everyday experiences as human beings outside of the analytic process.

Despite the current popularity of ethical constructs (e.g., mentalization, mutual recognition, conceptions of politics and social justice) in the analytic literature, I have no expectation that ethics will somehow become the primary frame of psychoanalytic practice. I have attempted here to offer one example of an ethical psychoanalysis, in the hopes that this will stimulate further reflection, exploration, and theoretical attention to the matters at play. In my view, by making our theories more *answerable and accountable* to the practically oriented experiences I have considered here—consciousness, behavior, altruism, dignity, freedom, the drive towards progress and change, the connection between ethics and psychological health—we will move towards a more down-to-earth and inclusive psychoanalytic vision, which might feel more relevant to a wider range of clinicians and patients. In this way, I see this project as contributing to the broader movement towards redefining psychoanalysis in a way that is more pragmatic, egalitarian, and expansive in its application (Altman, 1995, 2015; Aron & Starr, 2013; Renik, 2006; Wachtel, 2014). Aron and Starr (2013) thus invoke Freud's call for psychoanalysis to become *a psychotherapy for the people*—"a new psychoanalysis for the twenty-first century, a progressive psychoanalysis that moves beyond old polarities and adapts to our changed world, while remaining true to the revolutionary and humanistic spirit of Freud and his followers" (p. xix).

In arguing for the importance of this project, Aron and Starr (2013) offer what serves as possibly the most detailed and expansive history of psychoanalysis' attempts to define itself and answer the question—*what makes it psychoanalytic?* Along these lines, classical thought proposed various well-known criteria, including the analyst's stance of neutrality, anonymity, and abstinence; the use of less-structured, exploratory, free-associative techniques; the employment of interpretation as the primary technical tool, especially interpretation of the transference; the therapeutic aims of "insight," "making the unconscious conscious," lifting of repressions, and resolution of intrapsychic conflict; the practitioner's analytic training and the patient's basic capacity to engage in a more reflective exploratory process; and more "extrinsic" criteria such as increased session-frequency, extended treatment duration, and use of the couch. Highlighting classical theory's tendency to frame itself dichotomously, Aron and Starr (2013) also emphasize approaches traditionally seen as *non-psychoanalytic*, including a therapeutic stance that is more interactive, participatory, and expressive; technical interventions involving support, care, and efforts to influence or change the patient; and clinical goals of symptom remission and the strengthening of defenses (see chapters 4, 8, 17).

Given classical thought's longstanding history of conceptualizing behavior, interaction, and the environment as comparatively more "superficial" dimensions of human experience, it is ironic that so many of the above formulations of psychoanalysis are *behavioral* in nature, that is, focusing on the correct observable techniques (e.g., neutrality, interpretation, non-gratification, exploration rather than suggestion) the analyst must employ for the treatment to "count" as psychoanalysis. This method of psychoanalytic self-definition has of course felt constraining to many contemporary practitioners, leading relational theorists to offer conceptions of psychoanalysis that might encompass the broader array of technical approaches employed in daily clinical practice. Mitchell (1997) famously grounded psychoanalysis in the analyst's *intentions*, specifically the intention to remain as responsive as possible to the range of experiential possibilities within the dyad, "all of which then become the object of self-reflective scrutiny" (p. 193). Along similar lines, Cooper (2010) defines psychoanalysis by invoking the analyst's *dedication and aims*: "psychoanalysis [is] the sustained dedication to elaborating the content and structure of the patient's inner life that includes both how it shapes interaction with others and how it is shaped through interaction with others, including the analyst" (p. 103; my brackets). Similarly, Safran (2012) described psychoanalysis by highlighting the analyst's various *assumptions, interests, and emphases*, including "an assumption that all human beings are motivated in part by wishes, fantasies, or tacit knowledge that is outside of awareness," along with "an emphasis on using the therapeutic relationship as an important vehicle of change" (pp. 3–4). And Bromberg (2011) frames psychoanalysis in terms of *commitment*, in particular "the analyst's commitment to the joint processing of collisions between subjectivities," which "requires the analyst to be as attuned as possible to a patient's shifting equilibrium between affective safety and affective overload" (p. 53).

While all of these theories constitute distinct visions of the analytic process, they share the common conviction that psychoanalysis is most usefully defined not by the clinician's behavior or discrete techniques, but by the clinician's *subjective relationship to the process itself*, as exemplified by her intentions, aims, assumptions, and commitments. Mitchell (1997) summed up this position by remarking, "*What* is done in psychoanalysis is ultimately less important than the effort made and the intentions expressed in that effort" (p. 170). This approach allows for a more flexible and inclusive conception of psychoanalysis—even if the practitioner employs interventions that would formerly have been dubbed "non-analytic," the treatment could qualify as psychoanalytic in nature, as long as the aforementioned subjective conditions are met. However, I worry that these formulations still suffer from a subtler version of the same binary tendencies that have dominated psychoanalysis throughout its history, since—as we see from terms like reflection, scrutiny, elaboration, and joint processing—they continue to affirm *exploration of the non-conscious and unformulated dimensions of the patient's psychological world* as the hallmark of therapeutic work. By privileging these forms of interaction, when we are drawn towards non-exploratory interventions more associated with patients' conscious lives (e.g., developing a safety plan for a patient who is suicidal, helping a homeless person find a place to stay for the night, giving advice about parenting strategies), we are apt to feel like we are departing from a truly psychoanalytic ideal. This can constrain clinical experience, creating a cultural pressure towards some techniques over others, and inhibiting our freedom to comfortably and authentically respond to what we think the patient might need from us in the moment. "Sure, maybe this *treatment* counts as psychoanalytic because I possess the requisite intention to elaborate the patient's internal world, but this *intervention* is not really psychoanalytic. I may 'get a pass' for the moment, but I better throw in an interpretation or exploratory question sometime soon, to make sure that this doesn't become a superficial, subpar treatment." And then the subtext here: "To make sure that *I* don't become a superficial, subpar clinician."

This cultural pressure can have a powerful impact on analytic discourse more generally. Through my friendships and professional relationships with dynamically oriented clinicians, I am aware that most of them, from the classically trained ego psychologist to the traditional Kohutian to the self-proclaimed contemporary "intersubjectivist," regularly employ more practical interventions in clinical work—transparently expressing their opinions about patients' potentially maladaptive tendencies, and often taking active steps (e.g., advice giving; problem solving; sharing ideas about alternative approaches; inviting reflection about the potential consequences of different behavioral options; expressing frustration and concern about some tendencies, expressing hope and encouragement about others) to curb such processes. However, such interventions are rarely discussed openly in public settings, and they are even less frequently presented in the analytic literature, except as interesting and atypical "departures" from traditional technique. This is a problem—not just because we are inaccurately representing what psychoanalysis actually looks like in everyday practice, but because such portrayals become instantiated in our collective consciousness as ideals of analytic interaction. We can thus fail to sufficiently appreciate our patients' reality-based needs and desires, or even if we do "see" such needs, we feel inhibited in our ability to comfortably respond to them with a clear clinical conscience. From this perspective, our overly narrow descriptions of psychoanalysis might be limiting the dissemination of psychoanalytic knowledge *and* the efficacy of our treatments.

The narrowness of our psychoanalytic models can also inadvertently contribute to what Altman (1995) calls *psychoanalytic elitism*—that is, psychoanalysis' history of favoring wealthier, higher-functioning, psychologically minded patients who have the luxury of remaining consistently focused on their "internal" worlds. By implicitly devaluing more practical, consciously oriented interventions, psychoanalysis has been less hospitable to those patients who require regular attentiveness to their functioning in the "real world," for example people struggling with marginalization related to issues like race, poverty, gender, sexuality, psychosocial situation, and level of psychiatric impairment.

Our definition of psychoanalysis plays a foundational role in determining our sense of self-esteem in therapeutic work. Every distinct conception of psychoanalysis establishes a range of explicit and implicit conditions for our self-worth as clinicians, which, as I have attempted to illustrate throughout this book, directly affects the conditions under which we value our patients as well. *As long as we continue to define psychoanalysis in terms of the elaboration of non-conscious dynamics, we will remain hindered in our efforts to develop a more inclusive, pragmatic psychoanalytic model. Whether we notice it or not, the pressures and demands of reality—involving symptomatic improvement, psychosocial functioning, the experiences of other subjects—will inevitably begin to encroach on the therapeutic process, and we will then be forced to "choose" between maintaining our psychoanalytic ideals (along with the culturally conditioned sense of self-worth associated with them) and responding to the reality-based needs and experiences of our patients.*

It is at this point that our inquiries in this book offer a possible solution to the longstanding problem of psychoanalysis' self-definition. I have suggested that, by bringing psychoanalysis into closer communication with ethics, we arrive at a more integrated psychoanalytic vision that affirms the essential principles of psychoanalysis while simultaneously reflecting our everyday ethical commitments as human beings. I have argued for a dialectical approach to this project, specifically suggesting that we attempt to maintain a handful of paradoxes central to human experience:

- The dialectic between subjectivity and behavior
- The dialectic between unconsciousness and consciousness
- The dialectic between Self and Other
- The dialectic between determinism and freedom
- The dialectic between multiplicity and individuality
- The dialectic between exploration and change.

In closing, I want to observe that all of the "first terms" in these polarities are more traditionally associated with the *non-conscious* dimensions of subjectivity, while the "second terms" are more aligned with the *conscious, reality-based* dimension of human life. Here, it is possible that the tensions between psychoanalysis and ethics are reflective of perhaps a more fundamental tension at the heart of human experience, namely the tension between non-conscious process, the "bread and butter" of psychoanalysis, and conscious phenomenology, or the traditional province of ethics. Just as we have employed a dialectical method to bridge the gulf between psychoanalysis and ethics, rather than conceptualizing psychoanalysis primarily in terms of non-conscious process, we can attempt to bring consciousness into a dialectical relationship with the unconscious world. *On this view, the signature feature of psychoanalysis might be the clinician's deep appreciation of the dynamic, irresolvable dialectic between conscious experience and unconscious process, and a foundational commitment to using this dialectic technically—with patients, in the analytic relationship, and in ourselves—as the main vehicle for therapeutic change.*

From this standpoint, Freud's great discovery was not the notion of the dynamic unconscious, as he himself presumed, but of the *dialectic* between consciousness and unconsciousness. Thomas Ogden (1994) was perhaps the first analytic theorist to make this point in his seminal *Subjects of Analysis*:

> The Freudian conception of the process by which the subject is constituted is fundamentally dialectical in nature and involves the notion that the subject is created and sustained (and at the same time

> decentered from itself) through the dialectical interplay of consciousness and unconsciousness.
>
> (p. 30)

Ogden suggests this dialectical conception is largely implicit in Freud's writings, embedded within his more linear and binary presentations. As Ogden observes, Freud (1938) conceives of consciousness and unconsciousness as different, simultaneously existing "qualities of what is psychical" (p. 161), remaining in such a state of intimate communication with each other that it becomes nearly impossible to provide "a schematically clear-cut distinction between the two psychical systems" (Freud, 1915c, p. 190). Rather, Freud (1915c) suggests that unconscious operations "are even incapable of carrying on their existence" without the activity of consciousness (p. 187), such that the two dimensions of mind are truly "complementary" with one another (Freud, 1938, p. 159).

This dialectical reading of Freud is abundantly supported throughout all of Freud's writings, which betray a deep and foundational attentiveness not simply to unconscious process, but to the complex ways in which consciousness and unconsciousness mutually interact to produce the intricate vicissitudes of human subjectivity. We see this in Freud's various formulations about the nature of mind (Sandler, Holder, Dare, & Dreher, 1997), starting with the affect–trauma model, in which mind is constituted by the dialectic between conscious, ego-based operations (e.g., attention, perception, motility, morality) and unconscious phenomena (e.g., memories, ideas, and "dammed up" affects) that are incompatible with the person's conscious self (Breuer & Freud, 1893–1895); in the topographical model, in which mind is comprised by the tension between conscious "secondary process" operations (e.g., logic, decision-making, reality-testing, self-preservation, moral values), preconscious mechanisms like censorship and defense, and unconscious, infantile sexual and aggressive impulses and their repressed derivatives (Freud, 1900); and in the structural model, in which mind contains the irresolvable conflict between the conscious, reality-oriented ego and unconscious processes including the instinctual drives (*the id*), the demands of morality (*the super-ego*), and the defensive and self-regulatory operations of the ego (Freud, 1923a).

The dialectical nature of mind finds particularly clear expression in Freud's pivotal construct of compromise formation, which he employs to explain a wide range of psychic operations including dreams, symptoms, personality traits, and general behavioral patterns. As Freud (1923c) describes them, such phenomena entail

> a struggle between two trends, of which one is unconscious and ordinarily repressed and strives towards satisfaction—that is, wish-fulfillment—while the other, belonging probably to the conscious ego, is disapproving and repressive. The outcome of this conflict is a *compromise-formation* ... in which both trends have found an incomplete expression.
>
> (p. 242)

This dialectical conception is also supported by Freud's comments about the *shibboleths* of psychoanalysis, or the boundary markers that distinguish psychoanalysis from other types of treatment (Aron & Starr, 2013, chapter 17). Interestingly for our purposes, Freud (1923a) cites the communication between consciousness and unconsciousness as the "first shibboleth of psychoanalysis," proclaiming that "the division of the psychical into what is conscious and what is unconscious is the fundamental premise of psycho-analysis" (p. 13). This formulation reverberates throughout Freud's three other shibboleths—sexuality (1919a), dream theory (1933), and the Oedipus complex (1905)—all of which involve the dialectical tension between the conscious, reality-based dimensions of experience and the corresponding unconscious dimensions of human life. For Freud, sexuality is constituted by the tension between the person's overt sexual behavior and developmental phases *and* the presuppositions of instinctual libido and libidinal fixations. The dream is comprised of the dialectic between manifest content *and* repressed latent content consisting of unconscious, infantile wishes. And, perhaps most famously, the Oedipus complex is composed of the dialectic between the child's conscious attitudes towards parental figures (e.g., involving love and aggression) *and* non-conscious processes of repression, identification, and castration anxiety.

In light of the above, I suggest that, *at the experiential level*, Freud always appreciated the fundamental dialectic between consciousness and unconsciousness, but given his more binary, dichotomous philosophical orientation, he was forced to *explicitly frame* psychoanalysis by invoking unconscious dynamics. This was also probably a necessary rhetorical stance on Freud's (1917) part, given the longstanding historical tradition of equating "mind" with consciousness, as well as the Victorian notion of willpower positing the ego as "master in its own house" (p. 285), which he was actively and provocatively seeking to undermine. However, I propose that Freud overcorrected in his approach, ultimately arriving at an unnecessarily dichotomous psychoanalytic conception and clinical technique, which failed to sufficiently appreciate the conscious dimensions of the analytic subject.

I view this overcorrection on Freud's part as the ancestral forebear for the "gap between theory and life" that has reverberated throughout the history of psychoanalysis. In fact, many of the theoretical innovations proposed by the various analytic schools—ego psychology's focus on ego functionality and environmental adaptation; Melanie Klein's and Fairbairn's reformulations of the unconscious in terms of relationships; Sullivan's emphasis on interactional patterns and interpersonal relationships; Winnicott's and Kohut's explorations of the vicissitudes of self-experience; the increased emphasis on subjectivity and affects (as compared to experience-distant "drives") in contemporary psychoanalysis—can be seen as attempts to bring some previously underappreciated aspect of consciousness into a position of greater prominence in the therapeutic process. Naturally recognizing the inability of previous models to sufficiently reflect the conscious experience in question, these authors were intuitively working towards a more dialectically constituted vision of psychoanalytic practice. However, each new model mistakenly identified some *aspect* of consciousness as "the missing piece of the puzzle," while I am suggesting that consciousness *itself* has been the missing piece of the puzzle, or more specifically—the irresolvable dialectic between conscious experience and unconscious process.

This formulation helps to explain what has been so uniquely galvanizing and unifying about the relational turn in psychoanalysis. While earlier theorists tended to emphasize either the intrapsychic *or* the interpersonal spheres of human life, by recognizing the necessity of both internal *and* external relational configurations (Aron, 1996a; Greenberg & Mitchell, 1983; Mitchell, 1988), relational thought has offered a psychoanalytic perspective that is able to express, in a manner perhaps more fully than any previous analytic orientation, the fundamental polarity between consciousness and unconsciousness. On this view, consciousness encompasses our experiences of ourselves and our subjective realms, including our thoughts, beliefs, affects, longings, and fantasies; other subjects as we perceive them, and as they exist independently of us; and the real, bidirectional interactional patterns unfolding between ourselves and others. The unconscious includes analogous processes (e.g., representations of Self, Other, and the characteristic interpersonal patterns between Self and Other), unfolding variously as non-conscious, unformulated, and potentially repressed and dissociated dimensions of our subjectivity. By elaborating these various domains with diverse emphases and theoretical constructs, relational thinkers have offered a highly expansive and multi-faceted vision of human experience, one that expresses a broader range of conscious phenomena (e.g., agency, the multiplicity of self-states, the messiness and unpredictability of intersubjective life, the ethical commitments we have considered here) while simultaneously illuminating the complex tapestry of our internal worlds.[1] We have begun to learn that *we do not have to choose* between consciousness and unconsciousness in order to implement a disciplined, creative, relevant, and still genuinely psychoanalytic clinical approach.

Nevertheless, by continuing to explicitly frame psychoanalysis in terms of exploration of the unconscious, we are inadvertently minimizing the conscious facets of human life, thus unwittingly retaining a version of Freud's more binary portrayal of the analytic process. I suggest that, in order for psychoanalysis to transcend its position of marginality in our culture, and to fully actualize its potential to become "a psychotherapy for the people," we need to develop, advance, and elaborate a conception of the analytic method as essentially involving the dialectic between consciousness and unconsciousness. This would enable us to move towards a psychoanalytic vision that is more accessible not simply to a wider range of patients and clinicians, but one that is also more inclusive of a greater diversity of patients' *experiences*, and a broader array of clinicians' experiences, including their impulses to respond to patients in a fashion not traditionally understood to be "psychoanalytic." Some examples of this sort of formulation have begun to emerge in the literature. While LaFarge (2014) proposes a seemingly more traditional understanding of psychoanalysis as defined by attentiveness to transference and phantasy, a closer inspection of her theory reveals a more dialectically constituted view:

> Every aspect of human experience—one's thoughts and memories; one's perceptions of the world and of others within it; all that one says and does; and the manner and sequence in which all these interwoven dimensions of experience unfold—may be seen to have a dual aspect, to be stimulated and shaped both by conscious, contemporary experience and by memories and phantasies residing in the unconscious. The psychoanalytic setting and method provide a unique arena in which the duality of mental life can emerge and be recognized.
>
> (p. 1265)

Along similar lines, while Cooper's (2010) aforementioned description of psychoanalysis often emphasizes the elaboration of the patient's "inner life," at other times he offers a more dialectical perspective, framing analysis by referencing the analyst's efforts "to inspire and elicit the patient's interest and curiosity in the patient's conscious *and* unconscious experience" (p. 116; my italics).

In closing, rather than attempt a comprehensive defense of my particular definition of psychoanalysis, I will briefly highlight some of its salient features, for the purposes of further exploration. First, this dialectical approach retains relational theory's method of defining psychoanalysis by way of the clinician's subjectivity, in this case highlighting the clinician's *deep appreciation* of the foundational tension between conscious experience and unconscious process. On this model, a central feature that unites psychoanalytic clinicians across diverse orientations is the simultaneous attentiveness to both dimensions of the psyche—without attempting to reduce or collapse one domain into the other, while recognizing the intricate ways these dimensions mutually enrich, define, and negate each other to generate the full complexity of human experience. While this dialectical conception is rarely reflected in our publicly endorsed formulations of psychoanalysis, I believe that it speaks to something important about the personal commitments or "worldview" of most analytically oriented practitioners.[2]

And yet this appreciation cannot simply be actualized subjectively; as classical theorists have argued, it must be reflected in what we actually *do* in our consulting rooms. As the second part of my definition, I propose that psychoanalytic practitioners employ the dialectic between consciousness and unconsciousness—with patients, in the dyad, and in themselves—as the main *technical* vehicle for therapeutic change. In my view, this description encompasses much of what happens in everyday clinical work. As Freud (1915c) himself observed, consciousness "forms the point of departure for all our investigations" (p. 172), since it "is the only characteristic of psychical processes that is directly presented to us" (p. 192). Most analytic clinicians thus spend a significant amount of time attending to patients' conscious experiences—their descriptions of past and present events in their lives; what they say and do in their relationships; their conscious thoughts, beliefs, emotions, desires, and attitudes towards themselves and others; and their conscious feelings about the therapeutic process itself. We are interested in such experiences for their own sake, to approach as closely as possible what it feels like to occupy our patients' perspective, while also hopefully employing these reflections and explorations to deepen and expand patients' access to the non-conscious, unformulated dimensions of their subjective worlds. Seen from this vantage point, the technical dialectic between consciousness and unconsciousness is *already* a defining feature of psychoanalytic technique, although once again it has not yet sufficiently found its way into our publicly endorsed conceptions of psychoanalysis.

Of note, I have added the further specification that we maintain the aforementioned dialectic *with patients, in the analytic relationship, and in ourselves*. When preserving this polarity with patients, we work technically to explore and elaborate patients' conscious and unconscious dynamics, and how they simultaneously enrich, define, and negate each other in patients' lives (see Chapter 7). When upholding this opposition in the dyad, we make sure to direct attention to patients' conscious experiences of the relationship, as well as the ways in which these experiences express, reveal, transform, and contradict the non-conscious and unformulated aspects of their subjectivity. And when affirming this dialectic in ourselves, we work to consider our conscious experiences of our patients—how we see them; how we feel with them; our desires and longings in connection with them; our formulations and interpretations of their relational patterns; how we think we "should" be interacting with them, in order to best help them—and how such experiences mutually interact with our own unconscious processes, as they relate to our patients but also to our broader personalities in general, our own "foundational templates for relatedness" that continuously inform our approach to clinical technique.

It is important to note that I am not saying anything about whether these dialectics must be maintained *explicitly*. For many patients and analytic dyads, we will have ample opportunity to consider the dialectical association between consciousness and unconsciousness, with our patients and also in their experiences of the therapeutic relationship, in other words to "work in the transference." For other patients or at other times, that may be less possible or advisable, given the individual's intellectual abilities, concreteness of thought, or the presence of particularly pressing psychological symptoms (e.g., imminent risk of suicidality or homicidality, severe emotional dysregulation, certain presentations of psychosis) or psychosocial needs (e.g., homelessness, lack of social support, impaired functioning in the community) demanding more immediate attention. In such cases, as long as clinicians remain deeply attentive to the mutually interacting conscious and unconscious processes unfolding in the patient, in the relationship, and in themselves, and as long as they feel like they are concurrently aiming at functional improvement *and* transformation of the person's unconscious dynamics, they would be expressing the tension between consciousness and unconsciousness and thus, on the present definition, working psychoanalytically.

The above model has several strengths as a definition of psychoanalysis. First, it appears to encompass empirical findings on the distinguishing features of psychoanalytic praxis, including our focus on patients' emotional lives, developmental history, interpersonal relationships, defensive operations, fantasies, transference experiences, and patterns in "actions, thoughts, feelings, experiences, and relationships" (Blagys & Hilsenroth, 2000, p. 167; see also Shedler, 2010), domains that all transcend any binary distinction between consciousness and unconsciousness. This proposal also leaves space for the technical "controversies" that have beset different psychoanalytic schools, including the extent to which we should work primarily in the transference; the role that explicit interpretation should play in clinical technique; how warm, validating, and gratifying we should be with our patients; the place of transparency, self-disclosure, and self-expressiveness in our therapeutic approaches; and the amount of attention we should direct to the various dimensions of patients' experiences, such as interpersonal relationships, behavioral patterns outside of the treatment, the past versus the present, and patients' conscious experience versus "deeper" unconscious processes. Wherever we stand in these debates, if we are fundamentally committed to utilizing the dialectic between consciousness and unconsciousness *as the principal manner of helping our patients*, we will be employing a psychoanalytic approach. This amounts to a "big tent" vision of psychoanalysis, in which diverse technical methods can all be encompassed within a more inclusive model, as recently advocated by Aron and Starr (2013):

> Our commonality provides a "family resemblance" that allows abundant room for difference and disagreement while maintaining a common sensibility. Difference, conflict, and variety may then be studied and contained by the systemic application of "comparative psychoanalysis" rather than by defining psychoanalysis in a way that disowns members of the family.
>
> (p. 378)

One interesting implication of the above definition is that it expands the range of technical interventions that qualify as genuinely psychoanalytic. Consider some of the more "practical" interventions—for example, cognitive restructuring, behavioral scheduling, exposure-based strategies, problem solving, skills building, advice giving, support and nurturance, social work case management—that are geared towards altering patients' conscious beliefs or symptomatology, or towards directly improving psychological or psychosocial functioning in the community. According to relational formulations that define psychoanalysis in terms of unconscious exploration, these interventions might be entirely consistent with an analytic orientation, as long as the practitioner employing them possesses the requisite subjective intention to elaborate non-conscious processes. The present dialectical conception goes somewhat further on this front. Provided that the clinician employs such interventions as a technical expression of the dialectic between consciousness and unconsciousness, these interventions would be helping to *constitute* that dialectic, and thus they would be psychoanalytic in and of themselves, rather than simply "permissible" within the context of an analytic treatment. On this view, at least some consciously oriented interventions would be *necessary* in order to affirm the paradox between consciousness and unconsciousness, and so they would obtain some sort of technical and cultural "equality" with more exploratory, unconsciously oriented interventions.

Despite the relative inclusivity of the present model, it clearly delineates what might be regarded as *non-psychoanalytic* approaches. For example, in traditional cognitive behavioral therapies (e.g., CBT, DBT, ACT), the clinician usually considers the patient from a more conscious, functional, and behavioral perspective, while largely ignoring the transference and the clinician's own unconscious dynamics in the dyad. In such cases, the clinician is likely collapsing the dialectic between consciousness and unconsciousness, and so it would be difficult to see the treatment as psychoanalytic in nature. This point also applies to purportedly analytic treatments in which we shift to an exclusive focus on behavior change and functionality, without much (explicit or implicit) recognition of unconscious processes in the patient, ourselves, or the therapeutic relationship.

Perhaps more controversially, the present model also has some surprising implications for certain treatments that could serve as the stereotype of the quintessential "psychoanalytic" technique. I am thinking of those treatments, for example Jonathan's relationship with his analyst discussed in Chapter 7, where the clinician is primarily interested in the patient's unconscious dynamics, employing a more interpretive, past-focused, and transferential technical stance, while directing comparatively minimal attention to the patient's conscious experiences, symptomatology, behavioral patterns, current quality of life, and overall level of functionality outside of the treatment. In my view, by substantially overvaluing patients' unconscious realms, such treatments threaten to collapse the dialectic between consciousness and unconsciousness, and thus, based on the present dialectical vision of psychoanalysis, would be paradoxically *less* psychoanalytic, regardless of the analyst's training, pedigree, and culturally sanctioned "analytic" approach.

This dialectical formulation has potentially important implications for psychoanalytic theorizing considered more generally. If we conceptualize psychoanalysis as a discipline that, at its heart, affirms and explores the dialectical nature of mind, then we must begin to seriously consider some fundamental questions about the nature and phenomenology of conscious experience. *What is consciousness? How do we understand its functions, processes, and distinctive mechanisms of stasis and change? How might we think about the various dimensions of consciousness (e.g., belief states, emotions, longings, values, deliberation and choice)—their interaction with each other, as well their complex, bidirectional relationship with unconscious motivation? What can we say about the phenomenology of freedom, and the foundational role this experience plays in our identity as agents and subjects in the world? And where do health and illness come into all of this? What are the conscious and unconscious expressions of such processes, the ways that psychological well-being and pathology express and reveal themselves across multiple levels of subjective and relational life?*

From a technical perspective, as I have suggested, many of us are already embracing a more dialectical stance, and yet apart from some notable exceptions (Bateman & Fonagy, 2016; Wachtel, 2014), our theories of technique primarily emphasize the elaboration of non-conscious processes. On the present dialectical view, we are called upon to articulate our operative technical principles about how to explore and elaborate unconscious *and* conscious processes, as well as their dynamic connection with one another. In clinical writing, we would start to communicate more transparently about what it actually *looks like* to employ a technically dialectical method, including openly discussing our employment of interventions geared mainly towards conscious experience. We can no longer dismiss more active, consciously oriented, "evidence-based" modalities by saying, "That's not psychoanalysis." Such models are actually expressing an incomplete *part* of psychoanalysis, and our task is to selectively integrate these interventions with our principles of unconscious exploration to arrive at a more encompassing, expansive technical approach that is able to represent, explore, and evolve these dual aspects of our patients' subjective worlds.

In this book, I have outlined a particular conception of the psychoanalytic subject centering on the notion of human dignity—our natural sense that we possess an unconditional, intrinsic worth as persons, independently of anything we do, say, think, feel, desire, or achieve, but simply in virtue of *who we are* as human beings. Due to our reflexive awareness of ourselves as free agents, we all have something of a window into this dignity, a feeling that we ourselves are a *source* of meaning and value in our lives, rather than merely a receptacle for other people's meanings and values. However, the multiplicity and contextuality of human experience throw a wrench into the works here. Like all people, our caregivers ascribe diverse, often contradictory values (e.g., unconditionally positive, unconditionally negative, conditionally positive, conditionally negative) to a wide range of internal and external configurations of Self and Other, such that they naturally value *themselves and us* in a manner that does not fully reflect our unconditional worth as human beings. We thus come to value ourselves and others conditionally—*I am only worthwhile if I take certain actions, possess specific qualities, achieve these observable things, engage in my relationships in particular ways, receive distinct types of responses from other people. You are valuable only under certain conditions as well, and especially when you are helping me feel good about myself in the ways that I need.* We also ascribe conditional *negative* value to ourselves and others—*I am bad and unworthy if I take certain actions, possess specific qualities, fail to achieve these observable things, engage in my relationships in particular ways, receive distinct types of responses from other people. You are bad under certain conditions as well, but especially when you are making me feel bad about myself and who I am.* Finally, we also ascribe unconditional *badness* to ourselves and others. We thus feel shame: *I am bad, worthless, and defective in an essential way. If you were to truly know me, you would be disgusted with who I am. You would never love me, and you would never want to be close to me.* And we feel hatred: *You are a worthless piece of shit who is unworthy of love. I want to destroy you, to make you suffer, to expose you in all of your badness.*

On this view, there is a fundamental paradox at the heart of human experience—the tension between our natural sense of intrinsic worth and our conviction that we are actually only *conditionally* valuable, and perhaps even inherently bad. As I have proposed, when we are able to deeply engage in a formative relationship in which the caregiver is able to value herself and us unconditionally, then we develop the capacity to value ourselves and others intrinsically and unconditionally, simply in virtue of "who we are" as people (see Chapters 3 and 4). We are thus able to "stand in the spaces" between a shared recognition of dignity and all of those other forms of valuing mentioned above. *Even if I fail in this way, and even if you withdraw your love from me, I might still be worthwhile as a person. And even if* you *lack the qualities that I value, or if you fail to give me what I need from you, you could still be worthwhile as a person. I might sometimes feel like I do not deserve love and care from you, or that you deserve only my hatred and disdain, but I can continue to hold on to an experience of us together as truly mattering, to each other but also as human beings in general, who are worthwhile and deserving of love in this world.*

On the other hand, when the caregiver is unable to value herself and the child unconditionally (e.g., in cases of trauma and neglect), the aforementioned forms of valuing become not just one of many relational possibilities for the child—they become the experiential *truth* about the child's sense of value. This is the realm of severe pathology—in that state, some specific factor (e.g., physical attractiveness, professional success, certain forms of interpersonal engagement) is the unequivocal *source* of the person's value, and the basis for valuing others as well. The individual *is* bad when such conditions are not met, and other people are bad as well. And deep down in her bones, the individual *knows* she is worthless and defective, unworthy of the love and care from others that she desperately needs in order to survive.

This all amounts to an ethical vision of health and pathology. On this model, psychological well-being constitutes an ethical achievement—the ability to value Self and Other even in the face of our shared frailty and damagedness. And pathology always involves some ethical vulnerability—the tendency to enact violence onto ourselves and others, to undermine the basic worth of the person in the domains of psychology and behavior. Psychoanalysis thus becomes a project of ethical restoration, a collaborative process that enables both parties to value Self and Other under a wider range of conditions, thus becoming progressively more responsive to the essential value of the human person. One person at time, we are helping our patients attain a more just and humane relationship to themselves and other human beings, thus playing some part in healing the wounds that divide us from one another as people.

This ethical formulation offers one explanation of what makes psychoanalysis such a powerful, unique, and ultimately indispensable method of healing in human life. As traditionally implemented, most other sources of help and support (e.g., religion, political action, community service, case management, cognitive behavioral treatments, support groups, close friendships and family relationships) tend to operate primarily at the level of conscious and reality-based experience, devoting minimal explicit attention to "helping" at the level of the unconscious. In contrast, by employing the dialectic between consciousness and unconsciousness as the primary framework for helping our patients, psychoanalysis is able to apprehend the ways in which we are continuously enacting violence against ourselves and others in the conscious *and* nonconscious realms. And of course, when we are able to access and represent these forms of devaluation, we are then in a position to begin to transform and evolve them. By maintaining the dialectic between consciousness and unconsciousness in the therapeutic process, psychoanalysis is widening the scope of healing in human experience, offering a deeper, more expansive form of liberation in the lives of our patients, and in the broader relational world.

Notes

1 In partial support of this interpretation, it is interesting to note that one of the central dialectics repeatedly emphasized in Greenberg and Mitchell's (1983) revolutionary *Object Relations in Psychoanalytic Theory* is the dialectic between the innate and the experiential. Greenberg and Mitchell (1983) argued that, while the drive/structure model conceptualizes mind in terms of a priori motivational content that precedes experience, the relational/structure model views mind as deriving primarily from the unique contextual and developmental experiences of the specific person (see pp. 219–230). Since experience implies consciousness by definition, Greenberg and Mitchell (1983) were thus linking relationality with conscious experience, an association that has persisted and has likely contributed to many clinicians seeing relational theory as a more accessible and "experience-near" clinical orientation.

2 While it is difficult for me to imagine how someone would attain such an appreciation without *themselves* receiving analytic treatment, the present conception does not specify anything about the particular route that clinicians must take to arrive at such a position. In this way, I am shying away from the more "extrinsic" formulations of psychoanalysis, while also working against the tendency towards what J. H. Slavin and Rahmani (2015) call *psychoanalytic exceptionalism*, or the viewpoint that analysis constitutes the exclusive vehicle for genuine self-development and healing in human experience.

References

Abend, S. M. (2009). Freud, transference, and therapeutic action. *Psychoanalytic Quarterly, 78*, 871–892.

Aggarwal, N. K. (2011). Intersubjectivity, transference, and the cultural third. *Contemporary Psychoanalysis, 47*, 204–223.

Aldao, A., Nolen-Hoeksema, S., & Schweizer, S. (2010). Emotion-regulation strategies across psychopathology: A meta-analytic review. *Clinical Psychology Review, 30*, 217–237.

Allen, J. G. (2013). Psychotherapy is an ethical endeavor: Balancing science and humanism in clinical practice. *Bulletin of the Menninger Clinic, 77*, 103–131.

Altman, N. (1995). *The analyst in the inner city: Race, class, and culture through a psychoanalytic lens*. Hillsdale, NJ: Analytic Press.

Altman, N. (2015). *Psychoanalysis in an age of accelerating cultural change: Spiritual globalization*. London, UK: Routledge.

Anderson, F. S. (Ed.). (2008). *Bodies in treatment: The unspoken dimension*. New York, NY: Analytic Press.

Argyris, C., & Schön, D. A. (1974). *Theory in practice: Increasing professional effectiveness*. San Francisco, CA: Jossey-Bass.

Aron, L. (1991). The patient's experience of the analyst's subjectivity. *Psychoanalytic Dialogues, 1*, 29–51.

Aron, L. (1995). The internalized primal scene. *Psychoanalytic Dialogues, 5*, 195–237.

Aron, L. (1996a). *A meeting of minds: Mutuality in psychoanalysis*. Hillsdale, NJ: Analytic Press.

Aron, L. (1996b). Symposium on the meaning and practice of intersubjectivity in psychoanalysis: Introduction. *Psychoanalytic Dialogues, 6*, 591–597.

Aron, L. (1999). Clinical choices and the relational matrix. *Psychoanalytic Dialogues, 9*, 1–29.

Aron, L. (2000). Self-reflexivity and the therapeutic action of psychoanalysis. *Psychoanalytic Psychology, 17*, 667–689.

Aron, L. (2005). The tree of knowledge: Good and evil: Conflicting interpretations. *Psychoanalytic Dialogues, 15*, 681–707.

Aron, L. (2015, November 16). Re: The politics of enigma [Online forum comment]. IARPP Online Colloquium on the work of Galit Atlas, *Turning up the heat: Enigmatic and pragmatic registers of sex and desire*. Retrieved from http://iarpp.net/colloquium/turning-up-the-heat-enigmatic-and-pragmatic-registers-of-sex-and-desire/

Aron, L. (2016a). Ethical considerations in psychoanalytic writing revisited. *Psychoanalytic Perspectives*, *13*, 267–290.

Aron, L. (2016b). Mutual vulnerability: An ethic of clinical practice. In D. M. Goodman & E. R. Severson (Eds.), *The ethical turn: Otherness and subjectivity in contemporary psychoanalysis* (pp. 19–41). London, UK: Routledge.

Aron, L., & Anderson, F. S. (Eds.). (1998). *Relational perspectives on the body*. Hillsdale, NJ: Analytic Press.

Aron, L., & Starr, K. (2013). *A psychotherapy for the people: Toward a progressive psychoanalysis*. New York, NY: Routledge.

Atlas, G., & Aron, L. (2017). *Dramatic dialogue: Contemporary clinical practice*. London, UK: Routledge.

Atwood, G. E., & Stolorow, R. D. (1979). *Faces in a cloud: Intersubjectivity in personality theory*. Northvale, NJ: Aronson.

Ayer, A. J. (1936). *Language, truth and logic*. New York, NY: Dover.

Bacal, H. A. (Ed.). (1998). *Optimal responsiveness: How therapists heal their patients*. Northvale, NJ: Aronson.

Bacal, H. A. (2011). *The power of specificity in psychotherapy: When therapy works and when it doesn't*. Lanham, MD: Aronson.

Bacciagaluppi, M. (1989). Erich Fromm's views on psychoanalytic "technique." *Contemporary Psychoanalysis*, *25*, 226–243.

Badcock, C. R. (1986). *The problem of altruism: Freudian-Darwinian solutions*. Oxford, UK: Blackwell.

Bader, M. J. (1996). Altruistic love in psychoanalysis: Opportunities and resistance. *Psychoanalytic Dialogues*, *6*, 741–764.

Balint, M. (1968). *The basic fault: Therapeutic aspects of regression*. New York, NY: Brunner/Mazel.

Barsness, R. E. (Ed.). (2018). *Core competencies of relational psychoanalysis: A guide to practice, study, and research*. London, UK: Routledge.

Bass, A. (2012). Negotiating otherness: The analyst's contribution to creating new ways of being and relating in the analytic process: Commentary on paper by Frank Summers. *Psychoanalytic Dialogues*, *22*, 162–170.

Bateman, A., & Fonagy, P. (2004). *Psychotherapy for borderline personality disorder: Mentalization-based treatment*. Oxford, UK: Oxford University Press.

Bateman, A., & Fonagy, P. (Eds.). (2012). *Handbook of mentalizing in mental health practice*. Washington, DC: American Psychiatric Publishing.

Bateman, A., & Fonagy, P. (2016). *Mentalization-based treatment for personality disorders: A practical guide*. Oxford, UK: Oxford University Press.

Beebe, B., Knoblauch, S., Rustin, J., & Sorter, D. (2005). *Forms of intersubjectivity in infant research and adult treatment*. New York, NY: Other Press.

Beebe, B., & Lachmann, F. M. (2002). *Infant research and adult treatment: Co-constructing interactions*. Hillsdale, NJ: Analytic Press.

Benjamin, J. (1988). *The bonds of love: Psychoanalysis, feminism, and the problem of domination*. New York, NY: Pantheon Books.

Benjamin, J. (1995). *Like subjects, love objects: Essays on recognition and sexual difference*. New Haven, CT: Yale University Press.

Benjamin, J. (1997). Psychoanalysis as a vocation. *Psychoanalytic Dialogues, 7*, 781–802.
Benjamin, J. (1998). *Shadow of the other: Intersubjectivity and gender in psychoanalysis*. New York, NY: Routledge.
Benjamin, J. (1999). Afterword to "Recognition and destruction: An outline of intersubjectivity." In S. A. Mitchell & L. Aron (Eds.), *Relational psychoanalysis: The emergence of a tradition* (pp. 201–210). Hillsdale, NJ: Analytic Press.
Benjamin, J. (2000). Intersubjective distinctions: Subjects and persons, recognitions and breakdowns: Commentary on paper by Gerhardt, Sweetnam, and Borton. *Psychoanalytic Dialogues, 10*, 43–55.
Benjamin, J. (2002). The rhythm of recognition: Comments on the work of Louis Sander. *Psychoanalytic Dialogues, 12*, 43–53.
Benjamin, J. (2004). Beyond doer and done to: An intersubjective view of thirdness. *Psychoanalytic Quarterly, 73*, 5–46.
Benjamin, J. (2009). A relational psychoanalysis perspective on the necessity of acknowledging failure in order to restore the facilitating and containing features of the intersubjective relationship (the shared third). *International Journal of Psychoanalysis, 90*, 441–450.
Benjamin, J. (2010). Where's the gap and what's the difference? The relational view of intersubjectivity, multiple selves, and enactments. *Contemporary Psychoanalysis, 46*, 112–119.
Benjamin, J. (2011). Acknowledgment of collective trauma in light of dissociation and dehumanization. *Psychoanalytic Perspectives, 8*, 207–214.
Benjamin, J. (2018). *Beyond doer and done to: Recognition theory, intersubjectivity and the third*. London, UK: Routledge.
Bentham, J. (1988). *A fragment on government*. Cambridge, UK: Cambridge University Press. (Original work published 1776.)
Ben-Ze'ev, A. (2000). *The subtlety of emotions*. Cambridge, MA: MIT Press.
Besser-Jones, L. (2014). *Eudaimonic ethics: The philosophy and psychology of living well*. New York, NY: Routledge.
Besser-Jones, L., & Slote, M. (Eds.). (2015). *The Routledge companion to virtue ethics*. New York, NY: Routledge.
Bion, W. (2013). *Los Angeles seminars and supervision*. London, UK: Karnac.
Blagys, M. D., & Hilsenroth, M. J. (2000). Distinctive features of short-term psychodynamic-interpersonal psychotherapy: A review of the comparative psychotherapy process literature. *Clinical Psychology: Science and Practice, 7*, 167–188.
Bok, H. (1998). *Freedom and responsibility*. Princeton, NJ: Princeton University Press.
Bok, S. (1995). *Common values*. Columbia, MO: University of Missouri Press.
Boston Change Process Study Group. (2002). Explicating the implicit: The local level and the microprocess of change in the analytic situation. *International Journal of Psychoanalysis, 83*, 1051–1062.
Boston Change Process Study Group. (2005). The "something more" than interpretation revisited: Sloppiness and co-creativity in the psychoanalytic encounter. *Journal of the American Psychoanalytic Association, 53*, 693–729.
Boston Change Process Study Group. (2007). The foundational level of psychodynamic meaning: Implicit process in relation to conflict, defense and the dynamic unconscious. *International Journal of Psychoanalysis, 88*, 843–860.

Boston Change Process Study Group. (2008). Forms of relational meaning: Issues in the relations between the implicit and reflective-verbal domains. *Psychoanalytic Dialogues, 18*, 125–148.

Boston Change Process Study Group. (2010). *Change in psychotherapy: A unifying paradigm*. New York, NY: Norton.

Bowlby, J. (1969). *Attachment and loss: Vol. 1. Attachment*. New York, NY: Basic Books.

Bowlby, J. (1973). *Attachment and loss: Vol. 2. Separation: Anxiety and anger*. New York, NY: Basic Books.

Bradley, B. (2006). Two concepts of intrinsic value. *Ethical Theory and Moral Practice, 9*, 111–130.

Bråten, S. (1998). Infant learning by altero-centric participation: The reverse of egocentric observation in autism. In S. Bråten (Ed.), *Intersubjective communication and emotion in early ontogeny* (pp. 105–124). Cambridge, UK: Cambridge University Press.

Braude, S. E. (1991). *First person plural: Multiple personality and the philosophy of mind*. London, UK: Routledge.

Breuer, J., & Freud, S. (1893–1895). Studies on hysteria. In J. Strachey (Ed. & Trans.), *The standard edition of the complete psychological works of Sigmund Freud* (Vol. 2). London, UK: Hogarth Press.

Brink, D. O. (2006). Some forms and limits of consequentialism. In D. Copp (Ed.), *The Oxford handbook of ethical theory* (pp. 380–423). Oxford, UK: Oxford University Press.

Bromberg, P. M. (1980). Sullivan's concept of consensual validation and the therapeutic action of psychoanalysis. *Contemporary Psychoanalysis, 16*, 237–248.

Bromberg, P. M. (1998). *Standing in the spaces: Essays on clinical process, trauma, and dissociation*. Hillsdale, NJ: Analytic Press.

Bromberg, P. M. (2006). *Awakening the dreamer: Clinical journeys*. Mahwah, NJ: Analytic Press.

Bromberg, P. M. (2010). Minding the dissociative gap. *Contemporary Psychoanalysis, 46*, 19–31.

Bromberg, P. M. (2011). *The shadow of the tsunami and the growth of the relational mind*. New York, NY: Routledge.

Canestri, J. (Ed.). (2006). *Psychoanalysis: From practice to theory*. Chichester, UK: Wiley & Sons.

Celenza, A. (2007). *Sexual boundary violations: Therapeutic, supervisory, and academic contexts*. Lanham, MD: Jason Aronson.

Choi-Kain, L. W., Albert, E. B., & Gunderson, J. G. (2016). Evidence-based treatments for borderline personality disorder: Implementation, integration, and stepped care. *Harvard Review of Psychiatry, 24*, 342–356.

Coburn, W. J. (2002). A world of systems: The role of systemic patterns of experience in the therapeutic process. *Psychoanalytic Inquiry, 22*, 655–677.

Cooper, S. H. (1996). The thin blue line of the interpersonal-intrapsychic dialectic: Commentary on papers by Gerson and Spezzano. *Psychoanalytic Dialogues, 6*, 647–669.

Cooper, S. H. (2000). *Objects of hope: Exploring possibility and limit in psychoanalysis*. Hillsdale, NJ: Analytic Press.

Cooper, S. H. (2010). *A disturbance in the field: Essays in transference-countertransference engagement*. New York, NY: Routledge.

Cooper, S. H. (2016). *The analyst's experience of the depressive position: The melancholic errand of psychoanalysis*. London, UK: Routledge.

Copp, D. (1995). *Morality, normativity, and society*. Oxford, UK: Oxford University Press.

Crisp, R. (1992). Utilitarianism and the life of virtue. *Philosophical Quarterly*, *42*, 139–160.

Crumbley, A. (2011). A conversation with Jay Greenberg. *Psychoanalytic Psychology*, *28*, 175–182.

Dancy, J. (2004). *Moral particularism*. Oxford, UK: Oxford University Press.

Darwall, S. L. (1983). *Impartial reason*. Ithaca, NY: Cornell University Press.

Davies, J. M. (1994). Love in the afternoon: A relational reconsideration of desire and dread in the countertransference. *Psychoanalytic Dialogues*, *4*, 153–170.

Davies, J. M. (1996). Linking the "pre-analytic" with the postclassical: Integration, dissociation, and the multiplicity of unconscious process. *Contemporary Psychoanalysis*, *32*, 553–576.

Davies, J. M. (2004). Whose bad objects are we anyway? Repetition and our elusive love affair with evil. *Psychoanalytic Dialogues*, *14*, 711–732.

Davies, J. M. (2006). The times we sizzle, and the times we sigh: The multiple erotics of arousal, anticipation, and release. *Psychoanalytic Dialogues*, *16*, 665–686.

Davies, J. M. (2015). From Oedipus complex to Oedipal complexity: Reconfiguring (pardon the expression) the negative Oedipus complex and the disowned erotics of disowned sexualities. *Psychoanalytic Dialogues*, *25*, 265–283.

Denis, L. (2001). *Moral self-regard: Duties to oneself in Kant's moral theory*. New York, NY: Routledge.

Dennett, D. C. (1984). *Elbow room: The varieties of free will worth wanting*. Cambridge, MA: MIT Press.

Dewald, P. A., & Clark, R. W. (Eds.). (2001). *Ethics case book of the American Psychoanalytic Association*. New York, NY: American Psychoanalytic Association.

Donnelly, J. (2013). *Universal human rights in theory and practice* (3rd ed.). Ithaca, NY: Cornell University Press.

Drozek, R. P. (2010a). "Finding the value" in intersubjective and clinical process: Towards a valuational model of relational motivation: Reply to commentaries. *Psychoanalytic Dialogues*, *20*, 582–596.

Drozek, R. P. (2010b). Intersubjectivity theory and the dilemma of intersubjective motivation. *Psychoanalytic Dialogues*, *20*, 540–560.

Drozek, R. P. (2015a). The dialectics of dignity: Clinical applications: Reply to commentaries. *Psychoanalytic Dialogues*, *25*, 472–480.

Drozek, R. P. (2015b). The dignity in multiplicity: Human value as a foundational concept in relational thought. *Psychoanalytic Dialogues*, *25*, 431–451.

Drozek, R. P. (2018). Psychoanalysis as an ethical process: Ethical intersubjectivity and therapeutic action. *Psychoanalytic Dialogues*, *28*, 538–556.

Eagle, M. N. (1984). *Recent developments in psychoanalysis: A critical evaluation*. New York, NY: McGraw-Hill.

Fairbairn, W. R. D. (1952). *Psychoanalytic studies of the personality*. Hove, UK: Brunner-Routledge.

Fairbairn, W. R. D. (1958). On the nature and aims of psycho-analytical treatment. *International Journal of Psycho-Analysis*, *39*, 374–385.

Fenichel, O. (1941). *Problems in psychoanalytic technique*. New York, NY: Psychoanalytic Quarterly.

Ferenczi, S. (1988). *The clinical diary of Sándor Ferenczi* (M. Balint & N. Z. Jackson, Trans.). J. Dupont (Ed.). Cambridge, MA: Harvard University Press. (Original work published 1932.)

Foa, E. B., Yadin, E., & Lichner, T. K. (2012). *Exposure and response (ritual) prevention for obsessive-compulsive disorder: Therapist guide* (2nd ed.). New York, NY: Oxford University Press.

Foehl, J. C. (2010). The play's the thing: The primacy of process and the persistence of pluralism in contemporary psychoanalysis. *Contemporary Psychoanalysis, 46*, 48–86.

Foehl, J. C. (2014). A phenomenology of depth. *Psychoanalytic Dialogues, 24*, 289–303.

Fonagy, P. (1991). Thinking about thinking: Some clinical and theoretical considerations in the treatment of a borderline patient. *International Journal of Psycho-Analysis, 72*, 639–656.

Fonagy, P., Gergely, G., Jurist, E. L., & Target, M. (2002). *Affect regulation, mentalization, and the development of the self.* New York, NY: Other Press.

Fonagy, P., & Target, M. (2003). *Psychoanalytic theories: Perspectives from developmental psychopathology.* New York, NY: Routledge.

Fosshage, J. L. (1995). Countertransference as the analyst's experience of the analysand: Influence of listening perspectives. *Psychoanalytic Psychology, 12*, 375–391.

Fosshage, J. L. (1997). Listening/experiencing perspectives and the quest for a facilitating responsiveness. *Progress in Self Psychology, 13*, 33–55.

Frankfurt, H. G. (1988). *The importance of what we care about.* Cambridge, UK: Cambridge University Press.

Frederickson, J. (2009). Multiplicity and relational psychoanalysis: A Heideggerian response. In R. Frie & D. Orange (Eds.), *Beyond postmodernism: New dimensions in clinical theory and practice* (pp. 52–68). London, UK: Routledge.

Freud, A. (1946). *The ego and the mechanisms of defense.* New York, NY: International Universities Press.

Freud, S. (1900). The interpretation of dreams. In J. Strachey (Ed. & Trans.), *The standard edition of the complete psychological works of Sigmund Freud* (Vols. 4–5). London, UK: Hogarth Press.

Freud, S. (1905). Three essays on the theory of sexuality. In J. Strachey (Ed. & Trans.), *The standard edition of the complete psychological works of Sigmund Freud* (Vol. 7, pp. 123–246). London, UK: Hogarth Press.

Freud, S. (1910a). Five lectures on psycho-analysis. In J. Strachey (Ed. & Trans.), *The standard edition of the complete psychological works of Sigmund Freud* (Vol. 11, pp. 1–56). London, UK: Hogarth Press.

Freud, S. (1910b). Leonardo da Vinci and a memory of his childhood. In J. Strachey (Ed. & Trans.), *The standard edition of the complete psychological works of Sigmund Freud* (Vol. 11, pp. 57–138). London, UK: Hogarth Press.

Freud, S. (1911). Freud–Putnam correspondence. In N. G. Hale (Ed.), *James Jackson Putnam and psychoanalysis: Letters between Putnam and Sigmund Freud, Ernest Jones, William James, Sandor Ferenczi, and Morton Prince, 1877–1917* (pp. 83–202). Cambridge, MA: Harvard University Press.

Freud, S. (1912). Recommendations to physicians practising psycho-analysis. In J. Strachey (Ed. & Trans.), *The standard edition of the complete psychological works of Sigmund Freud* (Vol. 12, pp. 109–120). London, UK: Hogarth Press.

Freud, S. (1913). Totem and taboo: Some points of agreement between the mental lives of savages and neurotics. In J. Strachey (Ed. & Trans.), *The standard edition of the complete psychological works of Sigmund Freud* (Vol. 13, pp. 1–161). London, UK: Hogarth Press.

Freud, S. (1914). On narcissism: An introduction. In J. Strachey (Ed. & Trans.), *The standard edition of the complete psychological works of Sigmund Freud* (Vol. 14, pp. 67–102). London, UK: Hogarth Press.

Freud, S. (1915a). Freud–Putnam correspondence. In N. G. Hale (Ed.), *James Jackson Putnam and psychoanalysis: Letters between Putnam and Sigmund Freud, Ernest Jones, William James, Sandor Ferenczi, and Morton Prince, 1877–1917* (pp. 83–202). Cambridge, MA: Harvard University Press.

Freud, S. (1915b). Repression. In J. Strachey (Ed. & Trans.), *The standard edition of the complete psychological works of Sigmund Freud* (Vol. 14, pp. 141–158). London, UK: Hogarth Press.

Freud, S. (1915c). The unconscious. In J. Strachey (Ed. & Trans.), *The standard edition of the complete psychological works of Sigmund Freud* (Vol. 14, pp. 159–215). London, UK: Hogarth Press.

Freud, S. (1917). Introductory lectures on psycho-analysis (part III). In J. Strachey (Ed. & Trans.), *The standard edition of the complete psychological works of Sigmund Freud* (Vol. 16, pp. 241–496). London, UK: Hogarth Press.

Freud, S. (1918). From the history of an infantile neurosis. In J. Strachey (Ed. & Trans.), *The standard edition of the complete psychological works of Sigmund Freud* (Vol. 17, pp. 1–124). London, UK: Hogarth Press.

Freud, S. (1919a, May 27). Letter from Sigmund Freud to Oskar Pfister. In E. L. Freud (Ed.), *Letters of Sigmund Freud, 1873–1939* (p. 70). London, UK: Hogarth Press.

Freud, S. (1919b). The "uncanny." In J. Strachey (Ed. & Trans.), *The standard edition of the complete psychological works of Sigmund Freud* (Vol. 17, pp. 217–256). London, UK: Hogarth Press.

Freud, S. (1920). Beyond the pleasure principle. In J. Strachey (Ed. & Trans.), *The standard edition of the complete psychological works of Sigmund Freud* (Vol. 18, pp. 1–64). London, UK: Hogarth Press.

Freud, S. (1921). Group psychology and the analysis of the ego. In J. Strachey (Ed. & Trans.), *The standard edition of the complete psychological works of Sigmund Freud* (Vol. 18, pp. 65–144). London, UK: Hogarth Press.

Freud, S. (1923a). The ego and the id. In J. Strachey (Ed. & Trans.), *The standard edition of the complete psychological works of Sigmund Freud* (Vol. 19, pp. 1–66). London, UK: Hogarth Press.

Freud, S. (1923b). A seventeenth-century demonological neurosis. In J. Strachey (Ed. & Trans.), *The standard edition of the complete psychological works of Sigmund Freud* (Vol. 19, pp. 67–106). London, UK: Hogarth Press.

Freud, S. (1923c). Two encyclopaedia articles. In J. Strachey (Ed. & Trans.), *The standard edition of the complete psychological works of Sigmund Freud* (Vol. 18, pp. 233–260). London, UK: Hogarth Press.

Freud, S. (1925a). The resistances to psycho-analysis. In J. Strachey (Ed. & Trans.), *The standard edition of the complete psychological works of Sigmund Freud* (Vol. 19, pp. 211–224). London, UK: Hogarth Press.

Freud, S. (1925b). Some additional notes on dream-interpretation as a whole. In J. Strachey (Ed. & Trans.), *The standard edition of the complete psychological works of Sigmund Freud* (Vol. 19, pp. 123–138). London, UK: Hogarth Press.

Freud, S. (1930). Civilization and its discontents. In J. Strachey (Ed. & Trans.), *The standard edition of the complete psychological works of Sigmund Freud* (Vol. 21, pp. 57–146). London, UK: Hogarth Press.

Freud, S. (1933). New introductory lectures on psycho-analysis. In J. Strachey (Ed. & Trans.), *The standard edition of the complete psychological works of Sigmund Freud* (Vol. 22, pp. 1–182). London, UK: Hogarth Press.

Freud, S. (1938). An outline of psycho-analysis. In J. Strachey (Ed. & Trans.), *The standard edition of the complete psychological works of Sigmund Freud* (Vol. 23, pp. 139–208). London, UK: Hogarth Press.

Freud, S. (1939). Moses and monotheism: Three essays. In J. Strachey (Ed. & Trans.), *The standard edition of the complete psychological works of Sigmund Freud* (Vol. 23, pp. 1–138). London, UK: Hogarth Press.

Frie, R. (Ed.). (2008). *Psychological agency: Theory, practice, and culture*. Cambridge, MA: MIT Press.

Friedman, L. (2002). Psychoanalysis: Practice and technique. *Journal of the American Psychoanalytic Association*, *50*, 727–732.

Fromm, E. (1947). *Man for himself: An inquiry into the psychology of ethics*. New York, NY: Holt.

Fromm, E. (1950). *Psychoanalysis and religion*. New Haven, CT: Yale University Press.

Fromm, E. (1991). Causes for the patient's change in analytic treatment. *Contemporary Psychoanalysis*, *27*, 581–601.

Fromm, E. (1994). *The art of listening*. New York, NY: Continuum.

Gabbard, G. O., & Crisp, H. (2018). *Narcissism and its discontents: Diagnostic dilemmas and treatment strategies with narcissistic patients*. Washington, DC: American Psychiatric Association.

Gabbard, G. O., & Lester, E. P. (1995). *Boundaries and boundary violations in psychoanalysis*. New York, NY: Basic Books.

Gabbard, G. O., Westen, D. (2003). Rethinking therapeutic action. *International Journal of Psychoanalysis*, *84*, 823–841.

Gaztambide, D. J. (2012). "A psychotherapy for the people": Freud, Ferenczi, and psychoanalytic work with the underprivileged. *Contemporary Psychoanalysis*, *48*, 141–165.

Gentile, J. (2010). Weeds on the ruins: Agency, compromise formation, and the quest for intersubjective truth. *Psychoanalytic Dialogues*, *20*, 88–109.

Gerhardt, J., & Sweetnam, A. (2001). The intersubjective turn in psychoanalysis: A comparison of contemporary theorists: Part 2: Christopher Bollas. *Psychoanalytic Dialogues*, *11*, 43–92.

Gerhardt, J., Sweetnam, A., & Borton, L. (2000). The intersubjective turn in psychoanalysis: A comparison of contemporary theorists: Part 1: Jessica Benjamin. *Psychoanalytic Dialogues*, *10*, 5–42.

Gerhardt, J., Sweetnam, A., & Borton, L. (2003). The intersubjective turn in psychoanalysis: A comparison of contemporary theorists: Part 3: Darlene Bregman Ehrenberg. *Psychoanalytic Dialogues*, *13*, 533–577.

Ghent, E. (1989). Credo: The dialectics of one-person and two-person psychologies. *Contemporary Psychoanalysis*, *25*, 169–211.

Ghent, E. (1992). Paradox and process. *Psychoanalytic Dialogues*, *2*, 135–159.

Gibbard, A. (1990). *Wise choices, apt feelings: A theory of normative judgment*. Cambridge, MA: Harvard University Press.

Ginet, C. (1990). *On action*. Cambridge, UK: Cambridge University Press.

Glimcher, P. W., & Fehr, E. (Eds.). (2014). *Neuroeconomics: Decision making and the brain* (2nd ed.). London, UK: Elsevier.

Goodman, D. M., & Severson, E. R. (2016). *The ethical turn: Otherness and subjectivity in contemporary psychoanalysis*. London, UK: Routledge.

Goodwin, G. P., & Darley, J. M. (2008). The psychology of meta-ethics: Exploring objectivism. *Cognition*, *106*, 1339–1366.

Green, O. H. (1992). *The emotions: A philosophical theory*. Dordrecht, Netherlands: Kluwer Academic.

Greenberg, J. R. (1981). Prescription or description: The therapeutic action of psychoanalysis. *Contemporary Psychoanalysis*, *17*, 239–257.

Greenberg, J. (1991). *Oedipus and beyond: A clinical theory*. Cambridge, MA: Harvard University Press.

Greenberg, J. (1999). Analytic authority and analytic restraint. *Contemporary Psychoanalysis*, *35*, 25–41.

Greenberg, J. (2001). The analyst's participation: A new look. *Journal of the American Psychoanalytic Association*, *49*, 359–381.

Greenberg, J. (2008). Choice. *Journal of the American Psychoanalytic Association*, *56*, 690–707.

Greenberg, J. R., & Mitchell, S. A. (1983). *Object relations in psychoanalytic theory*. Cambridge, MA: Harvard University Press.

Grünbaum, A. (1984). *The foundations of psychoanalysis: A philosophical critique*. Berkeley, CA: University of California Press.

Harcourt, E. (2015). The place of psychoanalysis in the history of ethics. *Journal of Moral Philosophy*, *12*, 598–618.

Hare, R. M. (1963). *Freedom and reason*. New York, NY: Oxford University Press.

Harlem, A. (2015). Dignity in three acts. *Psychoanalytic Dialogues*, *25*, 452–462.

Harris, A. (2005). *Gender as soft assembly*. Hillsdale, NJ: Analytic Press.

Hartmann, H. (1958). *Ego psychology and the problem of adaptation*. New York, NY: International Universities Press.

Hartmann, H. (1960). *Psychoanalysis and moral values*. New York, NY: International Universities Press.

Held, V. (2006). *The ethics of care: Personal, political, and global*. Oxford, UK: Oxford University Press.

Herman, B. (1993). *The practice of moral judgment*. Cambridge, MA: Harvard University Press.

Hoffman, I. Z. (1995). Review of *Oedipus and beyond* by J. Greenberg. *Psychoanalytic Dialogues*, *5*, 93–112.

Hoffman, I. Z. (1998). *Ritual and spontaneity in the psychoanalytic process: A dialectical-constructivist view*. Hillsdale, NJ: Analytic Press.

Hoffman, I. Z. (2000). At death's door: Therapists and patients as agents. *Psychoanalytic Dialogues*, *10*, 823–846.

Hoffman, I. Z. (2006). The myths of free association and the potentials of the analytic relationship. *International Journal of Psychoanalysis*, *87*, 43–61.

Hoffman, I. Z. (2009a). Doublethinking our way to "scientific" legitimacy: The desiccation of human experience. *Journal of the American Psychoanalytic Association*, *57*, 1043–1069.

Hoffman, I. Z. (2009b). Therapeutic passion in the countertransference. *Psychoanalytic Dialogues*, *19*, 617–637.

Hoffman, I. Z. (2016). The risks of therapist passivity and the potentials of constructivist influence. *Psychoanalytic Dialogues*, *26*, 91–97.

Holt, R. R. (1989). *Freud reappraised: A fresh look at psychoanalytic theory*. New York, NY: Guilford.

Hooker, B. (2000a). *Ideal code, real world: A rule-consequentialist theory of morality*. Oxford, UK: Oxford University Press.

Hooker, B. (2000b). Rule-consequentialism. In H. LaFollette (Ed.), *The Blackwell guide to ethical theory* (pp. 183–204). Malden, MA: Blackwell.

Hooker, B., & Little, M. (Eds.). (2000). *Moral particularism*. Oxford, UK: Oxford University Press.

Ipp, H. (2010). Nell—A bridge to the amputated self: The impact of immigration on continuities and discontinuities of self. *International Journal of Psychoanalytic Self Psychology*, *5*, 373–386.

Jacobs, L. (2008). Dialogue, confirmation, and the "good." *International Journal of Psychoanalytic Self Psychology*, *3*, 409–431.

Jacobsen, E. (1964). *The self and the object world*. New York, NY: International Universities Press.

Jaggar, A. M. (2000). Feminist ethics. In H. LaFollette (Ed.), *The Blackwell guide to ethical theory* (pp. 348–374). Malden, MA: Blackwell.

James, W. (1950). *The principles of psychology* (Vol. 1). New York, NY: Dover. (Original work published 1890.)

Johnson, R. N. (2011). *Self-improvement: An essay in Kantian ethics*. Oxford, UK: Oxford University Press.

Kagan, S. (1989). *The limits of morality*. Oxford, UK: Oxford University Press.

Kamm, F. M. (2007). *Intricate ethics: Rights, responsibilities, and permissible harm*. Oxford, UK: Oxford University Press.

Kane, R. (1996). *The significance of free will*. Oxford, UK: Oxford University Press.

Kane, R. (2002a). Introduction: The contours of contemporary free will debates. In R. Kane (Ed.), *The Oxford handbook of free will* (pp. 3–41). Oxford, UK: Oxford University Press.

Kane, R. (2002b). Some neglected pathways in the free will labyrinth. In R. Kane (Ed.), *The Oxford handbook of free will* (pp. 406–437). Oxford, UK: Oxford University Press.

Kant, I. (1997). *Groundwork of the metaphysics of morals*. Cambridge, UK: Cambridge University Press. (Original work published 1785.)

Kant, I. (1998). *Religion within the boundaries of mere reason and other writings*. Cambridge, UK: Cambridge University Press. (Original work published 1793.)

Kant, I. (2012). *Lectures on anthropology*. Cambridge, UK: Cambridge University Press.

Kaplan-Solms, K., & Solms, M. (2000). *Clinical studies in neuro-psychoanalysis: Introduction to a depth neuropsychology*. Madison, WI: International Universities Press.

Kennedy, R. (1993). *Freedom to relate: Psychoanalytic explorations*. London, UK: Free Association Books.

Kennedy, R. (2010). Between subjects: Commentary on paper by Robert P. Drozek. *Psychoanalytic Dialogues, 20*, 561–568.

Kernberg, O. F. (1975). *Borderline conditions and pathological narcissism*. New York, NY: Aronson.

Kernberg, O. F. (1976). *Object-relations theory and clinical psychoanalysis*. New York, NY: Aronson.

Klein, G. S. (1976). *Psychoanalytic theory: An exploration of essentials*. New York, NY: International Universities Press.

Klein, M. (1975). *Love, guilt, and reparation, & other works, 1921–1945*. New York, NY: Delacorte.

Kohut, H. (1977). *The restoration of the self*. New York, NY: International Universities Press.

Kohut, H. (1981). On empathy. In P. H. Ornstein (Ed.), *The search for the self: Selected writings of Heinz Kohut: 1978–1981* (Vol. 4, pp. 525–535). Madison, CT: International Universities Press.

Kohut, H. (1984). *How does analysis cure?* Chicago, IL: University of Chicago Press.

Korsgaard, C. M. (1983). Two distinctions in goodness. *Philosophical Review, 92*, 169–195.

Korsgaard, C. M. (1996a). *Creating the kingdom of ends*. Cambridge, UK: Cambridge University Press.

Korsgaard, C. M. (1996b). *The sources of normativity*. Cambridge, UK: Cambridge University Press.

Korsgaard, C. M. (2009). *Self-constitution: Agency, identity, and integrity*. Oxford, UK: Oxford University Press.

Kriegman, D. (1990). Compassion and altruism in psychoanalytic theory: An evolutionary analysis of self psychology. *Journal of the American Academy of Psychoanalysis and Dynamic Psychiatry, 18*, 342–367.

Kuhn, T. (1977). *The essential tension*. Chicago, IL: University of Chicago Press.

LaFarge, L. (2014). How and why unconscious phantasy and transference are the defining features of psychoanalytic practice. *International Journal of Psychoanalysis, 95*, 1265–1278.

Layton, L., Hollander, N. C., & Gutwill, S. (2006). *Psychoanalysis, class and politics: Encounters in the clinical setting*. London, UK: Routledge.

Leary, K. (2000). Racial enactments in dynamic treatment. *Psychoanalytic Dialogues, 10*, 639–653.

Lebreton, M., Jorge, S., Michel, V., Thirion, B., & Pessiglione, M. (2009). An automatic valuation system in the human brain: Evidence from functional neuroimaging. *Neuron, 64*, 431–439.

Lemma, A., Target, M., & Fonagy, P. (2011). *Brief dynamic interpersonal therapy: A clinician's guide*. Oxford, UK: Oxford University Press.

Levinas, E. (1998). *Otherwise than being, or, beyond essence* (A. Lingis, Trans.). Pittsburgh, PA: Duquesne University Press. (Original work published 1981.)

Levy, D. J., & Glimcher, P. W. (2012). The root of all value: A neural common currency for choice. *Current Opinion in Neurobiology, 22*, 1027–1038.

Levy, D. J., & Glimcher, P. W. (2016). Common value representation: A neuroeconomic perspective. In T. Brosch & D. Sander (Eds.), *Handbook of value: Perspectives from*

economics, neuroscience, philosophy, psychology, and sociology (pp. 85–118). Oxford, UK: Oxford University Press.
Lichtenberg, J. D. (1989). *Psychoanalysis and motivation*. Hillsdale, NJ: Analytic Press.
Lichtenberg, J. D., Lachmann, F. M., & Fosshage, J. L. (1992). *Self and motivational systems: Toward a theory of psychoanalytic technique*. Hillsdale, NJ: Analytic Press.
Loewald, H. W. (1960). On the therapeutic action of psychoanalysis. *International Journal of Psycho-Analysis, 41*, 16–33.
Loewald, H. W. (1980). *Papers on psychoanalysis*. New Haven, CT: Yale University Press.
Loewald, H. W. (1988). *Sublimation: Inquiries into theoretical psychoanalysis*. New Haven, CT: Yale University Press.
Lyons-Ruth, K. (1999). The two-person unconscious: Intersubjective dialogue, enactive relational representation, and the emergence of new forms of relational organization. *Psychoanalytic Inquiry, 19*, 576–617.
Mahler, M. S., Pine, F., & Bergman, A. (1975). *The psychological birth of the human infant: Symbiosis and individuation*. New York, NY: Basic Books.
McWilliams, N. (1984). The psychology of the altruist. *Psychoanalytic Psychology, 1*, 193–213.
Meissner, W. W. (2003). *The ethical dimension of psychoanalysis: A dialogue*. Albany, NY: State University of New York Press.
Merriam-Webster's collegiate dictionary. (2014). (11th ed.). Springfield, MA: Merriam-Webster.
Mill, J. S. (1979). *Utilitarianism*. Indianapolis, IN: Hackett. (Original work published 1861.)
Mills, J. (Ed.). (2004). *Psychoanalysis at the limit: Epistemology, mind, and the question of science*. Albany, NY: State University of New York Press.
Mills, J. (Ed.). (2005). *Relational and intersubjective perspectives in psychoanalysis: A critique*. Lanham, MD: Aronson.
Mitchell, S. A. (1978). Psychodynamics, homosexuality and the question of pathology. *Psychiatry, 41*, 254–263.
Mitchell, S. A. (1987). Discussion. *Contemporary Psychoanalysis, 23*, 400–410.
Mitchell, S. A. (1988). *Relational concepts in psychoanalysis: An integration*. Cambridge, MA: Harvard University Press.
Mitchell, S. A. (1993). *Hope and dread in psychoanalysis*. New York, NY: Basic Books.
Mitchell, S. A. (1997). *Influence and autonomy in psychoanalysis*. Hillsdale, NJ: Analytic Press.
Mitchell, S. A. (1998). Fairbairn's object seeking: Between paradigms. In N. J. Skolnick & D. E. Scharff (Eds.), *Fairbairn, then and now* (pp. 115–135). Hillsdale, NJ: Analytic Press.
Mitchell, S. A. (2000a). Juggling paradoxes: Commentary on the work of Jessica Benjamin. *Studies in Gender and Sexuality, 1*, 251–269.
Mitchell, S. A. (2000b). *Relationality: From attachment to intersubjectivity*. Hillsdale, NJ: Analytic Press.
Mitchell, S. A. (2001). No search or getting down to business? *Psychoanalytic Quarterly, 70*, 183–199.
Mitchell, S. A. (2002). *Can love last? The fate of romance over time*. New York, NY: Norton.
Moll, J., Oliveira-Souza, D., & Zahn, R. (2008). The neural basis of moral cognition. *Annals of the New York Academy of Sciences, 1124*, 161–180.

Moore, G. E. (1912). *Ethics*. New York, NY: Holt.

Moore, G. E. (1922). *Philosophical studies*. London, UK: Routledge & Kegan Paul.

Moore, G. E. (1959). *Philosophical papers*. London, UK: Allen & Unwin.

Mor, N., & Winquist, J. (2002). Self-focused attention and negative affect: A meta-analysis. *Psychological Bulletin, 128*, 638–662.

Nagel, T. (1970). *The possibility of altruism*. Princeton, NJ: Princeton University Press.

Nagel, T. (1979). *Mortal questions*. Cambridge, UK: Cambridge University Press.

Nagel, T. (1986). *The view from nowhere*. New York, NY: Oxford University Press.

Natterson, J., & Friedman, R. J. (1995). *A primer of clinical intersubjectivity*. Northvale, NJ: Aronson.

Nichols, S., & Folds-Bennett, T. (2003). Are children moral objectivists? Children's judgments about moral and response-dependent properties. *Cognition, 90*, B23–B32.

Noddings, N. (2013). *Caring: A relational approach to ethics and moral education* (2nd ed., updated). Berkeley, CA: University of California Press.

Nucci, L. (2001). *Education in the moral domain*. Cambridge, UK: Cambridge University Press.

Nucci, L. P., & Turiel, E. (1978). Social interactions and the development of social concepts in preschool children. *Child Development, 49*, 400–407.

Nussbaum, M. C. (2001). *Upheavals of thought: The intelligence of emotions*. Cambridge, UK: Cambridge University Press.

O'Connor, T. (2000). *Persons and causes: The metaphysics of free will*. Oxford, UK: Oxford University Press.

Oddie, G. (2005). *Value, reality, and desire*. Oxford, UK: Oxford University Press.

Ogden, T. (1986). *The matrix of the mind: Object relations and the psychoanalytic dialogue*. Northvale, NJ: Aronson.

Ogden, T. (1994). *Subjects of analysis*. Northvale, NJ: Aronson.

Ogden, T. H. (2005). *This art of psychoanalysis: Dreaming undreamt dreams and interrupted cries*. London, UK: Routledge.

Orange, D. M. (1995). *Emotional understanding: Studies in psychoanalytic epistemology*. New York, NY: Guilford.

Orange, D. M. (2013). Those old wineskins: Greenberg and Mitchell on Heinz Kohut's "mixed model." *Contemporary Psychoanalysis, 49*, 103–112.

Orange, D. M. (2016). *Nourishing the inner life of clinicians and humanitarians: The ethical turn in psychoanalysis*. London, UK: Routledge.

Ornstein, P. H. (1993). Chapter 12: Chronic rage from underground: Reflections on its structure and treatment. *Progress in Self Psychology, 9*, 143–157.

Parfit, D. (1984). *Reasons and persons*. Oxford, UK: Oxford University Press.

Peters, J., & Büchel, C. (2010). Neural representations of subjective reward value. *Behavioural Brain Research, 213*, 135–141.

Pizer, S. A. (1998). *Building bridges: The negotiation of paradox in psychoanalysis*. Hillsdale, NJ: Analytic Press.

Quinn, W. (1993). *Morality and action*. Cambridge, UK: Cambridge University Press.

Rachels, J. (1998). Introduction. In J. Rachels (Ed.), *Ethical theory* (pp. 1–33). Oxford, UK: Oxford University Press.

Racker, H. (1968). *Transference and countertransference*. New York, NY: International Universities Press.

Radden, J. (1996). *Divided minds and successive selves: Ethical issues in disorders of identity and personality*. Cambridge, MA: MIT Press.

Radden, J. (2004). Identity: Personal identity, characterization identity, and mental disorder. In J. Radden (Ed.), *The philosophy of psychiatry: A companion* (pp. 133–146). Oxford, UK: Oxford University Press.

Radden, J. (2011). Multiple selves. In S. Gallagher (Ed.), *The Oxford handbook of the self* (pp. 547–570). Oxford, UK: Oxford University Press.

Radden, J., & Sadler, J. Z. (2010). *The virtuous psychiatrist: Character ethics in psychiatric practice*. Oxford, UK: Oxford University Press.

Rangel, A., Camerer, C., & Montague, P. R. (2008). A framework for studying the neurobiology of value-based decision making. *Nature Reviews Neuroscience, 9*, 545–556.

Rawls, J. (1971). *A theory of justice*. Cambridge, MA: Belknap.

Rawls, J. (2000). *Lectures on the history of moral philosophy*. Cambridge, MA: Harvard University Press.

Renik, O. (1993). Analytic interaction: Conceptualizing technique in light of the analyst's irreducible subjectivity. *Psychoanalytic Quarterly, 62*, 553–571.

Renik, O. (1996). The perils of neutrality. *Psychoanalytic Quarterly, 65*, 495–517.

Renik, O. (2006). *Practical psychoanalysis for therapists and patients*. New York, NY: Other Press.

Riker, J. H. (1997). *Ethics and the discovery of the unconscious*. Albany, NY: State University of New York Press.

Rizzolatti, G., Fogassi, L., & Gallese, V. (2001). Neurophysiological mechanisms underlying the understanding and imitation of action. *Nature Reviews Neuroscience, 2*, 661–670.

Roberts, R. C. (2003). *Emotions: An essay in aid of moral psychology*. Cambridge, UK: Cambridge University Press.

Rosen, M. (2012). *Dignity: Its history and meaning*. Cambridge, MA: Harvard University Press.

Ross, W. D. (1930). *The right and the good*. Oxford, UK: Oxford University Press.

Rovane, C. (1998). *The bounds of agency: An essay in revisionary metaphysics*. Princeton, NJ: Princeton University Press.

Ruff, C. C., & Fehr, E. (2014). The neurobiology of rewards and values in social decision making. *Nature Reviews Neuroscience, 15*, 549–562.

Russell, P. (1995). *Freedom and moral sentiment: Hume's way of naturalizing responsibility*. Oxford, UK: Oxford University Press.

Russell, P. L. (1973). *Crises of emotional growth (a.k.a. the theory of the crunch)*. Unpublished manuscript.

Rustin, J. (1997). Infancy, agency, and intersubjectivity: A view of therapeutic action. *Psychoanalytic Dialogues, 7*, 43–62.

Safran, J. D. (2012). *Psychoanalysis and psychoanalytic therapies*. Washington, DC: American Psychological Association.

Safran, J. D. (2016). Agency, surrender, and grace in psychoanalysis. *Psychoanalytic Psychology, 33*, 58–72.

Samuels, A. (2016). *The political psyche* (Classic ed.). London, UK: Routledge.

Sandler, J. (1976). Countertransference and role-responsiveness. *International Review of Psycho-Analysis, 3*, 43–47.

Sandler, J. (1983). Reflections on some relations between psychoanalytic concepts and psychoanalytic practice. *International Journal of Psycho-Analysis*, *64*, 35–45.

Sandler, J., Holder, A., Dare, C., & Dreher, A. U. (1997). *Freud's models of the mind: An introduction*. London, UK: Karnac.

Sandler, J., & Sandler, A.-M. (1998). *Internal objects revisited*. Madison, WI: International Universities Press.

Scanlon, T. M. (1998). *What we owe to each other*. Cambridge, MA: Harvard University Press.

Schafer, R. (1968). *Aspects of internalization*. New York, NY: International Universities Press.

Schafer, R. (1976). *A new language for psychoanalysis*. New Haven, CT: Yale University Press.

Schafer, R. (1983). *The analytic attitude*. New York, NY: Basic Books.

Scheffler, S. (1982). *The rejection of consequentialism*. Oxford, UK: Oxford University Press.

Scheffler, S. (1992). *Human morality*. Oxford, UK: Oxford University Press.

Schore, A. N. (1994). *Affect regulation and the origin of the self: The neurobiology of emotional development*. Hillsdale, NJ: Erlbaum.

Schore, A. N. (2003a). *Affect regulation and disorders of the self*. New York, NY: Norton.

Schore, A. N. (2003b). *Affect regulation and the repair of the self*. New York, NY: Norton.

Schwaber, E. A. (1981). Empathy: A mode of analytic listening. *Psychoanalytic Inquiry*, *1*, 357–392.

Schwaber, E. A. (1983). A particular perspective on analytic listening. *Psychoanalytic Study of the Child*, *38*, 519–546.

Schwaber, E. A. (1992). Countertransference: The analyst's retreat from the patient's vantage point. *International Journal of Psycho-Analysis*, *73*, 349–361.

Searles, H. F. (1979). The patient as therapist to his analyst. *Countertransference and related subjects* (pp. 380–459). Madison, WI: International Universities Press.

Seelig, B. J., & Rosof, L. S. (2001). Normal and pathological altruism. *Journal of the American Psychoanalytic Association*, *49*, 933–959.

Seligman, S. (2005). Dynamic systems theories as a metaframework for psychoanalysis. *Psychoanalytic Dialogues*, *15*, 285–319.

Shabad, P. (2001). *Despair and the return of hope: Echoes of mourning in psychotherapy*. Northvale, NJ: Aronson.

Shane, E., & Brothers, D. (2017). Prologue: The ethical turn. *Psychoanalytic Inquiry*, *37*, 357–358.

Shapiro, Y., & Gabbard, G. O. (1994). A reconsideration of altruism from an evolutionary and psychodynamic perspective. *Ethics & Behavior*, *4*, 23–42.

Shedler, J. (2010). The efficacy of psychodynamic psychotherapy. *American Psychologist*, *65*, 98–109.

Shengold, L. L. (1979). Child abuse and deprivation: Soul murder. *Journal of the American Psychoanalytic Association*, *27*, 533–559.

Siegel, D. J. (1999). *The developing mind: Toward a neurobiology of interpersonal experience*. New York, NY: Guilford.

Singer, P. (2011). *Practical ethics* (3rd ed.). Cambridge, UK: Cambridge University Press.

Slavin, J. H. (2010). Becoming an individual: Technically subversive thoughts on the role of the analyst's influence. *Psychoanalytic Dialogues*, *20*, 308–324.

Slavin, J. H., & Rahmani, M. (2015). "The legitimate guiding forces of one's behavior in the world": Discussion of "Generative enactment: Memories from the future" by Aron and Atlas. *Psychoanalytic Dialogues*, *25*, 325–334.

Slavin, M. O., & Kriegman, D. (1992). *The adaptive design of the human psyche: Psychoanalysis, evolutionary biology, and the therapeutic process*. New York, NY: Guilford.

Slavin, M. O., & Kriegman, D. (1998). Why the analyst needs to change: Toward a theory of conflict, negotiation, and mutual influence in the therapeutic process. *Psychoanalytic Dialogues*, *8*, 247–284.

Sletvold, J. (2014). *The embodied analyst: From Freud and Reich to relationality*. London, UK: Routledge.

Slochower, J. (2014). *Holding and psychoanalysis: A relational perspective* (2nd ed.). London, UK: Routledge.

Solms, M., & Turnbull, O. (2002). *The brain and the inner world: An introduction to the neuroscience of subjective experience*. New York, NY: Other Press.

Solomon, R. C. (1993). *The passions: Emotions and the meaning of life* (2nd ed.). Indianapolis, IN: Hackett.

Spence, D. P. (1982). *Narrative truth and historical truth: Meaning and interpretation in psychoanalysis*. New York, NY: Norton.

Spence, D. P. (1987). *The Freudian metaphor: Toward paradigm change in psychoanalysis*. New York, NY: Norton.

Spezzano, C. (1993). *Affect in psychoanalysis: A clinical synthesis*. Hillsdale, NJ: Analytic Press.

Stern, D. B. (1992). Commentary on constructivism in clinical psychoanalysis. *Psychoanalytic Dialogues*, *2*, 331–363.

Stern, D. B. (1997). *Unformulated experience: From dissociation to imagination in psychoanalysis*. Hillsdale, NJ: Analytic Press.

Stern, D. B. (2010). *Partners in thought: Working with unformulated experience, dissociation, and enactment*. New York, NY: Routledge.

Stern, D. B. (2012). Implicit theories of technique and the values that inspire them. *Psychoanalytic Inquiry*, *32*, 33–49.

Stern, D. B. (2015). *Relational freedom: Emergent properties of the interpersonal field*. London, UK: Routledge.

Stern, D. N. (1985). *The interpersonal world of the infant: A view from psychoanalysis and developmental psychology*. New York, NY: Basic Books.

Stern, D. N. (2004). *The present moment in psychotherapy and everyday life*. New York, NY: Norton.

Stern, D. N., Sander, L. W., Nahum, J. P., Harrison, A. M., Lyons-Ruth, K., Morgan, A. C., et al. (1998). Non-interpretive mechanisms in psychoanalytic therapy: The "something more" than interpretation. *International Journal of Psycho-Analysis*, *79*, 903–921.

Stevenson, C. L. (1944). *Ethics and language*. New Haven, CT: Yale University Press.

Stohr, K. (2015). Feminist virtue ethics. In L. Besser-Jones & M. Slote (Eds.), *The Routledge companion to virtue ethics* (pp. 271–282). New York, NY: Routledge.

Stolorow, R. D., & Atwood, G. E. (1992). *Contexts of being: The intersubjective foundations of psychological life*. Hillsdale, NJ: Analytic Press.

Stolorow, R. D., Brandchaft, B., & Atwood, G. E. (1995). *Psychoanalytic treatment: An intersubjective approach*. Hillsdale, NJ: Analytic Press.

Strachey, J. (1934). The nature of the therapeutic action of psycho-analysis. *International Journal of Psycho-Analysis*, *15*, 127–159.
Straker, G. (2011). Shaping subjectivities: Private memories, public archives. *Psychoanalytic Dialogues*, *21*, 643–657.
Strawson, P. F. (1974). *Freedom and resentment and other essays*. London, UK: Methuen.
Suchet, M. (2007). Unraveling whiteness. *Psychoanalytic Dialogues*, *17*, 867–886.
Sullivan, H. S. S. (1953). *The interpersonal theory of psychiatry*. New York, NY: Norton.
Sullivan, H. S. S. (1954). *The psychiatric interview*. New York, NY: Norton.
Summers, F. (2000). The analyst's vision of the patient and therapeutic action. *Psychoanalytic Psychology*, *17*, 547–564.
Tauber, A. I. (2010). *Freud, the reluctant philosopher*. Princeton, NJ: Princeton University Press.
Taylor, C. (1989). *The sources of the self: The making of the modern identity*. Cambridge, MA: Harvard University Press.
Teicholz, J. G. (2010). The Achilles heel of psychoanalysis: Meditations on motivation: Commentary on paper by Robert P. Drozek. *Psychoanalytic Dialogues*, *20*, 569–581.
Tenenbaum, S. (2007). *Appearances of the good: An essay on the nature of practical reason*. Cambridge, UK: Cambridge University Press.
Totton, N. (2000). *Psychotherapy and politics*. London, UK: Sage.
Tublin, S. (2011). Discipline and freedom in relational technique. *Contemporary Psychoanalysis*, *47*, 519–546.
Uhlmann, E. L., Pizarro, D. A., & Bloom, P. (2008). Varieties of social cognition. *Journal for the Theory of Social Behaviour*, *38*, 293–322.
Van Inwagen, P. (1983). *An essay on free will*. Oxford, UK: Oxford University Press.
Van Zyl, L. (2015). Eudaimonistic virtue ethics. In L. Besser-Jones & M. Slote (Eds.), *The Routledge companion to virtue ethics* (pp. 183–195). New York, NY: Routledge.
Wachtel, P. L. (1986). From neutrality to personal revelation: Patterns of influence in the analytic relationship (a symposium)—On the limits of therapeutic neutrality. *Contemporary Psychoanalysis*, *22*, 60–70.
Wachtel, P. L. (1997). *Psychoanalysis, behavior therapy, and the relational world*. Washington, DC: American Psychological Association.
Wachtel, P. L. (2014). *Cyclical psychodynamics and the contextual self: The inner world, the intimate world, and the world of culture and society*. London, UK: Routledge.
Wallace, R. J. (1994). *Responsibility and the moral sentiments*. Cambridge, MA: Harvard University Press.
Wallerstein, R. S. (2006). The relevance of Freud's psychoanalysis in the 21st century: Its science and its research. *Psychoanalytic Psychology*, *23*, 302–326.
Wallwork, E. (1991). *Psychoanalysis and ethics*. New Haven, CT: Yale University Press.
Waring, D. R. (2016). *The healing virtues: Character ethics in psychotherapy*. Oxford, UK: Oxford University Press.
Watson, G. (2004). *Agency and answerability: Selected essays*. Oxford, UK: Oxford University Press.
Weisel-Barth, J. (2009). Stuck: Choice and agency in psychoanalysis. *International Journal of Psychoanalytic Self Psychology*, *4*, 288–312.
Weisel-Barth, J. (2015). An ethical vision: Response to Drozek's "The dignity in multiplicity." *Psychoanalytic Dialogues*, *25*, 463–471.
Wheelis, J. (2010). Mending the mind. *Psychoanalytic Dialogues*, *20*, 325–336.

Wille, R. S. (2008). Psychoanalytic identity: Psychoanalysis as an internal object. *Psychoanalytic Quarterly*, *77*, 1193–1229.

Williams, B. (1973). A critique of utilitarianism. In J. J. C. Smart & B. Williams (Eds.), *Utilitarianism: For and against* (pp. 75–150). Cambridge, UK: Cambridge University Press.

Williams, B. (1981). *Moral luck: Philosophical papers 1973–1980*. Cambridge, UK: Cambridge University Press.

Williams, B. (1985). *Ethics and the limits of philosophy*. Cambridge, MA: Harvard University Press.

Winnicott, D. W. (1958). *Through paediatrics to psycho-analysis: Collected papers*. New York, NY: Brunner-Routledge.

Winnicott, D. W. (1965). *The maturational processes and the facilitating environment: Studies in the theory of emotional development*. Madison, WI: International Universities Press.

Winnicott, D. W. (1971). *Playing and reality*. London, UK: Routledge Classics.

Wolf, S. (1990). *Freedom within reason*. Oxford, UK: Oxford University Press.

Wood, A. W. (1999). *Kant's ethical thought*. Cambridge, UK: Cambridge University Press.

Wood, A. W. (2009). Duties to oneself, duties of respect to others. In T. E. Hill (Ed.), *The Blackwell guide to Kant's ethics* (pp. 229–251). Chichester, UK: Wiley-Blackwell.

Yeomans, F. E., Clarkin, J. F., & Kernberg, O. F. (2015). *Transference-focused psychotherapy for borderline personality disorder: A clinical guide*. Washington, DC: American Psychiatric Publishing.

Young-Bruehl, E. (2011). Psychoanalysis and social democracy: A tale of two developments. *Contemporary Psychoanalysis*, *47*, 179–203.

Zeddies, T. J. (2001). On the wall or in the ointment? The psychoanalytic community as a third presence in the consulting room. *Contemporary Psychoanalysis*, *37*, 133–147.

Index